GREAT NORTHERN RAILWAY
ENGINE SHEDS

ISBN 1 899624 22 8

IN MEMORY OF RON DYER

First Published in the UK by
CHALLENGER PUBLICATIONS
Printed and Bound by
Amadeus Press Ltd, Huddersfield
This edition reprinted exclusively for the Book Law / Railbus Publications
309 Mapperley Plains, Nottingham, NG3 5RG.

GREAT NORTHERN RAILWAY
ENGINE SHEDS

by
Roger Griffiths & John Hooper

Volume 2
The Lincolnshire Loop
Nottinghamshire & Derbyshire

INTRODUCTION TO VOLUME 2

First published in 1989, Volume 1 of *Great Northern Engine Sheds* covered the sheds northwards from King's Cross to Grantham including the various branches en route. This, the long awaited second volume covers those engine sheds found in Lincolnshire, around what was called "The Loop" line, those in neighbouring Nottinghamshire and also the solitary examples found in Derbyshire and Staffordshire. By their very nature many were small buildings serving single line branches in truly rural areas but nonetheless they were just as interesting as their larger counterparts found in the towns and cities served by the company. Lincolnshire was largely dominated by one railway company - the GNR which had its origins there - and its branch lines spread everywhere, especially in the Wolds and the flatlands of the south of the county.

Scale track plans, from various periods, have again been included to orientate the text and photographs with the shed histories. When the authors set about the task of compiling this book they had little idea of the magnitude of work that awaited them and neither did they realise that a history about the locomotive sheds of the GNR could not be produced, unless that history was more generally to encompass the entire activities of the GN's Locomotive Department. Hence to take the story that bit further than the sheds and engines, we have included a number of appendices which are set out at the rear of this volume to cover, in detail, aspects of the Great Northern Loco Dept. These include the development of the breakdown cranes and trains, repair facilities, turntables & other turning devices and, another bite at the all important subject of water which was first detailed in Volume 1.

Any opinions expressed are ours alone, as is the responsibility for any errors. We hope that any reader who would like to correct, or raise a query about, anything in these pages, will get in touch with us via the publishers.

Volume 3, which is to be published in the winter of 1996, will complete this trilogy of GNR shed history. Encompassed will be the engine sheds found in England's biggest county, Yorkshire, where some of the larger, and more complex, establishments were erected. Also included will be the sole Lancashire located engine shed. Further appendices will present details of the men who worked for the Loco Dept during the years of the GNR including the Loco Engineers. The numerous servicing and stabling points will be listed and detailed. Photographic material is still being sought for this final volume and if there are any interested possible contributors, the authors would welcome contact via the publishers please. *Roger Griffiths, Bristol. John Hooper, Oldham.*

Publishers note: The track plans contained within this volume are scaled in feet and are approximate only.

CONTENTS

Boston shed's main building is seen here on 29th April 1956, during its final rebuild. The 3-road portion at right displays the asbestos roof probably applied during the 30s and the corner buttress almost certainly added when the original arched entrances were replaced by wooden lintels and cast iron columns. *A.R.Goult*

BOSTON

If ever the GNR had a "Cinderella" location it was Boston, once known as St. Botolph's Town, and an East Coast seaport whose prominence was for a time, second only to London. Boston's port continued to prosper, especially after the 1884 expansion, but the town's importance as the centre of the GN's network was much more shortlived, blooming from the earliest days, only to diminish again within five years, relegating Boston to the long-term role of a quiet backwater.

The seaport and its associated River Witham Navigation were great boons during construction of the GNR's "Loop" line - pig iron was being landed as early as February 1847, for onward transport to the railway's foundry at Lincoln, where it was made into rail chairs. Then, in mid-1848 came a notable event, when no less than eight vessels docked and discharged Baltic sleepers simultaneously. However, construction in Boston itself did not commence until October 1847, when pile-driving began for the River Witham bridge, over which passed the first train - a ballast train - on 25th May 1848.

Buildings in Boston were already in hand by the time that first train ran, with Bury having completed plans for "the main engine house" on 4th May 1848. Even so, it is evident that some permanent buildings were not intended to be ready in time for the opening of public services; for example, the building of a 'permanent' station did not commence until May 1850. Accordingly, in August 1848, there began construction of a temporary station off West Street and on 31st of the same month, Bury recommended "hire of new premises" and "temporary wooden buildings". The latter included an engine shed, the erection of which was sanctioned, on a site adjacent to the temporary station.

First public trains to run were those of the GN-worked East Lincolnshire Railway, whose contractors, Messrs. Waring & Company, completed the last section from Firsby, on 20th September 1848. Services were commenced on the following 2nd October, starting with the 7.35 a.m. train to Hull (passengers travelling via the ferry of course), and fifteen days later, the first section of the GNR's "Loop" line, from Peterborough via Boston, to Lincoln, was brought into use. Just over a fortnight after that, it is evident word had got around that the GN was having water supply problems at Boston, as on 2nd November 1848, Boston Waterworks offered: "...to supply water to the Great Northern engine station...". If the reader refers to the chapter on "Watering Arrangements", it can be seen that not until December did the GN's Lincolnshire Committee note that the company was paying an exorbitant price for its water, but instead of accepting the Waterworks' offer the GN made provision to take water from the River Witham. Less than two years later the railway company were to regret that decision, as the 20th September 1850 issue of the *Stamford Mercury* reported: "*...The Boston Water Company have made arrangements with the GNR to supply their engines with water. The former company have hitherto been using the Witham water, but it is found to injure the engines...*".

Things must have been pretty chaotic all round at that time, with Bury reporting, on 23rd November 1848: "...I am sorry to state that the shops at Boston are not yet in so forward a state as the demands of the line require and it is desirable the contractors are urged forward with them...". Then, in December, Bury commented that: "...the temporary engine shed at the station is not yet ready...". However, on 21st December, the locomotive engineer was able to advise that the Locomotive Stores and its contents had just been insured for £1,500, signifying perhaps that some building work had at last been completed. Even so, with all the permanent buildings and temporary accommodation planned for Boston, it soon became clear Bury had not made provision for enough, as on 6th June 1849 he was asked to tender for construction of additional workshops.

Just when Boston's temporary engine shed came into use is not known, but it must have been early in 1849. Its layout, exact site and facilities are also unknown, though it may be assumed possibly to have been of galvanised iron construction, just like the temporary carriage shed in the town, which was reported as having been blown down in a "heavy storm", in February 1850. It is known that the carriage shed scaled 250 ft x 20 ft, so it is likely the engine shed was of about the same width and probably around 100-150 feet in length.

Bury faded from the scene early in 1850, to be replaced by Sturrock, one of whose early duties was to report, on 11th August 1850, that Boston's (permanent) engine shed was nearly ready. This apparently did not apply to the workshops, as on 1st September 1850 Sturrock unleashed the first of a flurry of requests for new buildings at Boston, and all the activity effectively concealed the date upon which the engine shed opened. The locomotive engineer's first requirement was that the temporary engine shed at Walton Junction (Peterborough) "...be moved to Boston Yard for the repair of engines...". That request seems to have been turned down, because on 24th September Sturrock reported to the Board, with drawings of a temporary shed which he recommended be erected in the yard at Boston, for "...the repair of engines...". Then, the Board resolved that: "...the Resident Engineer, Mr. Henry Fowler, be instructed to build the shed as per the plan submitted, at a cost not exceeding £150...". Next came two requests in October, the first on the 15th, when Sturrock asked for "...a temporary waggon shed at Boston, near to the present waggon shed, for repairs of carriages...". The estimated cost was £250 and the locomotive engineer also asked that the present carriage shed by the station "...be further enclosed at a cost of £50-60...". Was the existing shed a rebuild of that demolished in February's storm? Whatever, it was resolved both the works be carried out. The second request came on 22nd October, when Sturrock asked for additional sidings at Boston, "...as the accommodation in that respect is very deficient at present...". Approval was given accordingly.

Provision of the temporary workshops and the sidings was succeeded on 27th May 1851, when Sturrock requested "...alterations to the temporary shed at Boston, to admit of the two lathes authorised by the Board on the 14th of May, at an estimated cost of £300. The materials used would be recovered and made available again when the machines require to be removed to the permanent repairing shop. I request also that this work be carried out without delay..." This was authorised, but even then the locomotive engineer was not satisfied, as on 30th September 1851 he reported to the Board: "...the present stock of machines at Boston is insufficient for the engines employed and I request authority to order the following from Nasmyth & Company, of Manchester: 2 planing machines at £110 each; 2 planing machines at £75 each; 1 portable drilling machine at £45; 1 small slotting machine £65...".

In between all this, after a number of months' silence on the subject, the locomotive engineer returned to the matter of Walton Junction temporary engine shed. January 1851 saw Sturrock again ask that: "...it (the Walton Junction building) be

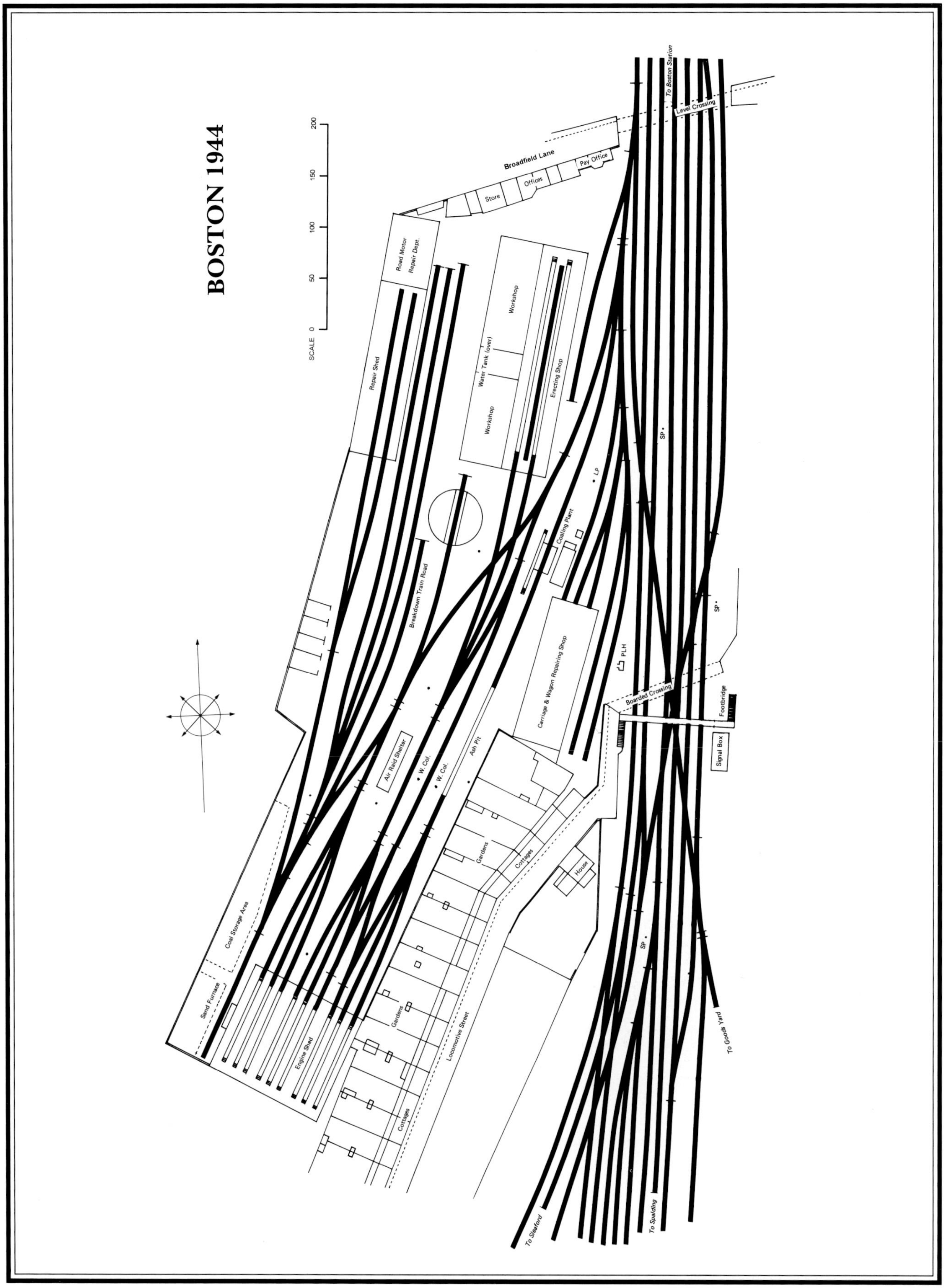
BOSTON 1944
SCALE 0 50 100 150 200
To Boston Station
Level Crossing
Broadfield Lane
Pay Office
Offices
Store
Road Motor Repair Dept.
Repair Shed
Workshop
Water Tank (over)
Workshop
Erecting Shop
Breakdown Train Road
Coaling Plant
LP
SP
SP
Carriage & Wagon Repairing Shop
PLH
Boarded Crossing
Footbridge
Signal Box
Air Raid Shelter
W. Col.
W. Col.
Ash Pit
Gardens
Cottages
House
SP
Coal Storage Area
Sand Furnace
Engine Shed
Gardens
Locomotive Street
Cottages
To Goods Yard
To Sleaford
To Spalding

moved to my yard at Boston, where it can be erected for £100-120, and used as a temporary shed for the repair of carriages..." This time it appears Sturrock got his way, as on 8th March 1851 he followed up by requesting the purchase of a small piece of land adjoining Boston Works, owned by Peto & Betts, that could be used for the erection of a temporary carriage shed "...which has been removed from Walton Junction. There is not enough room in my yard at present..." It would seem though that question of land ownership featured a "grey area!" During the early part of August 1852, Sturrock recommended: "...that an arrangement be made with a Mr. Brackenborough, for the rental at £25 per annum of a piece of land adjoining the works at Boston, which was formerly the property of a Mr. Ingram and at the same time part held by the Company, at £10 per annum and on which is erected a carriage shed..." So, the inference is that Peto & Betts had not been the owner of the land by the works and the GN had put up its temporary carriage shed - in part at least - on another party's land, without permission! Altogether an embarassing situation, but left with little choice, the Board resolved to accept Mr. Brackenborough's surprisingly good-natured and cheap offer, for a term not exceeding three years! (In fact, this was not an isolated case vis-a-vis the GNR in Boston - the Grand Sluice bridge had been partly built outside the limit of deviation!).

While all this was in progress there were two requests for provision of locomotive coking stages at Boston. That, of 1st April 1851, asked for a coke stage and engine pit at Boston station, to cost an estimated £280-15-0d, which was approved. Whether this was installed on the Up or Down line is not clear, but by the mid-1860's there were two stages and two pits at the station, one on each line; records of provision of the station's second set of facilities have not been traced. However, it is the other 1851 requirement for a coke stage that interests us most of all. On 25th February, J.Cubitt, the Engineer, submitted a letter to the Board that enclosed a tracing "...showing the position of the coke stage that I recommend be erected near the locomotive yard at Boston, at an estimated cost of £95..." It looks then as if Boston's permanent engine shed was still not fully functioning by February 1851. Perhaps the building was in use, even partially, while engines continued to visit the temporary shed for coke and possibly stabling? In the absence of all but the scantiest information, everything must be speculative, but this request for a coke stage is the best available indicator that Boston engine shed was probably finally completed, in every respect, by mid-1851.

The GN Locomotive Department's site at Boston covered some 3-4 acres adjacent to Broadfield Lane, and there are not infrequent references to "Broadfield Lane engine shed" in the archives; locally, the shed was always known by that name. The locomotive depot stood at the extreme southern end of the site and comprised a dead-end building in brick, measuring 115 ft in width, by 100 ft in length. Three slated gable roofs each provided cover over 3 roads, which all had arched entrances, ran the full length of the shed and were equipped with inspection

In a picture packed with detail we see two of the former Boston Works buildings that were later converted for loco running purposes: the smithy/turnery, with bricked-up entrances, and the adjoining one-time erecting shop. Note that the 54ft turntable, laid down in 1900, had been modernised by the fitting of vacuum traction, probably in 1935, when the 100 ton coaler was also provided. That coaler had to be given a general overhaul in 1948, which required special notices being sent to all sheds that rostered engines for workings to Boston. Every such loco had to be given sufficient coal for the round trip, while Boston's own allocation made temporary use of the depot's old coal stage, luckily still extant. 3rd April 1955. *B.K.B.Green.*

The afternoon sun highlights the grace of Stirling Single No.663 at Boston, in the early years of the 20th century. 663 was one of three Class A2 4-2-2 allocated to the shed at the time, for use on light passenger duties along the "Loop". *Authors collection.*

pits. Because the shed occupied virtually all the width of the narrow site at this point, the coke stage and 40 ft turntable stood about 260 ft to the north, positioned opposite each other, with access tracks to some of the nine shed roads passing between. The stage lay on the eastern side and just east of that were the depot offices, in a parallel row of brick buildings, all of which backed onto the extreme south western corner of a 150 ft x 50 ft wagon repair shop. It was not necessary to provide repair facilities at the engine shed, because at the north end of the Broadfield Lane site there were the permanent buildings of the GN's Boston Works, a facility which had been managed by Frederick Parker since 1848.

Quite when the Works' permanent premises came into use is yet another unknown, but this probably occurred during the first half of 1849. What happened at that time, to all the various temporary works buildings is also a mystery, but doubtless most were soon removed. The new works comprised, on the east side, a 2 road erecting shop, 205 ft x 43 ft. This was adjoined on its western side by a 2 road smithy/turnery - the smiths occupied the southern half of the building - that also scaled 205 ft x 43 ft. Positioned centrally atop the smithy/turnery was a 27 ft high brick tankhouse, supporting a 32,000 gallon water tank that supplied the locomotive shed as well as the workshops. Running along the north west boundary wall and separated from the erecting shop/smithy/turnery by several open tracks, was a 3 road building measuring 215 ft x 48 ft. Internally, the tracks extended for 155 ft, leaving a 60 ft area at the north end which formed the works' stores. Exactly what the southern portion was used for is not certain - tender shop, or paint shop, or perhaps a combination of both - or maybe some other function entirely? Whatever their purposes though, the works buildings were all constructed in brick, with slated gable roofs; the smithy/turnery had separate arched entrances whereas the erecting shop and 3 road building had the unusual feature of an overall archway, subdivided between the roads by use of cast iron and wooden columns respectively, with wooden fascia boards above. Finally, along the northern boundary wall were placed buildings that housed the works manager's office, the locomotive engineer's residence - until 1853, used as offices afterwards - and another stores.

This works complex provided the GN's sole heavy repair and overhaul facility until 1853, the time that Doncaster "Plant" opened and Frederick Parker and 300 men and their families left Boston for the new works. Boston shops continued to function, however, and be expanded upon. For example, on 18th December 1855, when a new lathe and planing machine were ordered and again, on 13th February 1857, when £65 was approved for purchase of a punching machine. Nevertheless, Boston's level of activity was much reduced and while things did pick up as a natural consequence of increasing traffic, the works never regained its early importance.

Boston's last new railway route opened on 12th April 1859, when the GN-operated Boston, Sleaford & Midland Counties Railway entered the town, on completion of the section of line from Sleaford. Originally, the Ambergate Nottingham Boston & Eastern Junction Railway had planned to run into Boston from the west, but after building its Nottingham-Grantham section, the financially strapped Ambergate Company's subsequent aspirations came to nought. Before it became clear that the Ambergate Railway would not reach Boston, a property speculator bought up land on the southern edge of town which supposedly lay on the Ambergate's proposed entry route. On that land, which lay immediately east of the engine shed and south of the wagon works, "Locomotive Street" grew up over the years of the late 1850's, to join nearby "Duke Street" and "King Street" as the main living area of Broadfield Lane's workers. In fact, "Locomotive Street" was peopled entirely by footplatemen and fitters, whose homes were separated from their place of work simply by a high wall. Alas for the property speculator, he did not make a handsome profit from the sale of land to the Ambergate Railway - or the BS&MCR, as the latter finally built its line slightly to the south! Nevertheless, the landowner must have made a profit - albeit over a longer period of time - from the rents extracted out of his railwaymen tenants.

Moving on to the final quarter of 1862, there comes a confused state of affairs over Boston shed's coke stage. On 14th October, the GN's Engineer reported that the stage was in need of repair, the estimated cost of which was put at £100, as against complete replacement by a brick-built stage at a cost of £591. As may be expected, the GN Board authorised money for repair rather than replacement. Then, towards the end of December 1862, Sturrock reported to the Board on a visit he had made to Boston, where he had found: "...the coke stage, a wooden structure, is in a most dilapidated state. It has been repaired frequently and is propped up in consequence of foundations sinking, and is beyond further economical repair. I request permission to seek prices for renewal, for which, if approved, I will produce a plan for a more convenient and better structure..." It would seem that the repair authorised in October 1862 had not been effected before Sturrock's visit and it is equally clear that the Engineer and Locomotive Engineer were working in isolation, as the latter seems not to have been aware of October's proceedings. Frustratingly, the GN Minutes do not record if the Board put Sturrock "in the picture" as it were, or what was the Directors reaction to the locomotive engineer's comments, which after all, amounted to a *fait accompli* with regard to replacement of the coke stage. Neither do the available records make any further comment upon the matter, but by the late 1880's at least, Boston had been provided with a brick-built coaling shed, equipped with half ton bucket cranes. This entailed alteration of the engine shed's approach roads, to run each side of the coaling shed. The date of the addition is unknown, but almost certainly was around 1863.

Problems with water supplies occurred again in 1867, with the *Stamford Mercury* of 15th November reporting: *"...Through the excessive dryness of the season and the extraordinary demands of the Great Northern Railway Company, the supply of water in the reservoir at the Boston Water Works Company has unhappily proved inadequate to the wants of the residents....The GNR Company have been consuming 180,000 gallons per day, but the Water Works Company have ceased to supply them now, so that the inhabitants need entertain no fear of being fully supplied..."* That reservoir was at Revesby, 40 acres in extent, opened in 1845 and notorious for its unreliability until well into the 20th century. But, it was soon supplying the GN again. A fortnight after the above report, the Stamford newspaper carried a follow-up article. This stated that the directors of the water company had asked the GNR to pay 5d. (2p) per 1,000 gallons, for a period of 10 years, which the railway's Board had to accept; what the GNR did about water supplies during those two weeks is not recorded.

A further renewal of an engine shed facility was made in 1868, when Stirling asked for authority to spend £220, "...to replace the worn out and useless turntable at Boston..." The cost was sanctioned and a new 40 ft table duly installed in the existing pit. There was no other engine turning facility available at Boston at that time, so during the period the shed's turntable was out of use, some special arrangements would obviously have been necessary, to keep tender-first running to a minimum: doubtless, carriage turnplates etc, would have been used whenever possible.

Expanding traffic was the reason put forward by Stirling in July 1870, when he asked for an additional machine tool for Boston Works. The locomotive engineer said: "...A new drilling machine is required, to cope with an increased workload, due to the additional mileage being run in the Loop District...". The Board resolved that suitable invitations to tender should be issued and the matter does not reapper in the Minutes.

After these few brief references, further mention of Boston Locomotive Department in the Minutes is even sparser, for the remainder of the 19th century. Except for the arrival, by 1881, of an 8 ton hand-powered breakdown crane, that was still to be found at the shed over 75 years later. Then, another instance comes from 30th September 1886, when the Engineer reported to the Board about a fire that occurred during the night of

Ivatt Class D3 4-4-0 No.4311 looks out from the old Boston erecting shop on 18th June 1933. Later, this building would be adapted for use by Boston's first diesels. *T.Henderson collection.*

25th/26th September "...which started due to the spontaneous combustion of the engine waste, destroying a workshop and its contents, valued at £7,000..." The engineer followed up by proposing to build a new workshop, plus some cottages, on a site nearer the station. The workshop referred to was in the old Engineer's yard at Stells Lane, opposite the goods yard. The fire was one of the fiercest in Boston's history and destruction of the goods shed was only narrowly avoided. The reference to spontaneous combustion of "engine waste" meaning the oily rags used for cleaning. Not until 1894 did a new Engineer's workshop complex open, on a site off Sleaford Road.

The only other 19th century mention of Boston comes from 1899, when Ivatt produced plans to resite and enlarge the turntable at the engine shed and provide a further turntable at the passenger station. Total costs for the scheme were £3,377 and it was December 1900 before Ivatt could report: "...the new (55 ft) turntable in the passenger yard is being fixed; foundations for the turntable in the locomotive yard are complete..." The engine shed table was of a non-GN standard size - 54 ft, and according to its 'worksplate', was actually constructed in 1899. The site chosen for it was directly outside the southern end of the smithy/turnery building, with the result that henceforward, the only means of access to that premises' westernmost road was via the turntable. Around the same time as the shed's turning device was moved, completion of Doncaster's large new Crimpsall shop brought to an end the need for heavy repairs to be carried out at Boston Works. Accordingly, Boston's workshop facility formally became part of the engine shed, thereafter being used for running repairs and locomotive stabling - the latter particularly in the three road building on the western side. In later years, the dates of which are unknown, both tracks accessing the smithy were taken out and the arched entrances bricked up, while the three road building became a repair shop, losing its westernmost road in the process, to give more working room.

Simultaneously with the above turntable works, the GN was trying to improve its supply of water, after Ivatt had reported, on 29th May 1900: "...Boston Waterworks, who supply water to the shed there, charge 4d per 1,000 gallons, which costs the Company about £500 per annum. Supplies are irregular and at dry times of the year are so scant as to cause inconvenience. I propose to pump water from the River Witham, at a point about half a mile north of Boston station. This will involve about 1,000 yards of 8 ft main, engine house, boiler and pump, the total cost of which would be under £2,000, and the saving will be at least £250 per year..." It is interesting to note that the price of water had decreased by 1d. per 1,000 gallons since 1867. The matter was referred to the GN's legal department and on 4th October 1900, after due investigation, the solicitor stated: "...It is my opinion that the company can draw water from the river for the purpose of watering locomotives, providing that they do not interfere with the navigation or the rights of ripairian owners..." Board approval was given, and the locomotive engineer had things move very fast, so that by December 1900 he was able to report the new water pumping house was complete and ready for fixing of the boiler and pumps. Even so, not all of Boston's 30 million gallons annual requirement came to be taken from the river - the waterworks continued to supply nearly 1 million gallons a year, presumably for 'domestic' uses.

However, the normally efficient Ivatt had not considered one important factor, which came to light during 1905's widespread chemical analysis of the Great Northern's water resources. This was that at the point where the GN extracted supplies from the River Witham, the water had such a degree of salinity as to make it quite unsuitable for boiler use. In short, Ivatt had not been aware of the GN's problems over 40 years earlier with taking water from the Witham. The analyst's report suggested water could be taken from the river, but this had to be above the tidal reach, with Langrick Ferry being the suggested location. Ivatt took the matter up, a little belatedly perhaps, in what seems to have been an attempt at camouflaging his error in originally recommending the taking of supplies from the Witham, at a point where it was still mildly seawater. It was not until 6th December 1906 that he told the Locomotive Committee the water supply at Boston needed to be increased and 'improved', and suggested that "...the pump house be moved 5 miles upstream on the River Witham, at an estimated cost of £5,000..." The Minutes do not record if, and how Ivatt had to justify such expenditure, as the only other comment made is that the Locomotive Committee recommended Board approval of the scheme. This was forthcoming and on 20th July 1907 the Minutes record: "the main is now in use and the pump house is being removed from Boston to Langrick." Despite this attempt at improving water supplies, the authors have been told that even in the 1950's salinity of the water was still experienced, causing the engines to prime badly. It seems that spring tides could result in seawater reaching Langrick Ferry, and presumably the problem persisted until the end of steam.

Following that 1907 job, Boston engine shed is absent from the Minute books for over a quarter of a century, so let us now look at Boston Locomotive Department/District, its locomotives and some of their duties. The town was the seat of a Departmental/District Locomotive Superintendent (DLS), from the creation of such posts, about 1858. Prior to that a locomotive foreman was in charge, with Charles Sacré being the first, before he moved on to Peterborough and eventually, the Manchester Sheffield & Lincolnshire Railway. Boston's DLS post seems to have disappeared though, before the end of the 19th century, as a list of GNR Locomotive Districts, carried in Vol.6 (1900) of the *Railway Magazine* does not detail Boston. Eighteen years later, in an article on Peterborough, the *Railway Magazine* shows Boston and its outstations of Spilsby and Wainfleet as part of the Peterborough Locomotive District. In LNER days, Boston re-assumed the title of "Locomotive Department" but with only a Foreman in charge, while in the BR era the shed was subordinate to Lincoln.

Spilsby and Wainfleet outstations mentioned above, were not Boston's only such sub-sheds. Others were: Horncastle: Opened August 1855; Closed ca.1918 - Normally one tank engine outstationed until closure, when engines were supplied by Boston on a daily basis. Sleaford: Transferred from Grantham 30th September 1930; Closed May 1964 - Usually two engines allocated until 1958, when steam finished. After that a single diesel shunter was supplied. Spalding: Transferred from New England 29th December 1957; Closed 7th March 1960 - 14 steam and 1 diesel 'on shed' on 29/12/57; after closure of the shed, diesels continued to stable at the station. Spilsby: Opened 1st May 1868; Closed ca.1941 - Normal allocation one small tank engine. Wainfleet: Opened 11th September 1871; Closed ca.1956(?) - Usually two engines outstationed; tanks initially, with tender types later - especially Ivatt 4-4-0.

The opening of the ELR and GN 'Loop' line in 1848 brought Sharps and Hawthorn Singles to Boston, with some of the former later being converted to 0-4-2 and seeing further service in the area. The early 1850's saw "Large Hawthorn" singles

K3 61936 leads the eye to a general view of the refurbished main shed, giving a good idea of the large amount of glasswork that had been let into the rear wall. Note also that the sand drier had been rebuilt along with the depot roof. The date is 4th September 1960 and a solitary B1 is visible among the by then, ubiquitous, Ivatt Class 4 2-6-0. *Authors collection.*

The third works building turned over to running shed use - actually as a repair shop - lay on the west side of the Broadfield Lane site. Originally served by three tracks this shed's exact purpose during its workshops days remains unclear - in part at least, as the northern portion seems always to have been used as a stores. This 4th September 1960 picture shows how the four open roads separating the old works structures provided much needed stabling space in the awkwardly laid out shed yard. *Authors collection.*

A view inside the repair shop during GN days. Notice the overhead crane runs on the east wall; these no doubt date from the days when Boston was the main locomotive works. Between the two engine pits, another set of rails were laid in to facilitate movement of heavy items. *Authors collection.*

and Sturrock-designed 0-6-0 arrive and by 1855, the GNR's Rule Book was displaying the following duties being worked by Boston engine shed:

Down
Boston to Doncaster - 69 miles
Gainsborough - 48 miles
Grimsby - 48 miles
Lincoln - 31 miles
Louth - 34 miles
New Holland - 64 miles
Retford - 51 miles
Up
Boston to London - 107 miles
Peterborough - 31 miles

With development of the GN's "Towns" line and expansion into Derbyshire, Staffordshire, West Yorkshire etc, the emphasis fell away from the Loop and Boston's share of traffic declined. So much so that by 1889, there were only two main line goods and mineral workings and their return empties, being operated by the depot. However, there was one interesting working from Boston in the first years of the 20th century, involving a lodging turn to Stoke-on-Trent, via the GN's Derbyshire and Staffordshire Extension and running powers over the North Staffordshire Railway. On 1st May 1902, the GN's Way & Works Committee read a report from Ivatt in which he passed on a request from the Boston men working through to Stoke that they be allowed to book on at Stoke for the return journey, after 8 hours instead of the normal 9. Ivatt supported the mens' appeal and the Committee gave its approval.

Sturrock and Stirling 0-4-2, 2-4-0, 0-6-0 and small tank engines were quite adequate for the shed's tasks, until the depot got a considerable uplift of power when Ivatt's 4-4-0 arrived in 1898. His D1 and D2 were prime power until BR times. One engine in particular, D1 1395 (LNER D2 4395), was resident at Boston for 27 years, 1920-1947 except for a six week period at Woodford in the summer of 1929. Other passenger power was provided by 0-6-0's of course, with one Stirling Class J4 (LNER J3) still being present at the Grouping. There were also seven Class E1 2-4-0 at Boston at the time of the LNER's formation and they saw out their days on the easy services of East Lincolnshire until September 1927, when the last survivor of the class, No.3814, was withdrawn.

Earlier, in 1928, Ivatt's Class C2 "Small" Atlantics were based at Boston, seeing service on Peterborough and Lincoln trains until moved away again around the middle period of the Second World War. 4-4-2 re-appeared late in 1947 with the graceful ex-GC Class C4; within a year nine were allocated, but all had gone

Boston shedmaster's office, still standing on 3rd July 1983, some 135 years after it was built as the first headquarters of the GN's locomotive engineer. Bury and Sturrock both used this building until the centre of operations moved away to Doncaster in 1853. *L.Perrin.*

again by the end of 1950. Further significant passenger - or rather, mixed-traffic engines came, in the shape of K2 Moguls. They appeared in the latter half of the 1930's and gradually increased in number, to peak at 12 in 1954, before fading in the very early 1960's.Thompson's ubiquitous B1 4-6-0 seem to have evaded allocation to Boston - a considerable achievement - but of course, Boston men used to drive Immingham-based examples, between Boston and Kings Cross. With closure of the M&GNR in 1959, Broadfield Lane received large numbers of LMS Ivatt Class 4 2-6-0 and it was those machines that saw out the depot's last days.

On the goods side, 0-6-0's seem to have been the largest type to have worked from Boston; Ivatt and Gresley GN types became LNER Classes J2, J3, J4 and J6, being joined by ex-GE J17 for a few years in the late 1930's. Then, no fewer than seven ex-NER Class J21 came to Broadfield Lane in the latter half of 1938, with the last one leaving in the Spring of 1941. The year 1938 seems to have been of some significance 0-6-0-wise, as three LNER Class J39 also arrived, to stay until almost the end of the war. The type returned in the latter 1950's, with a maximum of seven being allocated in December 1958, reducing to three in the next year and disappearing for the last time in February 1960. The K2 mentioned earlier also participated in goods work, especially the fast night-time turns to Doncaster, and for a two year period, 1955-7, K3 No.61943 was a Boston engine, for use on an afternoon parcels train.

Successors to Sturrock's tank engine rebuilds of early GN singles were Stirling's 0-6-0 saddle tank classes, of which 10 were still working from Boston at the Grouping: eight J54 and one each of Classes J55 and J56. Their use seems to have kept Ivatt's numerous J13 (LNER J52) away from Boston, except apparently, for a single example, which was resident for about eighteen months during 1939-40. As in many instances, the ex-GNR saddle tanks succumbed to an invasion of ex-GE 0-6-0T quite early in LNER days. Boston was a prime example, with J66, J67, J68 and J69 all arriving at the end of the 1920's. Of the J66, Nos.7313 and 7321 saw only a few months use on shunting duties in Boston Docks before moving on to pastures new, but J68 survived on the same work until 1953. However, J67/9 were resident even longer - and more numerous, there being eight allocated in 1954, before the class finally died out in 1960. Other tank engine oddities for shunting work were a pair of ex-NER J76 in the mid-late 1920's and a single ex-H&B J75 - No.2528 - for most of the 1930's. A further example of 0-6-0T was provided during BR times, when "Austerity" Class J94 spent some time working from Boston. Lastly, mention must be made of the "Departmental" Y3 Sentinels that operated within Boston (Hall Hills) Sleeper Depot; they seem to have been officially allocated to Broadfield Lane only by BR, but naturally they were seen at the shed in LNER times, paying visits for maintenance purposes.

Early passenger tanks included Stirling 0-4-2 and 0-4-4 varieties, these largely being swept away by C2 4-4-2T that came to Boston in the first part of the 20th century; as ever, the Atlantic tanks' stay was a long one, the last specimen not leaving until the early 1950's - 67350 seems to have been that machine. Other types were latecomers and spent varying times at Boston. For example, Class A5 4-6-2T from 1948 to 1949, then three, 69808, 69818 and 69819, from 1950 to 1958; 69808 was used on the last ordinary passenger train to Horncastle. In addition came ex-GE N7, of which four were allocated in the first year of BR, being used on local passenger, branch and goods workings, until 1950. Altogether, a quite small participation by passenger tank types - yet another indication of Boston's generally quiet existence.

The earliest allocation details for Boston District come from 1905, when 43 engines were stationed, including four at the sub-sheds. In 1912 the District housed the same number of locomotives, a figure that had fallen by 1918 to 41, subdivided: Boston 38; Wainfleet 2; Spilsby 1. By the Grouping there had been an amazing 50% jump in locomotives allocated - 62. What had occasioned this increase is not known, but by January 1931 the allocation had decreased again, to the following 50 engines:
C2 3250, 3259; **C12** 4502, 4504, 4518, 4537; **D2** 3045, 4335, 4356, 4367, 4371, 4379, 4380, 4384, 4394, 4395; **D3** 4350, 4351, 4357, 4358, 4359, 4360; **J1** 3013, 3014, 3015; **J2** 3072, 3073; **J3** 4113, 4171; **J4** 4106, 4145; **J6** 3549, 3571, 3580, 3594, 3595, 3596, 3598, 3599, 3600, 3604, 3633, 3634; **J54** 3907; **J55** 3782; **J68** 7029, 7031, 7032; **J69** 7265, 7349.

A visit to the shed on Christmas Day 1937 - a day when most engines would have been "at home" - found only these 38 locomotives:
C12 4537; **D2** 3045, 4331, 4369, 4381, 4383, 4388, 4395; **D3** 4311, 4344*, 4357, 4359*; **J1** 3013; **J2** 3072, 3073; **J6** 3522, 3531, 3532, 3555, 3595, 3596, 3598, 3600, 3630, 3633; **J17** 8188; **J21** 806, 1569; **J66** 7304; **J68** 7029, 7031, 7033; **J69** 7350, 7367, 7385; **J75** 2528; **K2** 4630, 4639. Those marked * were stored. **J6** 3531 from New England, and **J17** 8188 from March, were the only 'visitors'.

Class K2 2-6-0 61759 stands at the head of Boston's antiquated breakdown train on 23rd June 1958 - the 8 ton hand-operated crane was by that time, no less than 77 years old! Note the WW2 air raid shelter at right and the wagon shop behind. *R.C.Riley.*

World War Two seems to have re-injected some more motive power to Boston, as by early 1947 there were 51 engines allocated once again; at that time, all were still of pre-Grouping origin: 45 GNR and 6 GER. Their duties are shown in a contemporary WTT, which details the daily despatch of engines and their workings, as shown in *table 1.*

It will be appreciated from the table that Boston shed really did not have all that much work. 42 turns, Monday-Friday, were covered by 39 engines from Boston, with two Pilots later working service trains and one Pilot duty being covered by a Grantham engine. On Saturdays there were 31 workings, requiring 30 engines, Grantham again covering a Pilot duty. Sunday was extremely quiet, with only one locomotive being required - that to work a changeover turn for an engine outstationed at Wainfleet. All this was typical of the "backwater" atmosphere mentioned right at the start of this history, but nevertheless, the allocation in BR times was little affected, with 49 engines in 1950 and 51 in 1959.

Despite Boston's appearance of being a bit of a sleepy place, the LNER had obviously thought the shed to be of some importance as in 1933, provision of a mechanical coaling plant was sanctioned. Construction was undertaken by Henry Lees & Co., during 1934 and the early part of 1935. As in other instances with Boston, a local newspaper proved more revealing than the railway company's Minutes. In this case it was the *Boston Guardian* which reported upon completion of the coaling plant in its issue of 19th January 1935 and the article is worth repeating here - if only as a typical example of 1930's provincial newspaper prose. The piece was entitled "Boston's New Landmark" and sub-titled "The mighty sixty-nine feet high coaling apparatus at the Boston Locomotive Department":

"Boston has now a new landmark. In fact, it has had this landmark for a considerable time, and during its erection in the..." (Here there seems to have been a line dropped in the original text. Probable wording was something like: "...past months, there has been much speculation in...") "...Boston LNER Locomotive Department by the uninitiated as to its real purpose. It is certainly a strange-looking erection, but has been built to serve a much-needed demand, namely the speedy filling with coal of engine tenders - a process which up to now has had to be performed in an antiquated and laborious manner.

In reality, it is a gigantic hopper, but there is really more to it than that. On Wednesday, a Guardian representative was shown over it by Mr. O. Travers, the Locomotive Department Foreman, but was so attracted by the wonderful view obtained from the top that he failed to grasp all the many technical details appertaining to it.

As might well be imagined, the structure is on very firm foundations, and the business of making these foundations occupied some considerable time. In fact, for over a year work in connection with the apparatus has been in progress, and it is expected that it will shortly be put into use.

It is built of reinforced concrete, and by an elaborate process, yet quite simple in principle, coal is brought alongside it in 20 ton wagons, and these self-same wagons are neatly tipped on one side, pouring their contents into a container. This container is raised and the coal is then tipped into the giant hopper, which has one hundred tons capacity.

Up to the present, the process has been for men to fill ten hundredweight tubs, and these have been hooked up by crane and then tipped into the engine tender.

The northern end of the shed yard on a sunny Sunday in the early 1950's. The 1935 coaling plant rivals 'Boston Stump' in the landmark stakes; its design was a 'one-off' and was custom built for the Boston site. The layout at Boston shed was awkward to say the least, with much toing and froing to get an engine from the west side of the yard to the eastern (exit) side. *N.E.Stead collection.*

With the new apparatus, engines will pass underneath it and the coal will be regulated by a shuffler, and as it emerges from the hopper, it is also sprinkled with water.

The coal will not be handled in any shape or form from leaving the wagon until it is placed in the tender.

The whole of the apparatus is run on electrical power, and there are numerous safeguards to provide for its smooth running and to minimise accidents.

Incidentally, it is the first plant of this design and type to be erected in the country."

The reference to the coaling plant being the first example of its type is misleading. What was meant was that it was the first of 100 tons capacity, a size not repeated anywhere else on the LNER's GN Section. All others of the type were of larger capacity, so the minimal size of Boston's example was another direct indicator to the shed's relative importance - a small coaler because it could cope with normal demand, and the small savings in wages, etc, made by its introduction.

After 13 years use, including the hard days of the Second World War, Boston's coaling plant was in need of attention and a general repair was carried out in June 1948. During this time, the old coaling shed, which had not been removed in 1935, was pressed into service for fuelling the depot's own locomotive stud. In addition, a general notice was circulated to all other sheds that had occasion to send engines to Boston, requiring all such locomotives to be coaled enough for a return trip.

Further major expenditure for BR was incurred in 1955 and 56, when the roof of the nine road engine shed was renewed. By then, the building was some 104 years old and although at an unknown time it had lost its arched entrances in favour of steel framed doorways, the original roof frame and columns remained. However, the 1850 slates had been replaced by asbestos sheets in LNER times - possibly in 1934/5, as part of a modernisation package that included the coaling plant. To be precise though, BR's works could hardly be described as a mere re-roofing. The shed's side walls were extensively refurbished, while the rear wall was almost totally reconstructed from the ground up, to incorporate a large area of glasswork. Overhead, the rebuilt roof comprised an all-new steel frame, retaining the triple gable style. It was supported by the 1850 columns, and had corrugated asbestos cladding and end screens and asbestos cement smoke ducts and vents.

The result was a virtually new building, completed just in time for the first arrivals of new diesels, an event which had been predestined at the end of September 1952. That was when two ex-GWR diesel railcars, Nos. 19 and 20, operated from Boston, on four days trial running over the Boston-Sleaford-Grantham line. The railcars were used singly and with ordinary coaches as trailers, and it is known they also worked Grantham-Lincoln services. Even so, it was originally intended that Lincoln would maintain the first diesels, so Boston remained a predominantly steam shed for a few more years, having the following 51 engines allocated in 1959:

Cl.4 43058, 43059, 43060, 43061, 43062, 43064, 43065, 43066, 43068, 43080, 43083, 43085, 43091, 43092, 43093, 43095, 43104, 43107, 43108, 43109, 43110, 43111, 43142, 43143, 43147, 43157, 43159; **J6** 64171, 64172, 64180, 64190, 64191, 64214, 64229, 64231, 64247, 64250, 64260;**J39** 64728, 64729, 64823; **K2** 61731, 61742, 61743, 61748, 61750, 61751, 61762; **J69** 68557, 68570, 68602.

When it did arrive at Boston, the new form of motive power was not housed in the refurbished nine road shed, as that was

Ivatt Class 4 43066 rests beside Boston shed on 23rd June 1958. The wall behind the locomotive shows the extent of rebuilding necessary for supporting the new roof. *R.C.Riley.*

still supporting steam. Instead, the two road former erecting shop was designated as the diesel shed and was equipped with the necessary fuelling point and specialised equipment.

Even so, despite the fact that the men would have greatly appreciated their improved working conditions, Boston's fine new steam shed can only be described as having been an unnecessary expense. That was because after it had been in use only for some seven years, diesels prevailed, and displaced steam from such duties as remained in East Lincolnshire, with the result that the entire depot was closed. Actual date of closure was Sunday, 5th January 1964, when all but 10 of the 68 staff remaining were declared redundant; those retained, to look after the five diesel multiple units that stabled at the station, were three fitters, three electricians and four craftsmens' assistants.

Following closure, the nine road engine shed was pulled down with almost indecent haste - except for parts of two walls, to a height of about 7 feet, within the angle of which a commercial building has recently (ca1990) been put up. In the year following closure, the coaling tower was demolished by explosives, at around 8.00 a.m. on a Sunday morning! Then, March 1967 saw removal of the turntable (its partly filled-in pit remains visible), the former erecting shop and turnery buildings and the water tank above the latter; the smithy was retained, finally to be demolished in February 1987, leaving only the chimney shaft. Also taken out in 1967 was the repair shop portion of the one-time three road works building on the west side, leaving just the 60 ft stores portion at the north end. Today that building still stands, in use as a video film rental shop, while a bungalow has appeared on part of the demolished section. Also still standing is the shedmaster's office - Sturrock's old HQ - which looks out over the remainder of the historic Broadfield Lane site.

The unmistakable Great Central lineage is seen in this portrait of a Class A5 4-6-2T at Boston in June 1958. No. 69808 and her sisters 69818/9 would soon be moved away, after 8 years at 40F, during which time this particular machine had the distinction of hauling the last ordinary passenger train over the Horncastle branch. *K.Cook.*

Table 1.

WEEKDAYS		
Dep. Shed	Arrive	Duties
3.35 am	Passenger Stn 3.40 am	Boston Stn No.1 Pilot: 3.45 - 4.45 am
4.45 am	Goods Yard 4.50 am	5.15 am Goods Boston - Skegness
4.50 am	Goods Yard 4.55 am	Boston Yard 'A' Pilot: Down road shunting, 6.00 am Monday - 6.00 am Sunday.
5.45 am	Goods Yard 5.50 am	6.05 am Goods Boston-Skegness
5.50 am	Passenger Stn 5.55 am	6.25 am Passenger Boston-Horncastle
5.50 am	Boston Dock 6.00 am	Boston Dock Pilot No.1: Shunting as required
5.50 am	Goods Yard 5.55 am	Boston Yard 'C' Pilot: Park Sidings shunting, 6.00 am Monday - 6.00 am Sunday
6.50 am	Passenger Stn 6.55 am	Boston Stn No.2 Pilot: 7.00 am - 1.10 pm; works 1.40 pm Passenger BostontoLincoln
7.15 am	Firsby 7.45 am	8.45 am Goods Firsby-Spilsby
7.20 am	Passenger Stn 7.25 am	7.45 am Passenger Boston-Lincoln
7.30 am	Engineers Yard 7.35 am	Ballast Train working
7.35 am	Goods Yard 7.40 am	8.00 am Goods Boston-Grimsby
8.40 am	Passenger Stn 8.45 am	9.20 am Passenger Boston-Peterborough
8.50 am	Goods Yard 8.55 am	Boston Yard 'B' Pilot: South End shunting, 9.00 am Monday - 3.00 am daily
9.30 am	Honington 10.25 am	12.00 pm Goods Honington-Boston
10.00 am	Passenger Stn 10.05 am	10.51 am Passenger Boston-Grantham
10.30 am	Passenger Stn 10.35 am	11.10 am Passenger Boston-Lincoln
11.45 am*	Alford Town 1.02 pm	1.40 pm Goods Alford Town-Boston
11.45 am SX*	Skegness 12.42 pm	2.30 pm Goods Skegness-Colwick SX
12.40 pm SX	Old Leake 1.15 pm	2.25 pm Goods Old Leake-King's Cross SX (suspended)
12.40 pm	Goods Yard 12.45 pm	1.00 pm Goods Boston-Louth
12.55 pm SO	Passenger Stn 1.00 pm	Boston Stn No.4 Pilot: 1.00 pm - 9.50 pm SO
1.00 pm	Goods Yard 1.05 pm	1.10 pm Goods Boston-Lincoln
1.00 pm	Passenger Stn 1.05 pm	Boston Stn No.3 Pilot: 1.10 - 2.30 pm
1.10 pm	Woodhall Jct 2.00 pm	5.20 pm Goods Woodhall Jct-Boston
1.15 pm SO	Kirton 1.25 pm	Kirton Pilot: 1.30 - 5.50 pm SO
3.10 pm SX	Old Leake 3.23 pm	4.25 pm Goods Old Leake-King's Cross SX
3.10 pm	Goods Yard 3.15 pm	3.20 pm Goods Boston-Sleaford
3.15 pm SX	Kirton 4.15 pm	Kirton Pilot 4.15 - 8.20 pm
3.30 pm SX	Sibsey 3.42 pm	4.45 pm Goods Sibsey-King's Cross SX
4.00 pm SX	Goods Yard 4.05 pm	4.15 pm E&B Boston-Hall Hills SX
4.15 pm SX	Passenger Stn 4.20 pm	Boston Stn No.5 Pilot: 4.15 - 7.34 pm SX; 4.25 pm Goods Old Leake-King's X SX (dep Boston 8.20 pm)
4.20 pm	Goods Yard 4.25 pm	4.30 pm Goods Boston-King's Cross
7.00 pm SX	Sleaford 7.30 pm	8.15 pm Goods Sleaford-Colwick SX
7.00 pm SX	Goods Yard 7.05 pm	2.30 pm Goods Skegness-Colwick SX
8.00 pm SX	Goods Yard 8.05 pm	4.25 pm Goods Old Leake-King's Cross SX
8.20 pm SO	Goods Yard 8.25 pm	8.30 pm Goods Boston-New England SO
8.30 pm	Goods Yard 8.35 pm	8.40 pm Goods Boston-Colwick
8.45 pm SX	Passenger Stn 8.50 pm	Boston Stn No.7 Pilot: 8.45 - 9.50 pm SX
8.50 pm SX	Goods Yard 8.55 pm	9.00 pm Goods Boston-Doncaster SX
9.35 pm SO	Goods Yard 9.40 pm	9.45 pm Goods Boston-Doncaster SO
10.20 pm SX	Goods Yard 10.25 pm	10.30 pm Goods Boston-New England SX
10.20 pm SX	Goods Yard 10.25 pm	10.30 pm Goods Boston-Doncaster SX
11.00 pm SX	Goods Yard 11.05 pm	11.10 pm Goods Boston-Colwick SX
????	Boston Dock ????	Boston Dock No.2 Pilot: Dock shunting as shipping requires. Transfer Pilot; Goods to Dock and vice versa#
SUNDAYS		
8.38 am	Wainfleet 9.23 am	9.41 am Passenger Wainfleet-Skegness

Legend:

* Light engines coupled SX
# Goods agent Boston to give suitable notice when required.

Note:

(a) Boston Stn No.4 Pilot 2.30 - 4.15 pm SX, provided by Grantham, engine arriving on 1.20 pm Passenger Grantham-Boston.
(b) Boston Stn No.6 Pilot 7.58 - 9.00 pm SO, provided by Grantham, engine arriving on 7.02 pm Passenger Grantham-Boston.

BOSTON (HALL HILLS) SLEEPER DEPOT

In 1887 the GNR purchased the Boston sleeper works of Messrs. Bethal, partly, possibly, as an act of appeasement towards Bostonians for the move of the company's main locomotive workshops to Doncaster. After some 16 years, Bethal's works were obviously no longer adequate because on 8th August 1903, the GN initiated a £14,150 project, using company employees, to build a new sleeper depot at Hall Hills, Boston.

Progress was rapid as, on Christmas Day 1903, the Engineer was able to report: "...the tank house has been built and tank fixed; the brickwork of the saw shed is completed and roof principles fixed. Brickwork for the offices is nearly completed, the derrick road has been laid in and the derrick engine and boiler house built. All sidings have been laid and the tramways are in hand..." The depot, which had a capacity for 470,000 sleepers, opened on 15th February 1904 and the reference to tramways will indicate that internal trackage at the works was considerable, and worthy of the stationing of a shunting engine there.

Whether the practice of 'permanently' allocating a shunter to Hall Hills was adopted at the outset is not known, but certainly, at some time, a small engine shed was built within the works complex, to house the locomotive sub-shedded from the main Boston depot. If the shed was not erected as part of the initial job, then perhaps it appeared towards the end of 1911, when electric lighting was installed and various ancillary building works were undertaken. Study of available photographs leads the authors to the conclusion that the locomotive shed was a later addition, as its building style differs from that of the remainder of the works.

Brick-built, with a slated gable roof covering its single road, the little dead-end shed had the most rudimentary of facilities - water came from a hose pipe fed by the Works' 13,000 gallon tank and coal was taken from a small dump on the ground, by the shed entrance. Early denizens are unknown, but may possibly have been limited to only a single locomotive, Stirling-design Class J19 0-6-0T No.470A, which was in occupancy on the last day of the GN's existence, had been sent to Hall Hills on 19th December 1921. This veteran was finally withdrawn in April 1927, six months after it was superseded by the LNER's second 4-wheel Sentinel, which arrived at Hall Hills Depot in October 1926. For the next nearly 38 years Sentinel locomotives and Hall Hills were synonymous, with (except for visits to works of course, when another Sentinel would be temporarily drafted in), only two machines being stationed there, for 20 years and 18 years, respectively.

The first Sentinel initially bore no number, simply having the legend 'Boston' painted on its side, but the Class Y1/1 later had a range of three numbers while at Hall Hills, viz: April 1930 - 4801; September 1937 - 4991 and September 1946 - 8132. Shortly after becoming 8132 the Sentinel left Boston for a period of store at Doncaster, being replaced by Class Y3 Sentinel 8166 (formerly delivered in September 1930 as No.49). No.8166 became 68166 in August 1948, to be renumbered yet again in March 1953, when it was christened Departmental No.7.

In 1929, Boston Sleeper Depot turned out 23,484 sleepers and timbers creosoted, 190,752 sleepers chaired, and consumed 993,223 gallons of creosote oil in the process. Only one year later, creosote oil consumption reached 1,222,332 gallons, indicating a greater throughput and both records illustrate that the works shunter must have been kept quite busy. When one pauses to consider, it is surprising that Sentinels were ever used in such a fire-prone place as a sleeper depot, because the locomotives were infamous for spark-throwing. However, they were, of course, fitted with spark-arrestors which evidently worked until perhaps, 14th April 1959. On that day there was a serious fire at Hall Hills, which destroyed timber stocks, a pump house and creosote plant, and some parked wagons. The cause of the blaze is unknown, but it might well have been a spark thrown by the depot shunter. Anyway, some repairs were quickly effected and the Sentinel continued to serve Hall Hills until the sleeper depot closed in the Spring of 1964. No. 7 was officially withdrawn in May 1964, at the same time as her sister Y3, Departmental No.40, the last two LNER Sentinels to remain in service. However, ex-footplatemen from Boston main shed have stated that in BR days at least, Hall Hills locoshed was not used, with the Sentinel having to stand in the open: when the engine shed was closed is not apparent.

Demolition of the sleeper works did not follow closure and the whole complex, including the partly bricked-up locoshed, was still largely intact, but semi-derelict in late-1982.

The former Boston Hall Hills Sleeper Depot lies defunct on 30th September 1982. Even though stabling of a locomotive at the works had ceased some time before final closure in 1964, the former engine shed was still visible - below the tall chimney. *L.Perrin.*

Following closure of the shed at Hall Hills, the resident Sentinel used to stable at Boston main depot. On 13th July 1958 Departmental No.7 was at the rear of the shed. *A.R.Goult.*

COLWICK

Nowhere better than Colwick mirrors the one-time importance to Britain of its coal trade - the rise, pre-eminence and decline of the industry was matched by similar stages in the life of what was eventually, the largest of all GN sheds, serving naturally, the company's most extensive marshalling yards.

But, Colwick engine shed had a late beginning. Rails first came to the district in the mid-1840's, when the Midland Railway's route from Nottingham to Lincoln was opened. Then, on 15th July 1850, the Ambergate, Nottingham, Boston & Eastern Junction Railway completed its 22$^1/_2$ mile line from Grantham, to join the MR route into Nottingham. The point at which the lines met was Carlton Junction, in the Parish of Colwick, the hamlet of Colwick at that time consisting of but six houses and a couple of farms. By 1852, the Ambergate Company had built a warehouse and some sidings at Colwick, with merchandise being carted to and from Nottingham. Hardly surprisingly, the venture was not too economic, so the warehouse was demolished after only 4 years and the sidings were taken up. In 1858, however, the Ambergate Railway constructed its own route into Nottingham, terminating at its own station, which was complete with a small engine shed. Three years later came the GN's leasing of the company, which was to last until the Grouping.

On 28th October 1862, came the first glimmerings of Colwick's future, when the GN's Assistant Manager called attention to: "...a survey made in 1860, for a line which would be a continuation of the Grantham to Nottingham route, into the Derbyshire coalfield. There appears to be no probability of the Great Northern gaining access to these fields on fair terms through the Midland Company, so therefore should the company not seek its own access...?" In time, this led to the Derbyshire & Staffordshire Extension Act of July 1872, which in turn, led to creation of the various Colwick Junctions. They were opened on 20th May 1873, in readiness for the drive westwards, with first services, as far as Pinxton, commencing over Colwick West Junction on 23rd August 1875.

This was preceded, on 18th January 1875, by a Locomotive Engineer's report that first states the need for an engine shed at Colwick. (At that time, just prior to the Derbyshire lines opening, the GN was annually taking 440,000 tons of coal through Colwick, all from MR-served pits). Tenders were called, to be opened on 19th February 1875, with that of J.Parnell & Sons succeeding, with a price of £8,514. This covered a number of other works, with the locoshed element being £7,664 and only 10$^1/_2$ months later, on 11th January 1876, the Locomotive Engineer was able to report the shed as being "nearly ready". But, there had been a cost overrun, due to works not in the original contract, to the tune of no less than £3,200. The Board voted that £2,000 extra should immediately be advanced to Messrs. Parnell, in addition to the £7,055 already paid. The whole Colwick project was completed not long after and the GN then had sidings for 650 loaded and 500 empty wagons, and an engine shed, for 12 engines.

Colwick engine shed was built to the GN's standard design of the period, a dead-end brick building, scaling 165 ft x 65 ft and having two hipped roofs covering its four roads. At the depot's eastern side were offices, shops, etc., and beyond, a 45 ft turntable, 61,000 gallon water tank and a coal stage, equipped with a crane and canopy over the coaling road. Shed facilities were completed later in 1876 by arrival of a breakdown train having a standard Doncaster-built 8 ton hand crane. The coming of the shed and sidings created a need for staff housing, so on 29th September 1876 it was resolved that 24 cottages be erected, 12 each for Loco and Traffic staff. The firm of R.Stevenson tendered a price of £2,376 for 12 cottages, to be erected in 12 weeks and the Board accepted this on the proviso that the contractor build the second 12 under similar terms. Thus were created "Locomotive Terrace" and "Traffic Terrace", which flanked the rear of the engine shed.

All these facilities were not to be adequate for very long, with the Derbys & Staffs lines coming fully into operation in 1878. A year later the GN was hauling 914,000 tons of coal through its yard at Colwick, of which 540,000 tons came from pits served by the company's own rails. 1879 also saw the beginnings of the GN/LNWR Joint line, connecting Market Harborough with Grantham, Newark and Nottingham, and North Western engines appeared at Colwick, to start transporting away that company's own share of the coal traffic.

That LNW arrival has caused the authors a minor problem! It is known that the GN temporarily housed LNWR engines, pending completion of the North Western's own engine shed, an 8 road northlight structure, situated about half a mile south of the GN depot. A Colwick resident, railwayman and local historian, Harold H. Mather, has written that the GN put up a

Early pictures of Colwick are extremely rare, hence inclusion of this less than perfect, but nonetheless valuable print. In a view from the coaling stage, most of the "Big" shed is seen, together with "New" and the adjoining wagon shop, in the early years of the 20th century. Also visible is Colwick's 8 ton accident crane, which served from 1876 to around 1914. *Authors collection.*

A view across Colwick yard on 14th August 1932 shows the repair shop, and "Big" and "New" sheds, with their longitudinal smoke vents, which had replaced the individual flues along each roof ridge some years before. The vents and roofs were to see an increasing decrepitude, until BR renewed the lot in the early 1950s. *Authors' collection.*

temporary engine shed for the LNW's use, but the authors have found no trace of this in any archive they studied. Sadly, Mr. Mather died just prior to this history being compiled, so the authors were unable to take the matter of his sources any further. Suffice it to say that the GN did have the North Western's engines to contend with for a while, but how exactly this was done will probably remain unresolved.

Besides its 'guests', the GN had enough to grapple with regarding its own engines overcrowding Colwick shed. Burgeoning traffic was the cause and by 1881, with the first section of the Company's Leen Valley line under construction (opened in October, that year), yet more traffic was in prospect. So much so, that on 29th March 1881, Stirling produced a report for the Board, in which he asked for an extension to Colwick engine shed, to house a further 40 locomotives, with a repair shop, all requisite sidings and a coke (!) stage; he estimated the entire job would cost £20,220. Tenders were duly invited and the firm of E. Wood won the contract to build the engine shed extension and repair shop, with a bid of £11,310. Three months later, on 28th June, Stirling gave details of the costs of equipment to be supplied for the repair shop, as follows:

Steam engine, boiler, shafting and pulleys: £400
25-ton hand powered travelling crane for lifting locomotives - complete: £600

Stirling opined that these two items should be made in the company's own workshops, with the machine tools detailed next, coming from outside suppliers:

Wheel lathe: £550
14 inch lathe for pistons: £205
6½ inch lathe: £110
Radial driller: £90
Planing machine: £140
Burrows Patent screwing machine: £100
Smiths Fan for blowing fires: £20 *Total: £1,215*

As was usual for those days, construction was rapid and the soon to be aptly named "Big" shed opened in June 1882, the first depot then being called the "Old" shed. The new building was big! Measuring 275 ft x 115 ft it had a northlight roof, to the new GN standard, (launched a month previously at Leicester Belgrave Road shed), that covered 8 roads. It was connected to the Old shed by the 2 road repair shop, that could accommodate four engines under its lofty hipped roof, and itself scaled 275 ft x 40 ft. The original turntable and water tank were retained, but a larger (100 ft x 45 ft) coal stage was built at the top end of the yard, where it could serve engines going to either shed. While talking about Belgrave Road above, that depot became a sub-shed of Colwick about 1916, joining earlier sub-sheds at Derby Friargate (from 1878), Pinxton (1876), Nottingham, London

Three GNR employees are captured for posterity by an Edwardian photographer, in this view of the rear of Colwick shed, taken from the railway village. The smoke vents and roof pitches of the Old shed are just visible, as are parts of the roofs over the Big shed and the repair shop. Pictures from this period tend to present a vista of well-tended neatness, but one wonders at what cost in human terms. Hindsight tells us that those three proudly posing men would have led lives that were dirty, hard and sometimes even dangerous, for precious little reward.

The "Old" shed at Colwick is seen here around 1910, when it still had doors and the hipped roofs with their apex skylights still sported the original lofty smoke vents. Note how the row of vents on the far right is taller, so as not to catch the lee of the workshop's roof. *Authors' collection.*

Road (Low Level) (1876), and Stafford Common (for part of 1881, LNWR shed thereafter). Lastly, there was the engine stabling/servicing point at Ilkeston (1891).

Just prior to the Big shed's construction, the GN had a problem with Colwick's water arrangements. To obtain water for the first depot, the company had constructed a weir in the adjacent Carlton Beck, creating a reservoir from which supplies could be drawn. In late 1880, early 1881, the weir caused flooding of the surrounding area, which damaged a Nottingham Corporation sewage works, crops and field drains. The Corporation successfully sought damages so, to prevent any repeat of the incident, the GN Board instructed that a borehole be sunk within the confines of the shed. The work was probably carried out coincident with building of the Big shed and when completed, the well had struck good quality water at 181 ft; the shaft was 11 ft in diameter and the bore pipe itself was 14 inches. This well, immediately east of the Old shed, was supplemented in later years by a second bore and served until closure of the depot, even supplying domestic users in the railway 'village', until local health inspectors made mains connections mandatory. Anyway, the well enabled the company to dismantle the weir and then to have the last laugh, when on 2nd June 1896, Nottingham Corporation sought permission to route a water main through the GN's premises at Colwick, to serve the County Asylum. The GN Board (somewhat gleefully it may be imagined) agreed, in return for an annual rental of £75 and a connection to that main!

With its locomotive facilities suitably enhanced, the GN next turned its attention to employee amenities. On 13th June 1884, tenders were opened for construction of a clubhouse for the staff. Messrs. Partington won the contract with a bid of £1,256-19-2d, but when completed, the clubhouse finally cost £1,803-13-3d. The reason for the cost overrun is not known, but the club certainly provided good facilities, with the normal recreation, smoking and reading rooms and eventually sporting four 25 yard indoor, and one 50 yard outdoor rifle ranges. The indoor ranges were provided by a quadrangle of wooden coach bodies, open inside. Normally, some 70-80 of the men were members of the rifle club at any time and their preoccupation with shooting doubtless stood them in good stead when many of them were called to the colours in World War One. Eventually, the club became the Colwick branch of the Railway Institute and still today, the site of the quadrangle of coaches is occupied by the British Rail Staff Association clubhouse.

Returning to January 1884, a further six goods sidings were authorised for Colwick yard which, with site preparation, were estimated to cost no less than £13,000. The money was well spent though, because coal traffic continued to increase by leaps and bounds, so that by 1887, one and a half million tons were passing through the yard each year, of which 30% was hauled away by the LNWR. Such traffic caused another expansion of the yard, between April 1888 and October 1889. The cost of that particular operation has not been ascertained, but it must have been considerable, because the GN had to widen the yard to accommodate the new sidings and that involved land purhcases. Then, within 2 years, yet another widening scheme was carried through, being completed in November 1891.

Sure enough, the booming coal carryings required more and more engines to move it, so that in July 1892, Stirling reported to the Board that of the 100 locomotives stationed at

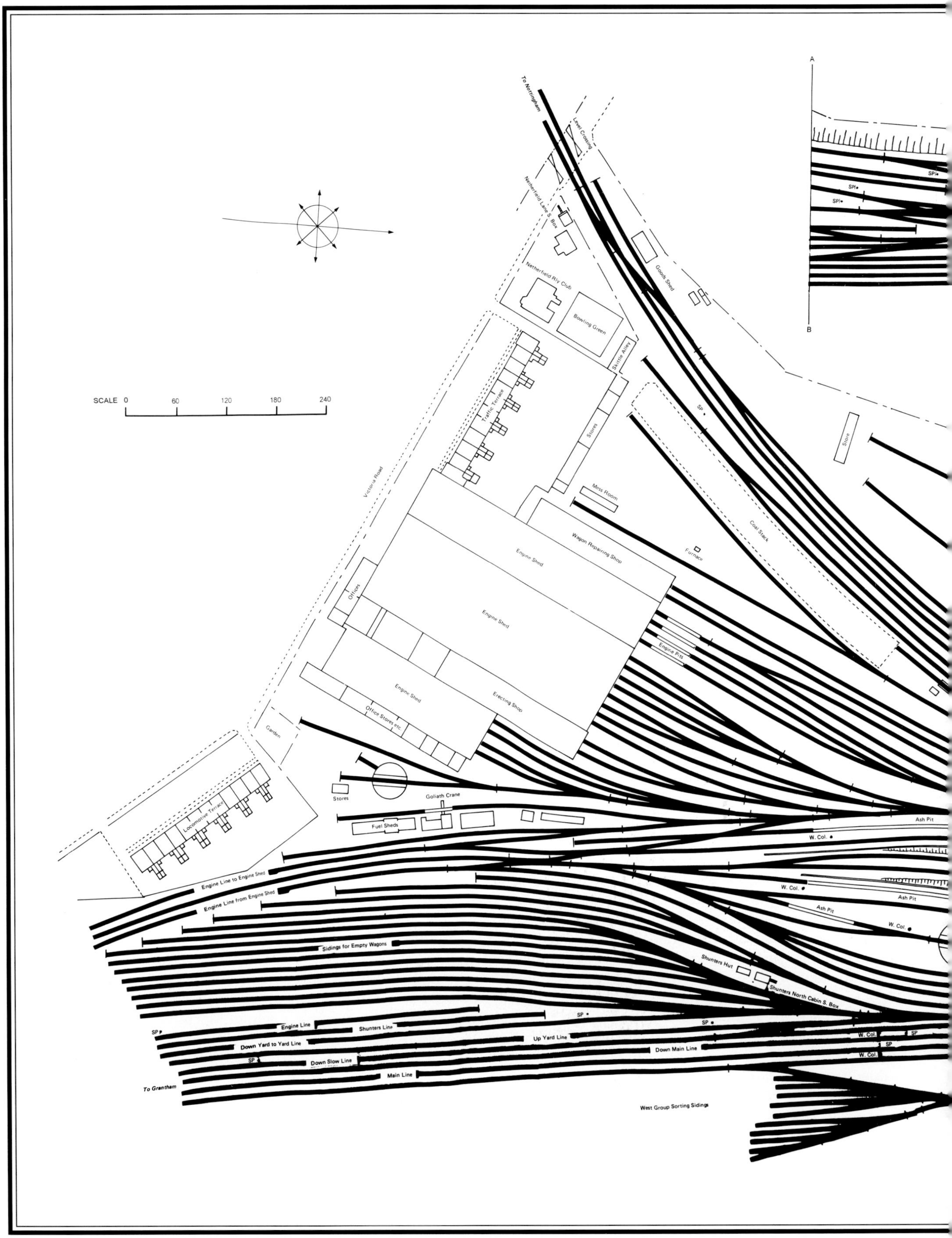
SCALE 0 60 120 180 240
To Nottingham
Level Crossing
Netherfield Lane S. Box
Netherfield Rly Club
Bowling Green
Goods Shed
Skittle Alley
Traffic Terrace
Stores
Victoria Road
Mess Room
Wagon Repairing Shop
Furnace
Coal Stack
Store
Engine Shed
Offices
Engine Pits
Engine Shed
Erecting Shop
Office Stores etc.
Garden
Locomotive Terrace
Stores
Goliath Crane
Fuel Sheds
Ash Pit
W. Col.
Engine Line to Engine Shed
Engine Line from Engine Shed
Ash Pit
Sidings for Empty Wagons
Shunters Hut
Shunters North Cabin S. Box
SP
Engine Line
Shunters Line
Down Yard to Yard Line
Up Yard Line
Down Slow Line
Down Main Line
Main Line
To Grantham
West Group Sorting Sidings
A
B
SPl

COLWICK 1911

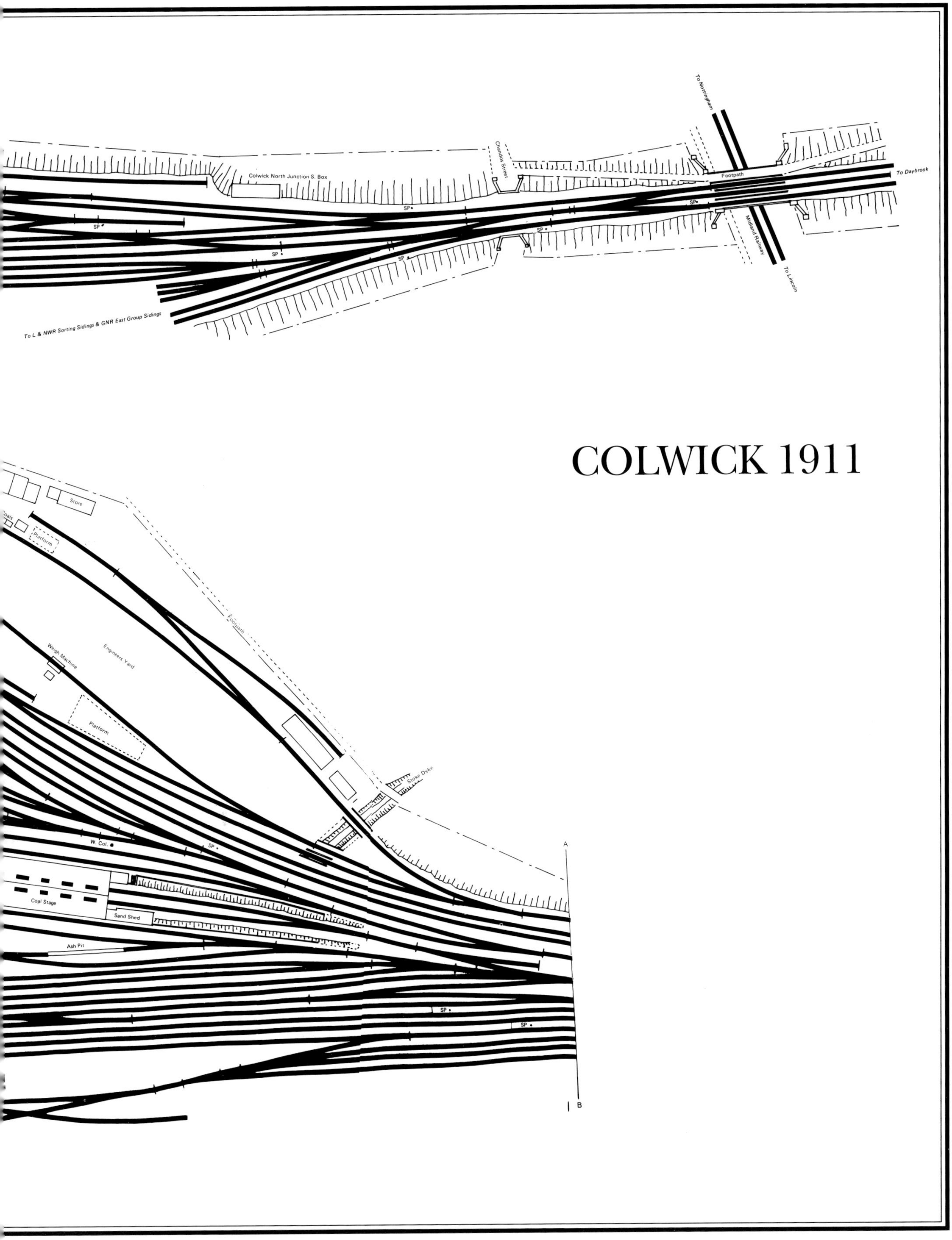

The north side of Colwick 'New' shed yard in 1928 with a host of GN types filling the stabling roads. Amongst them are J52 1206, R1 3131, J6 3573 and C12 4517. Notice that the R1 heads a line of five sister engines. *Authors collection.*

Colwick, "40 have to stable outside". He requested an extension of the depot, plus construction of a small wagon shop to hold 20 wagons, with siding space for another 100 outside. Stirling was given the go-ahead to produce plans for his proposals, which he duly presented to the Board on 3rd November 1892. The plans showed: "...how the shed may be extended and, if necessary, a further shed be built by diverting Netherfield Lane. This, however, would require purchase of 25 acres of land between the engine shed and the Nottingham Branch, and closure of a level crossing, for which Parliamentary Powers would be required. Replacement by a bridge would cost £5,000...". Stirling was asked to report further on the matter, but not until 22nd June 1896 does the subject come up again. On that day, Ivatt displayed a plan for the extension of Colwick shed, to provide additional cover for 36 engines, together with the wagon shop and sidings mentioned four years previously. Estimated costs were broken down as: shed expansion - £19,630; wagon shop - £1,450; sidings - £760; total: £21,840. The costs were approved by the Board, tenders were invited, Messrs. Dennett & Ingle's very precise figure of £15,481-1-10½d. secured them the contract and work commenced straightaway.

By June 1897, Ivatt was able to present this brief report on the work at Colwick: "...fair progress has been made during the past month, considering the very wet weather. The whole of the brickwork of the south and west walls of the engine shed and offices is up to about 8 ft above rail level...". Work proceeded well during that summer and what finally materialised, to be brought into use late in 1897, was not quite as Stirling had envisaged. First, the "Old" and "Big" sheds were extended at the rear, by 50 ft and 55 ft, thereby making them 215 ft and 330 ft long, respectively. The repair shop sandwiched between was also extended to 330 ft, with the extra space being utilised to enlarge the smithy and fitter's shop. In this way, additional covered shed room was provided for 12 of the 36 engines mentioned by Ivatt, with the remaining 24 not being housed in "a further (separate) shed" as suggested by Stirling, but in a four road extension to the western side of the Big shed. The extension, christened the "New" shed, measured 330 ft x 63 ft and had a northlight roof, to the same pattern as its neighbour. In the loco yard, a second 100 ft x 45 ft crane-equipped coal stage was installed, to the north west of that provided with the Big shed, but still the Old shed's turntable and water tank were not enhanced in any way. Inside the depot, all roads now had 315 ft pits, but unlike the two earlier structures, the New shed also had 50 ft pits in each of its 4 roads, just outside its portals; the locomotive repair shop's 145 ft pits were not extended, however. Lastly, adjoining the west side of New shed and occasioning the demolition of No.12 Traffic Terrace, came the 210 ft x 39 ft two road wagon shop, which also featured a continuation of the northlight roof, but devoid of smoke vents of course. In time, wagon repairs carried out by the shop's staff, albeit of a light nature, reached the amazing proportions of 350 a week!

During construction of the latest shed extension, 1896/7, further sidings were laid in the marshalling yard. Also, on 22nd February 1897, at a Way & Works Committee meeting, Ivatt asked that the company build some houses for the locomen, who had presented a petition to the engineer, describing the "great scarcity" of accommodation in the district. The Committee asked the company's surveyor: "...to investigate if anything can be done to encourage the building of houses...". Seems the company were reluctant to spend money on house building, but while the outcome of the surveyor's "investigations" is not clear, more houses were added to the railway village, in several phases.

During March 1898, it seems Messrs. Dennett & Ingle carried out "repairs" at Colwick shed. What was the nature of those repairs is not stated in the archive, but their cost to the GNR was £437-8-5d. However, 1899 was a year of much greater expense to the company, after an initial 3rd January request for £1,795, for a 15 ton steam breakdown crane, was turned down. Two days later, Ivatt pointed out that Colwick's locomotive yard, coaling and turning facilities were inadequate and causing delays in the general "dealing with locomotives". He asked for additional sidings to be laid in the loco yard, a large double-sided ramp coaler to replace the two stages and a second turntable, of 55 ft diameter. Estimated costs of £17,000 were approved on 6th July 1899 and the large undertaking was quickly put in hand.

Construction naturally had to go hand-in-hand with the continued operation of the locoshed, so even by December 1900, Ivatt could not quite report completion. At that time, the engineer said: "...The new coal stage is nearly finished and ready for roofing. The loco yard west of the stage is complete and in use; turntable foundations (to the east of the stage - *Authors*) are ready for the table to be fixed...". The job was finally finished early in 1901 and immediately the benefits were felt, with greatly increased turnround of engines and consequent reduction in delays to trains.

The Colwick breakdown train stands ready for business in its usual stabling position on the north side of the shed yard in about 1910. One of the depot's numerous L1 0-8-2T's, no.139, stands at its head. In the left background can be seen the wagon shop alongside the engine shed. The right background reveals the tops of a variety of locomotives, coaled and stored for the weekend, in the sidings alongside the coal stack near Netherfield Lane signal box. *Authors collection.*

It is worth mentioning the ramp coaler requested by Ivatt, which followed the pattern laid down some years before, at Ardsley. Measuring 175 ft x 55 ft overall, the structure had stone walls to the elevated rail level, with brick above, to the twin pitched roofs. Two sets of rails passed through the elevated coaling floor, each of which could hold sixteen 20 ton wagons. Six coal tips were provided, three per side, served by half ton trollies, which had a theoretical maximum throughput of 900 to 1,000 tons per day. Such a figure was never even closely approached, with the shed's all-time maximum consumption of coal being of the order of 350-400 tons daily, in the period around the First World War. Colwick's coal supplies incidentally, all came from local pits, such as Annesley, in the Leen Valley - except when the renowned "Raleigh Specials" were run. Named after the famous Nottingham bicycle manufactory, the specials were run for the Raleigh Company's staff, usually in May, often during the Whitsun Holiday, but always on a Saturday. By LNER days there were as many as ten trains, running as far as London or Blackpool. Colwick provided the locomotives for these workings, which were looked upon as something of a prestige job, and on those occasions only, some 10 wagons of Yorkshire coal were imported to Colwick, presumably to ensure optimum performance from the specially-prepared engines.

The latest improvements came just in time, as, coincident with work at the engine shed, the GN was making its largest and, as it happened, last expansion to Colwick marshalling yards. No fewer than 29 new sidings, for 1100 vehicles, were laid in during 1900, the culmination of a quarter of a century of growth of a facility that made a large contribution to the company's prosperity. In their final guise then, Colwick yards contained 68 Up sidings and 67 Down, capable of holding 6000 wagons. Further growth was not required and as such, the yards served the GNR, LNER and BR, until the process of winding down began, in 1958.

Back at the loco depot, the Big shed's northlight roof was already giving trouble and on 11th April 1902, a contract was let to Messrs. Mellowes who, with assistance from GN employees, were to carry out repair work. It would seem that once work commenced, the problem was found to be much more serious than originally realised, because for a job estimated to cost-in at £1,200, when finally completed, on 23rd December 1902, the GN ended up forking out £4,399! What caused such a dramatic increase is not clear, but the authors suspect that necessary repair work also had to be carried out on the hipped roofs of the Old shed.

Around the mid-1900's, an oil store was added to the depot, being built at the rear, adjoining the timekeeper's office. It was instigated by the then Superintendent, a Mr. Wilson, without Head Office approval - that came only after the building was completed! Oil was stored in 8,000 gallon overhead tanks and distributed to the locomen, whose lamps and oil bottles were kept neatly racked and individually labelled, at one end of the store. Service Locomotive 'H' was permanently placed at the back of the Big shed, on No.6 road, to supply steam and vacuum to the oil store - the latter facility being used to draw fresh oil supplies into the storage tanks. The oil store sufficed until replaced by the LNER during its 1930's modernisation progamme, at which time the room became a fitter's shop.

Gresley took over as Locomotive Engineer and in March 1912, started on the next phase of improvements to Colwick engine shed. At that time, Gresley noted the nature of the depot's traffic resulted in pooling of locomotives to a much greater extent than anywhere else on the company's system. Consequently, time taken for boiler washing-out was proving a limiting factor and he had studied the use of hot water for boiler washing and concluded that its use at Colwick would be of great benefit. Gresley then instanced the Economical Boiler Washing Company's products and recommended a unit be purchased

With the legend "GNR" still faintly visible on their tanks shortly after Grouping, venerable Stirling 0-6-0ST "twins" Nos. 681 and 689 rest between duties on the third road of Colwick New shed. The nearer engine was withdrawn in 1924, aged 42 years and never receiving its designated LNER number 3681. 689 however was rebuilt in 1927 and served its new owners until 1934. *W.L.Good cty W.T.Stubbs.*

for Colwick, at a cost of £2,415. This was approved and the apparatus was installed in the following October. To accommodate it, the rear of the wagon shop was used, reducing its length to 165 ft; to compensate, a 160 ft x 45 ft wing building was taken out at a right-angle to the wagon shop, to give greatly enhanced stores and office space. This wing utilised an existing loco stores block and in the process encroached slightly upon the rear gardens of Traffic Terrace. The wisdom of the loco engineer's scheme very quickly became apparent, with the following improvements in locomotive boiler washing being shown each week:

Cold Water
Cooling down: 6 hours
Washing out: 2 hours
Raising steam: 2 hours *Total:* 10 hours.
Hot Water
Blowing off and washing out: 2 hours
Raising steam: 1hour *Total:* 3 hours.
Time saved by using hot water: 7 hours per engine.
Average number of engines washed out, per day: 25
Water lost when washed out with cold water:1,670 gallons approx.
Water lost when washed out with hot water: 743 gallons approx
Total saving of: 927 gallons approx. per engine

Gresley soon followed this up when, in August 1912, he advocated provision of a gas producer plant. His report and recommendations were presented thus: "...the Suction Gas Plant (as Gresley called it) will be fuelled on char. At Colwick engine shed, which is the largest on the line, there are 240 engines, that produce 25 tons of smokebox ash per week. There are also two stationary boilers that supply steam for the pumps and a steam engine which drives the machines in the repair shop. The annual consumption of coal by the two stationary boilers is 980 tons. The whole of the shed and loco yard, including the coal stage, is lighted by gas obtained from Nottingham Corporation, at a cost of £830 per annum. If we had a gas producer plant which collects gas from char, we could use this to drive a gas engine and dynamos and light everything electrically. I consider we need a 120 bhp engine and an electric generator of 80 kW capacity, which will require the consumption of smokebox ashes at 2 lbs per bhp per hour, which at full load will amount to 12 tons per week. The Campbell Gas Engine Company, of Halifax, have quoted for a plant, total cost £3,300; the average saving of coal and gas, over the present system would be something of the order of £535 per year..." Purchase was finally approved on 6th December 1912, with the installation being completed in 1914. One of the first benefits was felt in the erecting shop, where a 33 horsepower motor took over the line-shaft drive of all the machine tools; the 25 ton engine hoist remained hand-operated though, to be replaced in later years by a 36 ton Royce electric overhead crane. The steam engine that drove the plant was removed, but its frame was so built-in that it lasted the life of the shed. The line shafting too continued to serve for all the depot's existence, except in the Blacksmiths shop, where the forges were provided with electric blowers from the start; the line shafting pulley that previously drove the Smiths fan remained until closure. In the blacksmiths shop incidentally, six hearths and anvils had been installed initially, together with a steam hammer and shearing/punching machine; these were still there when the shed was demolished, though at that time, only one hearth was in use.

A year after the suction gas plant was installed, a second gas engine was fitted at a cost of £56; the plant's make-up and capabilities were then:

Engine	No.1	No.2
Horsepower	100	160
Running speed (r.p.m)	300	260
Associated dynamo rating	75 kW	100 kW
Volts:	230	220
Amperes:	350	460
Associated electrical pump h.p	11-12	20
Operating speed (r.p.m.)	1,560	1,450
Gallons lifted per minute:	350	500
Head (inches):	50	50

Despite being superseded by submersible electric pumps, the steam pumps remained in situ to the end and saw very occasional use still. When called upon to substitute for their replacements, the steam pumps obtained steam from a locomotive parked in the stores siding, with a pipe coupled to the vacuum brake ejector feed. After closure of Colwick shed, the steam pumps were taken to the Industrial Museum at Wollaton Hall, Nottingham, where they may be viewed today, one of the few tangible remains of Colwick depot.

Around the time the suction gas plant was being installed, Colwick's ancient breakdown crane was replaced by the 15 ton steam crane from Peterborough. When not in use, the crane and its attendant vans were, in later years at least, stabled in the Old shed. It must be considered unusual that such an important depot as Colwick, the 'home' of a District Locomotive Superintendent, should have to wait so long for modern breakdown facilities, particularly as there was so much call upon them *(see section on Breakdown Cranes and Trains)*.

In 1916, the District Loco Superintendent of the time, one Charles Laverick, presided over the opening of a new classroom for the locomens' Mutual Improvement classes; Mr. Laverick had been instrumental in setting up M.I. classes at Colwick in the first place, in 1904. Unusually for such an occasion, the 1916 opening was not attended by Gresley - it is said that he and Laverick did not quite see eye-to-eye on a number of matters. (It had certainly been the intention for the Locomotive Engineer to open the new classroom, as 40 years later, in the loft of the Joiners Shop, an engraved copper plate was discovered, bearing the legend: "This room was opened by H.N.Gresley, September 1916"). This speaks volumes for the power that District Loco Superintendents wielded - one who served under Laverick describes him as a "benevolent despot!" It also shows that Gresley had his weaknesses and also his strengths, in allowing so influential a person as Charles Laverick to maintain his position and no doubt be difficult to handle in the process. Incidentally, the M.I. classroom had a slightly premature end, when in the early 1960's, O4 No.63707, manoeuvring from the ashpits, failed to stop and pushed some wagons into the classroom and old callers-up room! Destruction was not complete, but the classroom saw little further use.

The final GN-authorised improvement came on 6th April 1922, when expenditure of £1,137 was approved for extending ashpit facilities. By 31st December, the last day of the GN, it was recorded that concrete blocks for the job were being made on site, so it was left to the LNER to complete the work, during the first quarter of 1923. After that, it was not long before the new owners further increased Colwick's facilities when, in 1925, a wheeldrop was added. It was situated at the rear of No.1 road in the Old shed and was powered by a hydraulic pump situated in the machine shop, driven from the line shafting. The wheel drop provided much needed relief to the depot's very heavily used shearlegs. Apart from being a less efficient means of dropping wheels from locomotives, that shearlegs had a further disadvantage in that it was powered by a gas engine that drew its fuel from the Corporation mains. Thus, when involved in making a big lift, the shearlegs took the lion's share of gas, and neighbourhood housewives made many a complaint about being unable to cook lunch! Even though mains electricity was brought to the shed in the late 1920's, by way of a 440 volt three-core cable, taken under the Nottingham-Grantham line, the shearlegs remained gas-operated to the end.

It is now appropriate perhaps, to reflect upon the legion of locomotives that inhabited Colwick and the men who served them. Predominantly a mineral engine shed, Colwick's first tenants would have been surviving Sturrock, and the newer Stirling 0-6-0 and 0-4-2. Such types were steadily increased to meet traffic needs and as the depot was expanded in size, and remained the prime source of power for the first quarter of a century of Colwick's operation. Variety was provided from the start of the 20th century and one of the most famous new classes to be stationed at the shed was the L1 0-8-2T, known in the district as the "Baltics". The first 20 of the class arrived in 1905/6 and following the type's unsuitability for London's suburban workings, all 41 were at Colwick by early 1914. They were used on coal trains from the Erewash and Leen Valleys and Ilkeston, to Colwick Yard, and from there to Peterborough - the latter a round trip of nearly 100 miles. The class also undertook some passenger duties - mainly workmens' trains or, as they were known locally, "Paddy's Mails". Because of the L1's height, No.4 road in the New shed had the smoke troughs specially raised and 14 of the 0-8-2T could be stabled on that road, up to the water column. After the Grouping, L1 (LNER Class R1) were given Colwick-Annesley-Newstead-Colwick workings that could take over 12 hours to complete. Withdrawal of the big tanks commenced in 1927, to be completed in 1934.

The L1 was a tank engine version of Ivatt's "Long Tom" 0-8-0 of Class K1 (LNER Q1 and Q2) and these too were resident at Colwick for many years. First arrivals were in 1902, with the allocation reaching 22 by 1912 and by the mid-1920's many of the class were operating from the shed. They were used on local trips and duties over the main line to Peterborough, on which they handled 60 wagon trains. Withdrawals saw the class disappear from Colwick in the early 1930's, following a mass influx of Robinson designed O4 2-8-0, from 1924. The O4 soon became synonymous with Colwick, with nearly 50 being allocated by the end of 1939. Their numbers dwindled after the Second World War, but Robinson's reliable machines were to be seen at Colwick until 1966. They outlasted their sister GN 2-8-0's of classes O1 and O2, which came in 1914 and 1921 respectively. There were never many O1 on the roster, which saw them being used on 80 wagon goods trains to New England; after 1923, the class also took its turn on services to Woodford GC and March GE. O2 established themselves to the tune of over 40 being stationed at Colwick in 1944, but with the war's end, they started to move away, and all had gone by nationalisation. The war brought another class that was to become indelibly linked with Colwick, in the minds of all those 1950's shed-bashers - the WD 2-8-0. Mr. Riddles "Austerities" had been seen at the shed from the latter war period - along with USATC S160 2-8-0 for a while

8-COUPLED RESIDENTS AND VISITORS IN LNER DAYS.

(top) GNR 'Long Tom', LNER class Q2 no.3416, stands on No.1 road of the 'New shed' in May 1932.These engines were the prime motive power for the heavy coal train hauls to New England yards until the Robinson designed O4's superseded them in the early 1930's. 3416 was one of the last Q2's, hanging on at Colwick until 1935. The 'party wall' division between the Big and New sheds can be seen above the locomotive cab. *W.L.Good cty W.T.Stubbs.*

(centre) The Robinson 2-8-0's were long time residents of Colwick - 42 years. On the 13th March 1938, 5005 was one of nearly fifty such engines allocated to the shed. *W.L.Good cty W.T.Stubbs.*

(left) After the LMS had closed the former LNWR shed at Netherfield & Colwick in 1932, engines from that company were regular visitors to the LNER shed. Here, in June 1939, Stanier 8F 8102, with another of its ilk behind, rests on the Big shed yard, coaled and ready to return to its home district with another load of Notts coal. *W.Potter.*

- and the LNER bought so many 'de-mobbed' WD's (Class O7) that by 1947, nearly 50 were working from Colwick alone, a quantity that would persist into the mid 1960's.

Regarding the smaller goods engines, we must go back to the first few years of the 20th century, when some of the short-lived Baldwin Moguls were working from the shed; all had gone back to the West Riding though, by 1905. Ivatt's 0-6-0's were appearing in numbers at the same time, with J5 Nos. 165, 177, 180 and 192 all going to Colwick, new, in 1900. By Grouping 103 0-6-0's were allocated, 28 of them being Stirling engines, of classes J4 and J9; the remaining 75 were split between J5 (26), J21 (5) and J22 (44). This multitude of 0-6-0's saw use mainly on coal trains from the pits to Colwick Yard and on local passenger services. Some ran through to Peterborough, while J22 (LNER J6) did venture to London, returning on empties. J6 numbers dwindled to 16 by nationalisation, reducing to seven, by the early 1960's. The first series of J22 (LNER J5) - twenty engines, all ended up at Colwick by the latter part of World War Two; some passenger work was done, usually during the summertime, with a favourite working being the 7.30 p.m. Nottingham-Pinxton, returning on goods. The second series of J21 (LNER J2) were also used a great deal on Colwick's passenger duties, often being outstationed at the subsheds - Leicester was a common home for them. Strangely, the popular ex-GC J11 were never present at Colwick in any numbers - only one being allocated through the latter 1930's and 1940's, following a 1932-5 stint by a brace of J10; not until the late 1950's did a few more J11 arrive, to stay for a couple of years. J39 were also remarkably thin on the ground at first, with only No.2976 being on the roster in March 1933; numbers increased though, until the peak of about 25 was reached, in the early 1950's, falling to half that number before the end of that decade.

Passenger engines were probably not allocated to Colwick in any quantity until Nottingham London Road (Low Level) shed closed, around 1906. Earlier, however, a variation had been provided by MSLR Class D7 4-4-0 No.708, which was subshedded at Colwick, from Neepsend. 708 assisted on the Sheffield-Nottingham service, via the GN's Leen Valley route, until the MSL's London Extension opened, whence the Manchester company's presence at Colwick was ended.

On closure of Nottingham London Road depot, Ivatt's 4-4-0 classes descended on Colwick in some numbers, accompanied by surviving 2-4-0 classes. The 4-4-0 remained the major source of power into LNER days, with 8 D1 and 13 D3 being present at Grouping. These types were long stayers, with D2 (ex-GN D1) 62172 the last survivor of its class, being withdrawn in June 1951. D3 Nos. 4363 and 4365 were resident at Colwick for 24 and 26 years respectively, terms that were exceeded however, by sister 4353 (GN 1353) which arrived in 1905 and departed in 1936. During their time at the shed, Ivatt's 4-4-0's were used on Derby, Leicester, Grantham and Boston trains, and during the summer, to the East Coast resorts: consequently some were usually resident at the subsheds.

The 4-4-0's were joined in 1913 by 6 of Gresley's H2/3 Moguls (LNER K1/2), a figure that remained more or less constant until just before BR times, when 15 K2 were allocated. Their duties took them at first on braked goods trains to Manchester and Liverpool. They also ran over the lines to Derby, Burton-on-Trent (particularly on the beer trains), and Stafford. The increased numbers in the late 1940's was due to Manchester traffic being diverted over the North Stafford route to Uttoxeter and Macclesfield, owing to tunnel rebuilding works on the GC route. Some still survived into 1960, in use mainly on Colwick's local goods and summertime East Coast passenger turns; the last three were placed in store in October 1960, while 61759 was in use at that time as the depot's stationary boiler. Of Gresley's other 2-6-0, the K3 were latecomers to Colwick, arriving about 1937 and reaching about ten in number by BR times. Their duties were more or less the same as the K2, even down to 61943 replacing 61759 on stationary boiler duties in September 1962.

The GN's famous Atlantics also served at Colwick for a short time in the late 1930's, mainly seeing use on Grantham passenger workings. The C1 had been preceded by ex-GC C4 4-4-2, when 5360 and 6092 came in 1936. During the war years there were usually half a dozen allocated, but they were used mostly on GC line duties. The Atlantics worked alongside B17 4-6-0, of which a few had appeared in the early 1930's. The "Sandringhams" and "Footballers" stayed until about 1950, by which time Thompson's B1 were seeing much use at Colwick, also replacing the depot's C4's, 4-4-0, 2-6-0 and 0-6-0 on many local passenger duties, and especially on the summertime seaside extras. One of the shed's 'crack' B1's was 61188, and in 1953 she was loaned by Colwick to the Southern Region, together with sister 61192, to cover the emergency withdrawal of 'Merchant Navy' Pacifics. By 1961 over 20 B1 were stationed at Colwick, with 16 being among the last LNER types to leave the depot.

On the tank engine side, L1 have already been mentioned, with the next largest numbers being the various classes of Stirling and Ivatt 0-6-0ST used on Colwick's many shunting duties. Even so, given the shed's workload, relatively few shunting tanks were used - only 19-20 being allocated for example. This is presumably due to the fact that the major traffic, coal, was handled in trainloads that required little sorting; empties almost certainly occupied the shunters most, in making sure the many private owner wagons were sent back to their respective pits. Unlike a lot of ex-GN depots, Colwick retained its J52's (and J50's) until quite late in the day. Only by the late 1950's had the dwindling number of shunting turns been taken over by ex-GE J67/9 and J94's, though even then, a few J50 remained. Some 0-4-4 tanks were allocated to Colwick in early times, for local passenger duties, being joined by C2 4-4-2T in the period just before the First World War. The latter class saw much use on the Nottingham Suburban Railway, among other duties, with gradual replacement by GC A5 4-6-2T, during the 1939-45 war. N1 and N5 0-6-2T were also 1930's imports, joined in early BR days by N2 and N7. Only the N5 had any real measure of success, seeing use on local passengers and shunting - one of the latter duties being resident pilot at Burton, sud-shedded at the former MR shed there, into BR times. Greater success attended the 1955 allocation of Thompson's L1 2-6-4T to Colwick. The enginemen gave the class one of the best - if not the best - reception it gained from any depot and was almost immediately given prestige jobs like the 'Bogie' link to Derby, Grantham and Pinxton and taking over the lion's share of Nottingham-Leicester workings from J5/6. By the beginning of the 1960's, nearly 30 L1 were working from Colwick, but all were to be withdrawn by the end of 1962, after a gloomy period of cannibalisation, to keep as many of the class in action as possible.

The years after the Grouping saw other companies' engines come to Colwick. Some have already been discussed above, but a few more deserve a mention, to complete Colwick's cosmopolitan locomotive history. Early strangers were ex-NER J72 0-6-0T that took part in 1924 shunting engine coal consumption tests carried out by the LNER; but ex-GN 0-6-0ST

O4 class 6249 received attention under the shearlegs adjacent to the Old shed, about 1937. The shearlegs was powered by a gas engine that drew its fuel from the domestic mains and there is many a story from the railway village of Sunday roasts being spoiled because of the need for Colwick's fitters to carry out an urgent weekend "lift"! *W.Potter.*

remained in use at Colwick Yard, evidence presumably, that the interlopers did not prove so superior as to merit their replacing the 'home grown' product. Next, comes a major class, in the magnificent GC B8 4-6-0, which was used on fast goods to Manchester and Hull and on seasonal excursion passenger trains; normally six were allocated, between the years 1926 and 1942. An earlier and even stranger "regular" on the Hull trains for a few years was ex-NER B13 4-6-0 No.746. She was joined at Colwick in 1928, by some ex-GC D9 4-4-0, which came to work their former owner's line services from Nottingham, but did see use on ex-GN route workings to Grantham, Derby and Stafford. The latter two towns also saw ex-GE 2-4-0 of Class E4, during 1925, when 7447 and 7450 spent some time at Derby subshed. Lastly, comes the handsome 4-4-4T of LNER Class H2, bequeathed by London Transport in 1937, when all its workings north of Rickmansworth were taken over by the LNER. All seven of the Kerr Stuart locomotives came to Colwick around 1942, but were not liked, due to reputedly poor steaming capabilities. The necessities of wartime ensured the 4-4-4T's retention on light duties, but all had been withdrawn by 1947.

Moving to the men stationed at Colwick, the first reliable record of numbers working there comes from 1918, when an article in *The Railway Gazette* stated that about 900-1000 were employed in all grades. Apart from footplate staff, other work areas included machine and erecting shops, smithy, fitting shop, coppersmiths' and tin shop, joinery and wagon repair shop. The 30 or so clerical jobs covered typists, telegraphists and timekeepers, in addition to normal clerks. Footplate staff must have numbered nearly 800 and at that time they were covering the shed's basic 1037 weekly turns (907 ordinary and 130 relief).

J2 no.5018, minus its middle set of wheels, and J39 no.4988 await attention in the yard on the south side of the shed in September 1949. Behind stand the water tower, the rebuilt 'Old' shed and the lofty repair shop. *A.R.Goult.*

An unusual denizen of Colwick was the Class H2 4-4-4T. Ceded to the LNER by London Transport, the entire class of eight engines came to the shed in 1942. Reputedly unpopular with the footplatemen, the requirements of WW2 kept the engines in employment, albeit on light duties, but as soon as they could be done away with, they were. The class became extinct soon after this 12th July 1947 photograph was taken. *H.C.Casserley.*

More often than not though, these were increased to 1097 ordinary and 282 relief, a massive 1379 engine duties, or well over 200 each weekday, worked by an allocation of 263 locomotives. One duty no longer undertaken, however, was the outstationed engine at Pinxton, where the subshed had closed about the time the First World War commenced. As an exigency of that war, women engine cleaners were still a feature of Colwick shed when the magazine article appeared. The ladies had their own mess room and facilities, situated at the rear of the washout installation. The accommodation was created by building over the small yard that separated the shed's south western corner from the Traffic Terrace cottages; a cash room was added at the same time.

From the 1930's, more information comes from a former Colwick fitter, who has been of immeasurable assistance to the authors in their researches. Sid Checkley confirms that although engines allocated had dropped to about 212, there were still over 600 footplatemen and another 100-plus workshop hands. The latter's large numbers were dictated by the fact that Colwick carried out all the Locomotive District's engine repairs and also provided relief staff for the other sheds. Fitting staff included a Boiler Foreman, who had charge of the Boilersmiths, Tubers, Blacksmiths, Boiler Wash-out and Brick-arch men. His Mechanical Foreman colleague was responsible for the Machine Shop and the Fitters, of whom there were 52, with 7 apprentices and around 50 assistants in Craft grades. The fitting staff were distributed as follows: 1 Chargehand, Erecting Shop, 1 Chargehand responsible for safety valves, 1 Fitter, Shed Maintenance - coaling and washout plants and breakdown train, 3 Examining Fitters, 18 Running Work Fitters in three shifts: 6.00 a.m. to 2.00 p.m., 2.00 p.m. to 10.00 p.m. and 10.00 p.m. to 6.00 a.m., 1 Fitter specialising in lubricators, 1 Fitter specialising in brakes, including Westinghouse, 1 Fitter specialising in injectors, 1 Fitter on the drop-pit, 2 Fitters in Erecting Shop working individually or in concert, 2 Fitters for valve and piston exams - extra men used if Leicester or Annesley engines were in for examinations, 2 to 4 fitters for outstations, varying with the time of year - annual leave etc. The remaining fitters were employed on day to day repairs, with siderod re-bushing being a constant task, though no men were specifically allocated to it. Sid recalls that most of his time was spent on valve and piston exams on three-cylinder locomotives - A1/3 from Leicester mostly, but B17 and K3 were common too. After their introduction, B1 became regulars for valve chest liner work, when they started to give trouble. The main Fitters' Shop also housed the Tubers, who had a fire for annealing tube ends, also the Coppersmiths and in earlier days, a Whitemetaller. Most of the equipment they used was locally made, through the "chill", although in Gresley's time, a mould for crossheads came from Doncaster.

The Mechanical Foreman also had charge of Colwick's breakdown train and normally turned out with it and its crew of five labourers (including the crane driver), a fitter and a boilersmith - the latter to use the oxy-acetylene cutter: If the crane was attending a blocked main line, the Depot Master went along too. In later years, it became the practice for a maintenance fitter's mate to do the crane driving, while the fitter himself was with the breakdown gang. "Odd men out" among the shed's grades were the Joiner and Painter, who each had his own workshop. Then there was the Coppersmith grade, with two men being employed, one each on the day and night turns. Maintenance of all the depot's plant came under the Outdoor Machinery Department, which was overseen by an Outdoor Foreman. Included in all this of course, were the various Shift Supervisors.

On the footplate side, the Running Foremen "ran" the shed's engine duties and Sid recalls some details of enginemen's links as follows, and here we quote verbatim, from one of Sid's many letters to us: "...there was a group of 12 senior men that signed the Great Central line from Sheffield to Marylebone. Some sets of men ran to Marylebone nearly every day, often on special trains. On Saturdays there were football excursions to Sheffield (Wadsley Bridge) worked by this link. Another large link was the "GN Bogie Gang," though GN Bogies had gone years before; they worked the Grantham, Derby and Pinxton trains. In other links, men worked to Peterborough, King's Cross, Doncaster, Mexborough (a lodging turn), York and March. The trains were mostly mineral, but the King's Cross and York were fitted freight. One set of jobs was peculiar - Colwick to Immingham via Boston. In theory there was a balancing job from Immingham and the men changed over halfway. This did not always work and occasionally the signalman at Willoughby found his kettle in demand for the tea cans, while everybody waited! Colwick men did not sign the road beyond Willoughby, only up the Mablethorpe branch; many of the men signed that road and the one to Skegness, for the summer workings. For many years there was a job to Norwich (Wensum) with a Yarmouth train - this was in the days of the B17's. The shed's Manchester and Liverpool jobs ran to Trafford Park or Heaton Mersey, via both the GC and MR routes. (Sid has a special reason to remember

Colwick's massive 1901 coal stage forms a backdrop to Class J52 4274 and J4 3179 in 1932. The double-sided coaler had three tips per side and could accommodate sixteen 20t wagons on each of its two internal roads. Theoretical maximum fuel throughput was 900-1000 tons per day, but the highest recorded activity was during World War One, with 350-400 tons per day. *Locofotos.*

those turns, as two of his uncles were drivers in the link, one of them having 'Glenalmond' 5004 as his regular engine for many years). Lastly, a large link covered the collieries in the Erewash Valley and Stanton Iron Works; this included hauling the stone from Denton...". Another correspondent has enlarged upon these notes with mention of Colwick's workings over Woodhead to Mottram Yard. They resulted in Colwick engines being seen at Gorton shed in Manchester - B8, K2 and O4 classes are quoted as being regulars.

There was therefore, still much activity at Colwick in the Thirties, a situation which increased when the LMS closed its ex-LNWR Netherfield & Colwick engine shed. That was on December 4th 1932 and although all LMS engines were transferred away, ten sets of men came to Colwick LNER depot, from where they could continue to work coal trains to London, over the Joint line. LMS engines were supplied by Northampton and Market Harborough sheds and had two roads of the ex-GN shed formally reserved for their use, but in practice, they could rarely gain access to them! Also, it is significant perhaps that while LMS men and engines had this free access to Colwick LNER depot, it seems that LNER men were able to move LMS engines within the confines of the shed, but LMS staff were expressly forbidden to touch their host's machines!

Colwick was a thriving engine shed without doubt, to the tune of having the following allocation of 230 engines as at 31stDecember 1922, the last day of the Great Northern Railway:

C12 1511, 1515, 1517, 1519, 1520, 1523, 1524, 1526, 1530.
D2 1327, 1329, 1361, 1363, 1364, 1373, 1393, 1399.
D3 400, 1305, 1306, 1309, 1310, 1315, 1316, 1317, 1318, 1320, 1353, 1354, 1355.
E1 760, 818, 864, 897, 992.
G1 769, 824, 828, 830, 940.
J1 4.
J2 76,77,78.
J3 177, 303, 306, 308, 316, 343, 379, 1091, 1094, 1095, 1096, 1113, 1115, 1119, 1120, 1141, 1142, 1151, 1161, 1162, 1163, 1164, 1165, 1168.
J4 165, 179, 199, 318, 329, 334, 348, 352, 361, 396, 721, 849, 1031, 1033, 1034, 1035, 1040, 1041, 1111, 1112, 1116, 1117, 1143, 1144, 1166.
J5 27, 30, 33.
J6 521, 522, 524, 525, 526, 527, 528, 540, 541, 542, 543, 544, 545, 549, 550, 551, 552, 557, 558, 561, 562, 563, 564, 565, 566, 573, 574, 575, 576, 577, 580, 581, 583, 587, 588, 601, 626, 627, 628, 629, 630.
J7 156A, 188, 1021, 1023, 1024.
J52 1208, 1259, 1260.
J53 965, 966, 1055.
J54 673, 686, 689, 690, 906, 920.
J55 672, 674, 678, 851, 917, 918.
J56 613.
K1 1630, 1633, 1638, 1639.
K2 1631, 1635.
O1 464, 469, 470, 471.
Q1 401, 408, 409, 411, 412, 414, 415, 418, 425, 426, 427, 436, 437, 439, 443, 448, 449.
Q2 402, 410, 416, 417, 421, 450, 451.
R1 116, 118, 119, 120, 121, 122, 123, 124, 126, 127, 128, 129, 130, 131, 132, 133, 134, 135, 136, 138, 139, 140, 141, 142, 143, 144, 145, 146, 147, 148, 149, 150, 152, 153, 155.

Such quantities of engines were necessary to deal with the depot's workload, something which kept the numbers of locomotives 'at home' to a relatively low number - even on Sundays. Witness the following record of a visit to the depot, on Sunday 10th October 1937, that found *only* 139 locomotives and 1 steam railcar on shed:

By 1963, Colwick's new concrete roof covered a complement of engines that was somewhat reduced from only a few years earlier. So too had the number of types declined, as this picture, from 8th September that year shows. The once overwhelming numbers of GC 2-8-0 had dwindled to a single visible example, among a handful of WDs, B1 and Ivatt Class 4 2-6-0. *W.T.Stubbs collection.*

B7 5470; **B8** 5004, 5439, 5441, 5443, 5444; **C4** 6093; **C12** 4513, 4516, 4523, 4548; **D2** 3050, 4320, 4365, 4367, 4390, 4393, 4397; **D3** 4073, 4074, 4301, 4307, 4312; **D10** 5431; **J2** 3076, 3078; **J3** 4033, 4037, 4392, 4163, 4166; **J4** 4090; **J5** 3025, 3026, 3027, 3030, 3033, 3035, 3036, 3037, 3038, 3039; **J6** 3524, 3525, 3528, 3535, 3536, 3538, 3540, 3541, 3542, 3543, 3544, 3550, 3551, 3553, 3563, 3564, 3565, 3573, 3574, 3575, 3577, 3583, 3587, 3627; **J11** 5211, 5256, 5314, 6003; **J39** 1828, 1856, 1857, 2691, 2785, 2963, 2970, 2971, 2976; **J52** 3927, 3929, 3965, 3966, 4055, 4206, 4208, 4210, 4240, 4259, 4260, 4264, 4268, 4273, 4276, 4283, 4288; **K2** 4641, 4680; **N5** 5923, 5943; **O2** 3850; **O4** 5001, 5382, 5385, 5387, 5389, 6092, 6211, 6251, 6257, 6265, 6270, 6295, 6299, 6308, 6318, 6324, 6327, 6336, 6338, 6377, 6497, 6521, 6530, 6540, 6545, 6561, 6565, 6587, 6597, 6601, 6606, 6624; **O5** 5422; LMS 0-8-0's 8912, 9413, 9431 (all 2C Northampton), 9589 (2A Rugby); Steam railcar 51913.

Such was the depot's workload that it was natural for the LNER to allocate a considerable sum of money for the shed's modernisation. £35,000 was approved in 1936, for provision of:

(a) 500 ton mechanical coaling plant.

(b) 260 ft wet ash pit with ten travelling cages and 3 ton steam grab crane.

(c) 70 ft turntable (on the same site as the 55 ft specimen in the yard) .

(d) new artesian well, supplying the depot and yard, cottages, Railway Institute, and new water columns.

(e) new oil store, mess room and foreman's office.

The work took a long time to complete, not being finished until the early part of the Second World War. Part of the alterations concerned closure of the wagon shop from its original purpose, for use as a stores. Wagon repairs were afterwards carried out at the former LMS engine shed, a purpose served until after the war, when the building became a privately-owned engineering works, until it finally succumbed in the 1980's.

Colwick's involvement in World War Two needs little comment except to mention the demolition of the square of grounded coach bodies that formed the staff club rifle ranges; in replacement a staff canteen was erected. By the time the canteen appeared a man-made pond had been created near the rifle ranges, into which all the shed's pits drained; as a "nose-witness" has commented, eating in the canteen was accompanied by a smell that was "all its own!" Operationally, the shed would have been a hive of wartime activity, with an ever increasing battle to keep in traffic many engines that should have gone for repair or scrap long before. As alluded to above, the WD 2-8-0's of British and American designs must have brought much needed relief in the busiest last two years of the conflict. The shed does not seem to have received the attention of the Luftwaffe at any time, possibly because of its location away from Nottingham, but by the end of the war, the shed buildings were looking as if they had been raided a few times! Once again it was the northlight roofs that had fared worse and once again it was BR that was faced with their repair. The first attempt was made in the very early 1950's, when aluminium sheets were used. They lasted but a short time of unequal combat with engine smoke, completely rotting away to nothing. BR's second re-roofing was of a much more permanent nature, using the favoured materials of light steel supports and asbestos sheeting, with brick screens at the end. "Old", "Big" and "New" sheds were all treated, but the remaining roofs - repair shop. wagon shop and ancillary outbuildings, did not need attention. It was about the same time

Colwick's 500 ton coaler is complete and the 70ft turntable nearly so, in April 1939. The LNER was indeed fortunate that such new appliances were in place just in time to meet the rigorous demands of World War 2. New England O2 no.3477 takes advantage of the new facility. *National Railway Museum .*

A distinguished visitor to Colwick, but for an undistinguished reason. Top Shed's "Woodcock" had been hauling a 1961 railtour when she failed with vacuum brake problems and had to be "hidden away" in the re-roofed Old shed for attention! *Sid Checkley.*

as this second roof job that BR removed the original 45 ft turntable from its position beside the Old shed. It had served in that place for over 75 years, probably a record (for the GN, at least), but its latter decades would have seen it being used sparingly, given its limiting size and a location that was far less accessible than the 1901 turntable site by the coaling stage.

In April 1950, Colwick received the BR Eastern Region code of 38A, remaining a Locomotive District centre, with subordinate depots at Annesley (ex-GC) 38B, Leicester (ex-GN & GC sheds combined) 38C, Staveley (ex-GC) 38D, and Woodford (Halse) (ex-GC) 38E. Derby Friargate ex-GN shed remained as a Colwick sub-shed per se, but it, and Leicester GN, were both to close by the mid 1950's. Then, from 1st February 1958, Colwick became merely a subordinate shed itself, coded 40E, as part of the Lincoln District. Colwick's District Motive Power Superintendent, John Blundell, departed to staff the newly formed Sheffield District, taking with him his District Boiler Foreman, District Carriage & Wagon Foreman and District Outdoor Machinery Foreman; only the Chief District Locomotive Inspector, who was close to retirement, did not accompany the redoubtable Mr. Blundell, who was replaced at Colwick by a shedmaster. Such moves reduced Colwick's allocation, which was still near the 200 mark in the early 1950's, to less than 150 by 1959. A further contributory factor to that 1959 figure was decline of the coal industry and consequent gradual wind-down of Colwick sidings, which commenced on 9th August 1958, when the yard was closed on Saturday nights, for a 'trial period'. Next, on 1st March 1960, the first diesel went on trial on the Denton branch, to be followed by the first working of a timetabled train, on the following 25th April, when BRC&W Type 2 D5401 left Colwick on the 1.35 a.m. to Whitemoor. In 1963, the Saturday night closure of Colwick yard became 'permanent', a situation that was further extended in 1966.

That succeeded the 3rd January transfer of Colwick depot to the Midland Region, which gave it the code of 16B, although it is doubtful if any engines carried it, following the LMR's introduction of "Divisional" allocations from 16th January 1965. The new "management" moved out all ex-LNER group engines with indecent haste and replaced them with its own designs. Colwick yard closed from 2.00 p.m. on Saturdays with effect from 13th August and the Traffic Offices went the following 5th December, being transferred to the locoshed. That event was followed by formal closure to steam on 12th December 1966. Actually, the last 'active' steam engine left the shed on the last day of 1966, leaving a number of serviceable Stanier 8F's in store, until they too were moved away, in February 1967. Even then, that was not the end of steam at Colwick, because B1 61264 remained on stationary boiler duties until April 1968, being joined in such work for a while in 1967 by Standard Class 4 4-6-0 No. 75016. After working steam left, Colwick's buildings continued to serve as a diesel depot for another $4^1/_4$ years, which period witnessed the continued run-down of the marshalling yard, until final closure came on 18th April 1970 - the locoshed had reached the end of its career during the preceding week, on 13th April. Demolition inevitably followed, commencing on 17th October 1971, with the massive coaling tower being felled on 29th December 1971. Today, the shed site is given over on its western side to an industrial development of small factory units off a road called "Great Northern Way", while sweeping from the north, around and over the east side of the site is a new by-pass - the "Colwick Loop Road". Of the massive marshalling yard, only a few overgrown oil sidings remain, at the Grantham end; the yards' site is scheduled for building of the "Victoria Park" estate of retail and industrial units. Lastly, in Colwick railway "village", the cottages in Deabill Street and Godfrey Street still survive, along with some allotments further to the east.

Thus ends the story of the Great Northern Railway's biggest engine shed of which not a sign remains.

DERBY

Derby, population in 1893: 81,168 in addition to being the centre of the Midland Railway's empire is also close to the geographic centre of England. Even so the city saw a few invasions with that in 1745 by 'Bonnie' Prince Charles Stuart's Highlanders preceding the Great Northern Railway's assault by 133 years.

The GN obtained its Derbyshire & Staffordshire Extension Act on 25th July 1872. Part of the works was a contract for £40,000, awarded to Messrs. Kirk and Randall, for the erection of goods and locomotive sheds at Derby. The latter was not finished in time for opening of the line for goods and passenger traffic, in January and April 1878 respectively, but was reported complete and ready for use on 1st October, the same year. It is easy to understand why the shed was known as "Friargate" for all its existence as it was actually sited adjacent to Slack Lane which was hardly an auspicious choice of name, even for an engine shed. However the shed would probably have had a different name if it had been located as originally intended. The first site earmarked was on the opposite (south) side of the main line, facing west. A circa 1870 plan shows a four road building, 45 ft turntable, a 62 ft long coal stage that tapered in width from 20 ft to 6 ft and two 75 ft pits alongside the stage. All in all it was a more spacious site than that eventually used, but no reason has yet been found for the change of location.

Friargate depot was the fourth and last to be built to the pattern previously laid down at Retford, Colwick and Lincoln in having two tiled hipped roofs covering four dead-end roads, which at Derby could each accommodate two tender engines under cover. The shed scaled 120 ft by 65 ft and was constructed in brick with typical mid-Victorian decorative work at gutter level. Coaling was effected from a brick-built coal stage positioned adjacent to the northernmost shed road; it was equipped with a crane and bucket and had a canopy extending over the coaling area. The two storey high edifice was stoutly constructed as it formed a base for the shed's water tank, which had a capacity of 68,000 gallons i.e. when full, it contained over 300 tons of water. Situated by the shed's southern wall was a 44 ft 6 ins turntable which later had its operating capacity enhanced by the use of 2 ft extension rails placed at both ends. Nevertheless the turntable's site was so cramped that in time the increasing size of locomotives meant some types could be turned in one direction only to avoid their fouling the shed wall. Actually sited below the level of the aforementioned Slack Lane, access to the depot was gained via a staircase that entered the north-west corner of the shed. Originally the fitter's shop had been located below those stairs but it was later moved to one of the rooms along the inside of the shed's south wall, where were also sited the foreman's office and staff messroom.

Thus built the depot immediately settled into an existence which seems to have pertained throughout its life and has been described by one who worked there as being a "cathedral calm!". This makes it difficult to find any mention of happenings at Derby, especially in its earlier years. By 1900 though it was quite a busy place as evinced by the following table of services worked by Friargate locomotives that commenced or terminated at Derby.

The scene of disrepair visible at Derby ex-GN shed on 24th July 1949 was typical of the run down facilities inherited by British Railways in all of its regions. The new owners carried out extensive repairs to many of its engine sheds, but Friargate was not among them. It was in much the same condition when closed, in 1955. On shed on this July 1949 day were D2 - 2172, 2173, 2177; J5 - 65485, 65488, 65491; J67 - 8527; LM - 42561. *T.J.Edgington.*

WEEKDAYS

Train	Time	From/To
	a.m.	
6	12.50	Goods to Colwick MX
8	4.10	Goods from Colwick MX
23	5.05	Goods from Colwick MO
24	5.10	Light engine to Burton Goods
39	6.00	Passenger to Burton
53	6.50	LE to Burton to shunt GN goods MO
50	7.00	Light engine to Ilkeston
51	7.10	Empties to Stanton Jct
55	7.15	Passenger to Burton
69	9.05	Passenger to Stafford
91	10.38	Passenger to Grantham
110*	11.00	LE to Ilkeston to work empties to Pleasley
110#	11.15	Pass to Stafford
114	11.55	Express passenger to Newark
	p.m.	
139	12.48	Passenger from Stafford
121	1.02	Passenger from Grantham
133	1.22	Passenger to Stafford
145	1.35	Express passenger to Grantham
153	2.00	Fast cattle to Carlton Fields (Colwick). **
160	2.20	LE to Stanton Jct. and then on to Heanor to take over Ilkeston-Heanor passenger working
175	3.00	Express passenger to Grantham
186	3.38	Passenger from Stafford
163	3.48	Passenger from Nottingham (Victoria)
159	4.20	Light engine from Heanor
170	4.25	Passenger to Stafford
182	5.00	Light engine to Burton for shunting
196	5.05	Express passenger to Netherfield
177	5.08	Goods and coal from Colwick
183	5.20	Coal from Ilkeston worked by Stanton Branch Pt.
190	5.39	Passenger from Grantham
212	5.54	Passenger from Stafford
223	7.10	Passenger to Stafford
253	8.25	Goods to King's Cross
259	8.46	Passenger to Stafford
265	9.50	Empties to Ilkeston worked by Stanton Branch Pt.
268	10.00	Passenger to Nottingham (Victoria) WSO
274	10.30	Passenger from Burton
275	11.20	Light engine from Ilkeston
295	11.27	Empty coaches from Burton SX
276	11.34	Passenger from Nottingham (Victoria) WSO
296	11.53	Passenger from Burton SO

SUNDAYS

Train	Time	From/To
	a.m.	
16	5.30	Coal from Stanton Branch worked by S.B.Pilot
29	9.10	Passenger to Basford & Bulwell
	p.m.	
36#	12.28	Passenger from Netherfield
6	12.30	Goods to Colwick
36*	1.20	Passenger to Grantham
42	4.25	Passenger to Stafford
49#	7.40	LE to Etwall to work milk train to Eggington Jct
49*	8.36	Passenger from Stafford
52	9.28	Passenger from Grantham

Key:-
* Up;
** Runs when required;
# Down;
LE Light engine;
S.B Stanton Branch
SO Saturdays only;
SX Saturdays excepted;
WSO Wednesday and Saturdays only;

From the table it can be seen that Friargate was responsible for the majority of Burton and Stafford services, and men and locomotives were outstationed at those places for varying periods over the years. Such workings required an allocation of about 12/17 locomotives usually of the 0-6-0 and 4-4-0 varieties although for a while in 1925 ex GER Class E4 2-4-0s Nos.7447 and 7450 came to Derby for workings to Stafford. By December 1930 Friargate's allocation stood at 14 engines comprised of seven classes as recorded thus: **B8** 5444; **D2** 4363, 4375; **D3** 3400; **J3** 3361, 3362, 4033, 4161, 4162, 4164, 4166; **J6** 3626; **J52** 4259; **J54** 3688.

In 1933 Class Y3 Sentinel No.55 was stationed at Derby from 28th April to 2nd June and records show that it was trialled in the Engineer's Yard and on the brewery sidings shunt at Burton. The experiment was not successful and the Sentinel went back to Retford. Another of the class, No.98, had spent the previous March at Derby also. Yet a visit made to the depot eighteen months earlier on 8th November 1931 found a Colwick Y3 in residence together with the following 14 engines of eight other classes; what the Sentinel's duties were at that time has not been discovered. **B8** 5445; **D2** 4305, 4328, 4329; **D3** 4306; **J3** 3362, 4112, 4115, 4116, 4162; **J4** 4041; **J77** 199; **K2** 4640; **N5** 5748; **Y3** 96.

The number of engines allocated remained steady through to the mid-1930s after which it gradually fell to about ten, but the types of loco did not alter. In fact the last Class D3 4-4-0 in ordinary service, 2148, was sub-shedded at Derby when withdrawn in November 1950. Then, not long before the end of the shed's service life, in January 1954, a new class appeared when two N1 0-6-2T arrived to work the Derby - Nottingham section of the Grantham passenger service. They - condenser fitted 69451 and 69481, were first observed on 31st January four days after being transferred from Hornsey. Also on Friargate with the N1's were J6 64213, 64230, 64273, J52 68882 and N7 69621.

The reduction in locomotives mentioned above resulted in Friargate crews more and more finding themselves manning engines from the main shed at Colwick on widely varying duties. A typical diagram involving a Colwick K2 was the 10.10 a.m. all stations passenger, from Nottingham to Burton. This was followed by local goods working in the Burton/Derby area until taking a goods to Grantham returning from there to Derby arriving at 10.50 p.m. Next day the same locomotive and a Derby crew worked the 12.50 p.m. goods to Stafford Common returning on the 5.45 p.m. milk to Eggington Junction, there handing the train over to a Colwick Class J1 or J2 on to Grantham. After waiting until 10.50 p.m. the Colwick K2 and Friargate men then worked another milk train to Netherfield.

Of course the famous Burton beer trains were partly Derby's responsibility and provided at least one lodging turn, that was the Hull train leaving Burton at 7.45 p.m. Monday to Friday returning from Hull the next day at 7.55 p.m., it was a turn worked alternately day and day about with North Eastern locomotives and men.

Should extra engines be required at Derby - summer Fridays for Saturday specials were a case in point, they would be sent from Colwick. At that time Friargate's yard would be full of engines that had had their fires pulled to the back of the firebox and 'lumped up' in readiness for the next day's duty. Inevitably this caused a certain amount of smoke and equally inevitably there would be complaints about the nuisance. Records show that most of these emanated from the local fish and chip shop

DERBY 1930

Colwick J5 no.65490 was a familiar sight at Friargate shed right up to closure. *Authors collection.*

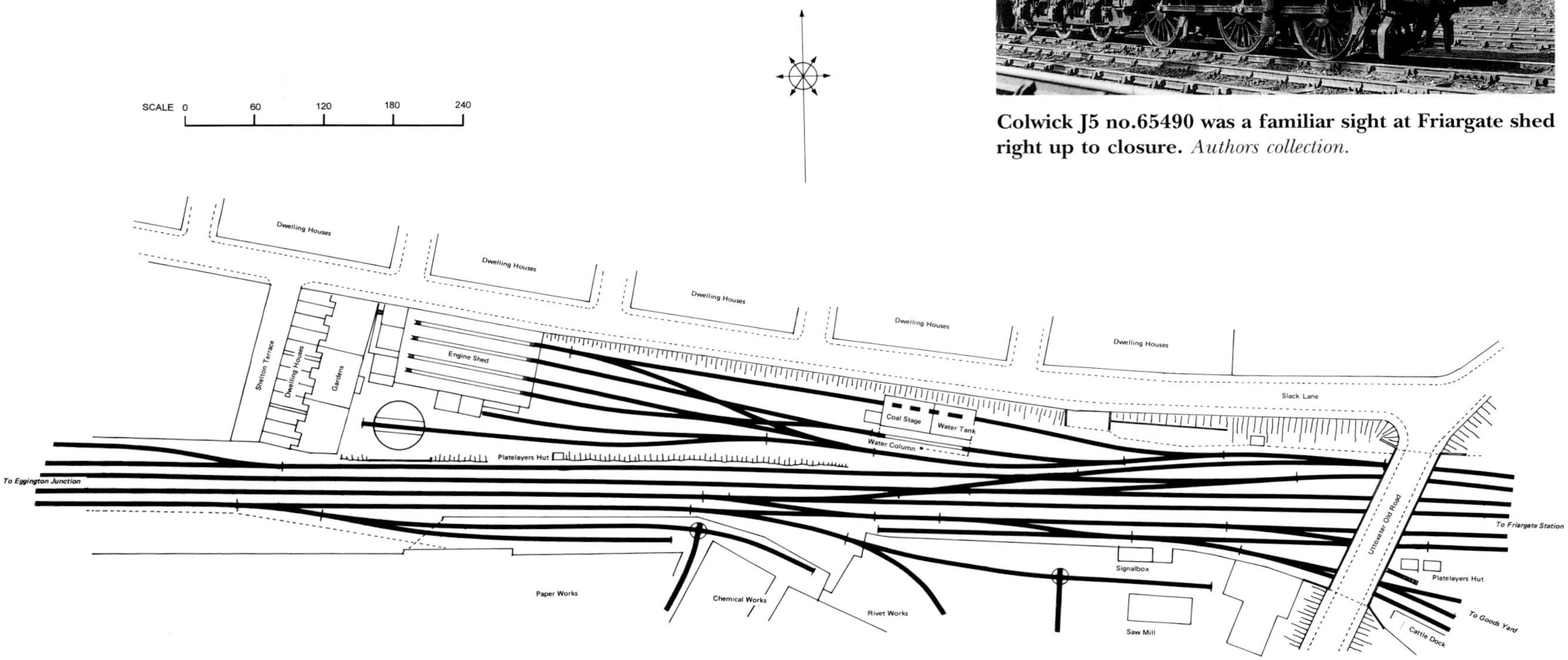

The dilapidated hipped roof does not seem to provide much in the way of shelter for the residents of Friargate in this 4th June 1950 view. BR had drawn up plans to rebuild the shed in the asbestos clad style used extensively on the LMS in the late 1940's but it was not to be. An unidentified A5 bathes in the sunlight streaming through the 'roof'. *H.C.Casserley.*

in Slack Lane evidently the social centre of the area during the late hours that these incidents occurred.

Staff at Friargate shed was never large in numbers. There was a shed foreman more often than not being a Premium Apprentice gaining his running shed experience, he reported to the District Locomotive Superintendent at Colwick. The foreman had one skilled fitter with a mate on each of the day and night shifts, with the latter being the busiest owing to the majority of the allocation being at home during these hours. The remaining staff comprised a number of labourers on coal stage and engine cleaning duties - these usually being youngsters who would graduate to become footplatemen. Of the latter there had been perhaps 20 sets in the early days, but the figure stabilised at about 20 men from the latter part of the GN's existence.

For a period prior to World War One Derby was the headquarters of the GN's Western Divisional Engineer but this had little effect upon Friargate's tranquillity. However, that placidity was disturbed on several occasions. One event that has been brought to the authors' attention was when the shed staff were somewhat detached observers of an accident close to the depot. That was when a empty coaching stock train was leaving the sidings adjacent to the shed. At the same time a Burton to Colwick train came in on a parallel track and the drivers being old friends struck up a conversation from their respective footplates. Unfortunately one of them overran signals and points and caused a meeting of engines. With no suitable equipment at Friargate to help with such a situation all the depot staff could do was call out the Colwick breakdown train!

On another occasion, the shed staff were more intimately involved. That concerned a certain J52 tank which was standing on the coaling road. Sated with coal and water the locomotive evidently needed to find relief so it set off on its own, passed through the shed and the rear wall, into the staff lavatories! Luckily nobody was caught literally with their pants down but the ensuing paperwork must have been quite painful.

With so little to commend its importance it is surprising that on 2nd March 1948 the Railway Executive produced plans for the replacement of Friargate's dilapidated roof with an asbestos covering on a light steel frame. It is *NO* surprise that this work was never carried out and Friargate shed closed, still gas-lit and in even more dilapidated condition in 1955. Just before that on 21st November 1954 the allocation which Colwick officially reported as consisting of six Class N1 was actually the following ten locomotives: **J5** 65483; **J6** 64212, 64215, 64230, 64238, 64257; **J39** 64832; **J52** 68768; **N1** 69441, 69467.

Such men as remained at closure were transferred to Derby Midland shed while the locomotive duties were assumed by Colwick. Even so the shed continued in use as a signing-on point for a number of years - being reported as such in April 1959 for instance - before the end finally came. But then against all odds the depot survived demolition and still stands today largely intact, in use by a chemical company, and sporting the last remaining example of the GN-style of hipped roofs. Except for a small wagon shed, the goods shed and a carefully maintained bridge over the main road no other trace remains of the GNR in the Friargate area of Derby.

A fine view of a typical GNR coaling stage/water tank facility, as seen on 4th June 1950 - the wooden shelter over the coaling road has survived in remarkably good condition, especially when one looks at the rest of the depot! Also evident is the cramped nature of the site; the turntable was located between the shed building and main line, just beyond the distant breakdown van. *H.C.Casserley.*

GAINSBOROUGH

Destined to be almost the shortest lived of GN engine sheds, Gainsborough's exact location and layout are unknown to the authors. This important Lincolnshire town on the River Trent was already being served by the MSLR when the section of the GN's "Loop" line from Lincoln to Gainsborough opened for traffic, on 9th April 1849. Ten months previously, on 1st June 1848 to be exact, the GN Board had approved the idea of using the MSLR station, as finding a site for their own station, convenient for the town, had been proving difficult. The proposal was ratified by a GN/MSLR Agreement dated 13th August 1848 whereby ... "all use by the GNR of Gainsborough MSLR station shall be payable for all descriptions of traffic, equal to 2 miles of the maximum charges of the MSLR who are TO FIND ALL STATION ACCOMMODATION" *(authors capitals).*

So the GN started to use the MSLR premises which involved a reversal over the latter's line from its junction with the GN, west of the station. It is known that the GN commenced using engine shed facilities from the date of opening, enabling closure and re-use of the temporary shed building at Lincoln, the former railhead. What is not clear is whether the MSLR provided a separate shed for the GN under the clause about that company finding all "station" accommodation, as both companies' archives make no mention. What probably happened was that the GN had use of the MSLR engine shed at Gainsborough, stationing men and machines there. The MSL's depot was a two road structure that stood at the south-west corner of the station, coming into use with the MSL line from Brigg, on 2nd April 1849.

However within a short while poor quality of the water supplies at Gainsborough shed was the cause of late running of GN services which resulted in public complaint. Reference was particularly made to locomotive No.54 a Hawthorn Single, which appears to have suffered far worse than any other, due it seems, to boiler tubes of faulty manufacture. An alternative water supply was found but the GN had already decided to move its locomotive facilities back to Lincoln. Accordingly during March 1850, operations ceased from Gainsborough shed except for "Cleaners and Firelighters" expenditure which continued until May 1850. Next month Sturrock was able to report to the Board that in discontinuing workings from Gainsborough a saving in excess of £800 per annum was being effected.

Thereby ended Gainsborough GN "shed" after a life of only 13 months and although the GN eventually did build their own station in the town, at Lea Road, no engine shed was ever located there.

HORNCASTLE

Situated on the River Bain, 21 miles east of Lincoln, Horncastle was an important market town, with a thriving trade in corn, wool, malting and brewing. Apart from its weekly market, Horncastle was the venue for three annual fairs, with the Horse Fair being one of the largest in Britain. In addition, the town was served by the Horncastle Navigation and in 1851, the Great Northern Railway built warehouses and a coal wharf on the canal, the merchandise coming by barge from Dogdyke.

With a presence in the town it was natural perhaps that the GN would be asked to run all services over the Horncastle & Kirkstead Junction Railway, which was sponsored by private local interests and incorporated on 10th July 1854. The request was acceded to by the GN Board on 19th August 1853 (Minute No.89), and a suitable agreement drawn up. This was based upon the "Estimate of Working Expenses" given in a letter from Mr. Seymour Clarke, to the Horncastle Company, on 18th August 1853. For interest's sake, that letter's full content is given here, as a typical specimen of how working agreements were struck by the GN and numerous independent companies. The association was not to be of the smoothest, however, and although in 1888, an attempt was made to fix a price, the H&KJR never was taken over by the GN, remaining nominally independent until the Grouping.

ESTIMATE OF WORKING THE LINE

Length of line: 7$^1/_2$ miles.
Two trains a day, each way.
One train each way on Sunday.
195 miles a week.
One engine to do all the work.
Cost of an engine including repairs - interest, depreciation, wages and stores: £13-12-0 per diem or £95-4-0d per week, which gives 20 ???? per mile for locomotive power (sic).
One first class - two second class and one Break at the Clearing House - Mileage cover to 2$^1/_4$ per mile for the Train.
195 miles a week or 9140 miles per annum, @ 1/10 $^1/_4$d = £848-7-11d
Goods wagons to be provided at the usual mileage rates. On through Goods rates the Horncastle Company to have the Terminals at their own station.
The staff at Horncastle and Roughton stations to be provided at the expense of the Horncastle Company - Guards to be paid by the Horncastle Company - also signal men.
The estimated cost of the Horncastle station: £6-5-0 per week or per annum £325 -

Lamps, Oil, Coals	*£85 0 0d*
Stationery and Tickets	*£20 0 0d*
Staff at Roughton Station	*£98 16 0d*
Stores	*£40 0 0d*
One Guard	*£54 12 0d*
Signal Man at Junction	*£54 12 0d*

These items will form the total expense of Working the Line save only parochial rates and maintenance of way.
Summary

Train Mileage	*£ 848 7 11d*
Horncastle Station	*£ 430 0 0d*
Roughton Station	*£ 145 16 0d*
Guard and Signal Man	*£ 109 4 0d*
	£1533 7 11d

Estimate for maintenance of way at £70 per annum per mile - £525.
Parochial Rates £100.
= £625
= £2158 7 11d
Added) If Roughton Station be dispensed with, it will reduce it by - £145 16 0
= £2012 16 11d
The Estimated Traffic as per included letter from Messrs Babington and Sketchley is £5000 for the Horncastle Branch - their Capital £45,000.
My Estimate of the Expense of working the line deducted from £5000 will leave £2841 12 1d for division, or about six per cent on the capital.
I contemplate no charge being made for the use of Kirkstead station as we shall save our present depot at Horncastle.
All the expenses of the alterations at Kirkstead to be paid by the Horncastle Company including the Signal Stations at the Kirkstead Junction and a small Engine House and Carriage Shed.
(Signed) Seymour Clarke.

Construction of the line was swift, with opening occurring on 11th August 1855 for an initial weekday service of 9 return trains, with 2 on Sundays - a considerable departure from Seymour Clarke's estimate of the service to be provided. There was a further change from Clarke's missive: the opening timetable shows the first train of the day being a Horncastle to Kirkstead service, leaving the terminus at 7.25 a.m. - the last train arrived back at Horncastle at 9.45 p.m. Both times suggest the engine was kept at Horncastle, and not Kirkstead. September 1857's GN WTT also clearly indicates an engine was stabling overnight at Horncastle, as the first of the 6 daily return mixed trains then left at 7.15 a.m., on its 20 minute trip to the junction. Sunday services had also been reduced from the initial two, to one return working, leaving Horncastle at 12.35 p.m.: this Sunday train was eventually discontinued from June 1868. On weekdays in 1857 there was an afternoon return goods working, as and when required - a feature that was shown as an afternoon Fridays only goods and coal train in the 1860 WTT. Later, a daily regular goods was run, eventually becoming two workings *(see below)*. Locomotives working these services were sub-shedded from Boston and would probably have been 0-4-2T and 0-4-4T, or even Hawthorn 0-4-2 and eventually Stirling 0-4-2 and 2-4-0. Engines were changed over when necessary, using the 6.25 a.m. Boston to Kirkstead goods and return.

Not everything about Horncastle locoshed is known for certain. What *IS* known is that it was single road, single-ended and scaled about 65 ft x 20 ft. Construction would seem to have been in brick - probably yellow in colour, like the station - with a single-pitch, tiled gable roof. It appears certain an engine turntable was never installed and coaling was carried out direct from a wagon, at Kirkstead. Water was stored in a 7,500 gallon tank near the station, the replenishment of which was the cause of some friction between the GN and directors of the Horncastle Company. Seemingly, by 3rd January 1874, the reservoir at Horncastle, used among other things for locomotive purposes, had had its source of supply cut off. No reason can be found for the cessation, but the GN asked the H&KJR to spend an estimated

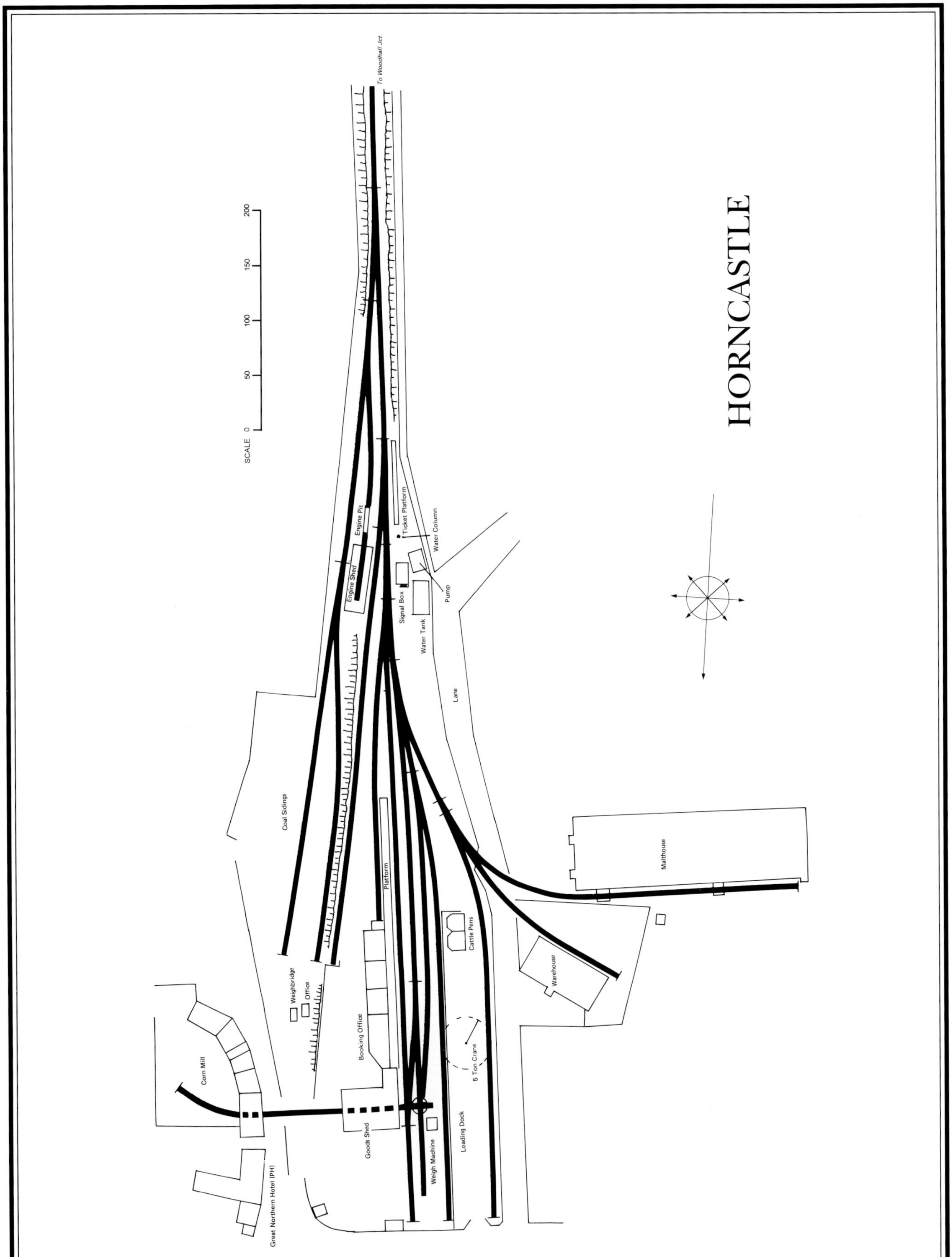
HORNCASTLE
To Woodhall Jct
SCALE 0 50 100 150 200
Ticket Platform
Water Column
Engine Pit
Engine Shed
Signal Box
Pump
Water Tank
Lane
Coal Sidings
Platform
Malthouse
Cattle Pens
Warehouse
Weighbridge
Office
Booking Office
5 Ton Crane
Corn Mill
Goods Shed
Loading Dock
Weigh Machine
Great Northern Hotel (PH)

Two colliers rest from loading their horse dray to watch Class J11 4284 leave Horncastle with its articulated 2-coach set, forming the 12.42 p.m. service to Woodhall Junction on 10th June 1947. The locomotive's home depot was Langwith Junction - typical of the several sheds whose duties included the supply of power for the branch after Horncastle shed closed, 23 years before this picture was taken. *W.A.Camwell.*

£335 to lay water pipes and restore a feed to the reservoir. Exactly three months later no less a person than Henry Oakley himself goes on record by saying that the water problem must be resolved when the GN's working agreement was next renewed. In June the General Manager advised the GN Board he had formally asked the Horncastle Co. for the new water pipes, but things obviously got worse, as by 5th September 1874, the GN were threatening to withold renewal of the working agreement until an adequate and reliable water supply was secured. Inexplicably, there the matter fades from both the GN and Horncastle Co. archives, until 9th September 1884 - ten years later - when the Horncastle Cos. Minutes record the directors approval for spending £45, to purchase fittings for the securing of a water supply from the mains. So, what happened 1874 - 1884? That the GN continued to work the line is undisputed so somebody must have compromised! Even then, trouble with water did not end, as the mains supply, from Horncastle Waterworks, proved most unsuitable for locomotive use and it would seem likely that in later years, engines used to fill up at Kirkstead whenever possible.

Before the problem over water arose, the GN had some trouble, in 1865, with the few enginemen stationed at Horncastle, which resulted in a widespread complaint from loco department employees. Upon investigation by Stirling, it was discovered that the Horncastle men had been receiving "improper earnings" by manipulation of the system of payment then in force. Understandably, the company had subsequently made alterations to stop the problem, but having been found out as it were, the Horncastle staff then instigated a general complaint from locomen, about alterations to an agreed system of payment! Doubtless the rebellion was quickly and firmly put down by the GN, although no further mention is made in the archive about Horncastle staff until 23rd January 1906. That was when the Locomotive Committee heard that one of the drivers at the branch terminus had recently suffered an epileptic fit, and with the customary attitude of the time, it was deemed the unfortunate individual was no longer capable of being employed by the company.

Traffic over the branch remained bouyant, necessitating extension of Horncastle goods shed and platform in 1873, and provision of a virtually new station at Woodhall Spa, in 1888. Then, on 1st November 1900, the GN's Traffic Committee approved work costing £4213, for 'improving facilities' at the terminus - the money having to be found by the Horncastle Company, however! The basic train service did not alter though, with 6 or 7 return workings a day still being a feature of the 1897 timetable. By 1910 there were two locomotives to be seen at Horncastle each weekday afternoon; the branch engine and that off the 2.40 p.m. goods from Kirkstead, which departed from the terminus on the 8.00 p.m. goods to Lincoln. This would have been the pattern of services that continued until around 1918, by which time Horncastle shed appears to have closed. Certainly, the WTT for 1921 shows no requirement for a locomotive to stable there overnight, or at weekends, with all power being supplied by Boston. One of the shed's last residents was Stirling 0-4-2 No.25A (condemned 8th April 1921); her

A view from the buffer stops at Horncastle, taken in the last few years of the branch's existence. Horncastle shed once stood to the left of the line, just about opposite the pitched roof building seen in the right distance. *A.Cartwright.*

driver, Harry Curtis, his fireman, and a cleaner named Wright, all lived at Horncastle. Mention should also be made of one Robert Billingham, the oldest driver on the GNR when he died. Born in 1826, this resident of Horncastle was still at work in the 1890's.

Thenceforward working of the branch could perhaps be described as complex! For example, in 1924 the first two return trips over the line were worked by an Atlantic tank that had brought the e.c.s. from Boston. The tank then went home, only to appear again at Horncastle with the last Down working of the day, which was through from Boston. The 4-4-2T then proceeded back to its shed again, double-heading the Lincoln engine on the 8.00 p.m. goods to Kirkstead, then light to Boston. On Fridays only, the 4-4-2T had an extra duty, working the 9.50 a.m. FO train from Horncastle to Kirkstead, then returning to Horncastle, light engine, to take the normal 10.50 a.m. train to Kirkstead, before proceeding light to Boston. That Lincoln engine departing Horncastle at 8.00 p.m. had arrived at 10.27 a.m., on a goods from its home town, and then worked the remaining four return branch passenger trains. In between those, a second Lincoln loco arrived at the terminus with another goods, at 2.22 p.m., quickly departing again, for Lincoln, at 3.55 p.m. So, from 'one engine in steam' the Horncastle branch then required one Boston 4-4-2T at each end of the day, and two Lincoln goods engines! Which hardly seems an economic way of running a service! It is worth mentioning that the branch train was made up of a pair of coaches formerly GN railmotors Nos. 5 and 6.

Nevertheless, that was the pattern which generally remained in force through the LNER period, reducing to five return workings in BR times, up to withdrawal of passenger trains, from Saturday 11th September 1954. During the later era locomotives of other than GN origin became commonplace, with ex-GC Class N5 0-6-2T virtually monopolising passenger services in the post-war period, assisted during 1948-50 by ex-GE Class N7 0-6-2T. Following the end of passenger trains, goods services continued to run, bringing to Horncastle more tender engines than hitherto was the norm. Classes K2, K3, J6, and other 0-6-0 types were seen, but perhaps the most notable visit occurred on 13th January 1955, when Lincoln sheds's ex-GC "Director", 62667 SOMME worked the afternoon goods. Another stranger came on the day the branch saw its last passenger train - and incidentally, the longest train ever to run over it - when, on 12th September 1964, Stanier Class 5 No.44918 hauled an eight coach RCTS special to Horncastle.

Latterly, goods trains were in the care of diesel locomotives; Class 31's, a Class 37 once and Class 08 'tripping' from Lincoln Holmes Yard. Even so, the traffic in agricultural and oil products dwindled to one trip a week and finally ceased on 5th April 1971, at which time the Woodhall Junction (formerly Kirkstead) to Horncastle branch was closed. The locomotive shed had disappeared many years before, at a date as yet unknown, but around the early-mid 1920's.

LINCOLN

Principal city of England's second largest county, Lincoln was the market centre of a large agricultural produce area, also being well known for the manufacture of farm machinery and later, small locomotives for industry and British Railways. Three principal railway companies other than the GN also served Lincoln. First was the Midland, which reached the city in 1846, to be followed on 18th December 1848, by the Manchester Sheffield & Lincolnshire Railway, which at first ran into the MR's station. Last of the 'competition' was the Great Eastern, a late-comer via the GN/GE Joint line, opened on 1st July 1882.

The GNR's plans for its own Lincoln installations were produced on 23rd April 1847. (It was in the same year that Lincoln assumed a two year importance, when the company purchased a foundry there, for temporary use as a workshop, pending completion of permanent facilities at Boston). For its station, the GN proposed two 500 ft platforms and associated buildings, two large carriage sheds, two sets of carriage and horse wharfs, a "spare engine" house, two coke and water depots, twelve turntables for carriages and one for locomotives and tenders. The Board authorised Benjamin Cubitt to proceed with all this, on the proviso that costs did not exceed £18,000. The engineer replied that he could meet this only "...by erecting the plainest of buildings..."

GNR services to Lincoln commenced on 17th October 1848 and the engine shed is thought to have been brought into use on the same day. Contemporary layout plans have eluded the authors, however, so there is much uncertainty about exactly where the depot stood. It is assumed to have been constructed of wood, but known that engines had use of a 16 ft turntable, which was placed nearby. While coke and water facilities surely were installed, it is not clear what form they took, or their situation. Certainly, it does not seem as if they were provided as originally planned (see next paragraph). Anyway, the engine shed served for only six months, being closed on 9th April 1849, when the line was extended to Gainsborough and GN locomotive facilities there were brought into use. After closure, Lincoln engine shed was taken down, later to be re-erected elsewhere (unknown), for use as a carriage shed. All further life history of the GN's shortest-lived engine shed is lost in the mists of time, except that its first inhabitants were probably Sharp Singles, Nos.3 and 4, that had arrived in the city in 1847, travelling over MR metals.

As related previously, Gainsborough GN 'engine shed' was closed in May 1850 and on the fifth of the following month, Sturrock reported to the Board that goods engines "...must now coke at Lincoln..." He sought approval for "...coke sheds on Up and Down lines and a two road engine shed, for an assistant engine and a pilot engine..." Plans for the engine shed were approved in August 1850, and a contract was awarded on 13th of that month, to the Lincoln firm of Messrs. Charles Ward, for £650; the building was brought into use early the next year. The shed stood on the north east side of the station and comprised a brick building, with arched entrances and a slated gable roof of unknown dimensions. A 40 ft turntable was provided, but it is not certain what coking facilities appeared initially - whether adjacent to the main lines and/or at the shed; water was available from a 19,000 gallon tank situated at the station.

Lincoln shed covered services to Gainsborough and Retford, and by February 1857, the locomotive allocation had grown to five and Sturrock noted that the shed was too small, accommodating as it did, only two engines. He continued: "...Consequently, the engines cannot be maintained as they ought and there have been occasions of delay to trains, because the engines have to stand outside and steam cannot be got up in time. I have invariably punished the drivers and firelighters

Lincoln engine shed in September 1911. This view, looking towards the station, from a signal at the end of the Holmes ticket platform shows the shed as it was handed over to the LNER. The spare land to the right was later utilised for locomotive stabling as the allocation grew. The apparent split in the picture is caused by a guy wire securing the signal post. Holmes goods yard stands on the left whilst the main line separates the shed from the goods facilities. *Authors collection.*

Lincoln shed on 7th July in the last year of LNER operation, with ex-GC locomotives much in evidence, following closure of that railway's engine shed in the city. Graceful Atlantics 2903 (left) and 2902, are seen with Class B2 1492 and C12 7381. *H.C.Casserley.*

(Sturrock was ever the martinet!), but delays still occur and this will only be alleviated by the creation of a bigger shed..." He recommended that the shed be lengthened, to house four locomotives, which was approved and completed late in 1857.

Traffic increased over the years and by the end of the 1860's, Lincoln station's position, between two busy level crossings, had already become a source of much bad feeling in the city. This was due to delays experienced by road traffic, because in addition to normal train movements, there was shunting and numerous light engine manoeuvres between shed and turntable, all of which entailed closing the level crossing gates. In fact, the problem had arisen as early as January 1850, with comments in the local press. Then in February that year the *Stamford Mercury* reported the following: "...The other day, Sir Montague Cholmeley was stopped for a considerable time whilst a row of trucks stood across the street; and it is understood that he vowed he would make the nuisance the subject of complaint before the House of Commons. The Company are perfectly incorrigible..." Later that same year exasperated locals took matters further, by climbing the crossing gates and assaulting the gatekeepers!

Such problems could not go on forever, so early in 1869 the Board of Trade gave notice to the GN that all shunting over the level crossings would be banned, with effect from 1st January 1870. This spurred the GN Board into precipitate action and £1,875 was authorised for relocation of the turntable, along with other works. On 17th July 1869, Stirling was able to report to the Way & Works Committee that: "...resiting of the turntable, removal of a coal depot and rearrangement of some sidings behind the Up platform will be completed within 10 days..."

This seems to have placated the Board of Trade, temporarily at least, and on 20th July 1870, came what was to prove a fortuitous offer. That was by one Mr. Tweed, on behalf of Lincoln Corporation, to sell to the railway 29 acres of land, west of the station, in an area known as the "Holme". The General Manager was asked by the Board to investigate the land's situation and value, and report back. The outcome was purchase of the ground on the Holme - and just in time, because on 29th October 1872, the citizens of Lincoln again applied through the Board of Trade, to: "...prevent shunting over High Street level crossing and standing of trains..." The Board recommended that: "... a water tank and crane be erected on the Holme, where goods work is done and that a couple of lines be put down, so that passenger trains can run outside the goods..."

A further problem for the GN arose on 1st September 1874, when Lincoln Corporation served 3 months notice of its

(left) **Stirling 5ft saddletank no.167 stands outside the shed c1900.** *Authors collection.*

Except for provision of a loco spur with pit, the mid-1930s scene at Lincoln was little different from 25 years earlier. Within a few years though, the shearlegs would disappear and further loco sidings would be laid down on the vacant land to the right of this picture. *W.A.Camwell.*

intention to cut off water supplies, unless the GN agreed to pay domestic rate. Such tribulations as the foregoing, plus the need for more locomotive accommodation, made the GN determine to relocate its engine shed and again the Holme was selected. Stirling had already submitted plans via the General Manager, on 7th January 1873, at an estimated cost of £10,860, for shed, coke stage, turntable, sidings etc. At first, the matter was deferred, but finally gained approval on 26th September 1873. The necessary tender was issued and a contract let early in 1874, to Messrs. Kirk & Parry, who completed the job in March 1875.

The GN's third Lincoln engine shed was to the company's standard design of the time - a four road dead-end building in brick, with two slated hipped roofs, measuring 163 ft x 69 ft and providing cover for 12 engines. Because ground at the Holme was generally of a soft, wet consistency, substantial foundations were required, so the building rested upon piers that went 18 ft-6 ins. into the earth. The area of land available for the shed was quite limited and caused the coal stage to be positioned beside the depot, between it and the main lines. In addition, the 45 ft turntable had to be accommodated beyond the coal stage, right at the rear of the shed; there, a short engine repair spur led off the turntable and ran behind the shed offices. To complete the shed's facilities (and no doubt, "cock a snook" at Lincoln Corporation!), water was obtained from the River Witham, to be stored in a 59,000 gallon tank, which stood at the rear of the depot, above the offices and stores.

With the increased engine accommodation available at its new shed on the Holme,it would be assumed the GN immediately closed and removed the locomotive depot at the station, but it appears this did not occur straightaway . The Appendix to the 1881 WTT gives two whistle codes for engines wishing to gain access to Lincoln sheds: a 'long pip' for the Holme and 3 'short pips' for the station depot. In view of all the furore raised over Lincoln's level crossings, it is very surprising the old shed remained in use. Quite how long that continued has not been ascertained, but by the last years of the 19th century the building had been removed, although the turntable remained at the back of the Up platform.

Lincoln's locomotives had surprisingly few long-distance workings - Grantham, Retford, Boston, Gainsborough and East Lincolnshire roughly bounded the shed's area of responsibility. For a time though, from 7th August 1850, there was a working to Sheffield, over MSLR tracks, a duty that with others, doubtless ceased when the Peterborough - Retford section of the 'Towns' line was opened, on 1st August 1852. But, Lincoln would have assumed extra duties when the Gainsborough to Doncaster line was completed, on 1st July 1867 and Lincoln engines commenced through working. The allocation was thus only about a dozen locomotives by the early 1860's, with the original Sharps and Hawthorns gradually being replaced by Sturrock's later designs. Stirling's first Doncaster products were well in evidence by the time Holme shed opened, but his most famous creation, the 8 ft Single, eluded Lincoln until the last years of their lives, when Nos.8 and 1008 arrived. Even then, the Singles spent most of their time allocated to Louth, which had become a sub-shed of Lincoln, following opening of the Louth & Lincoln

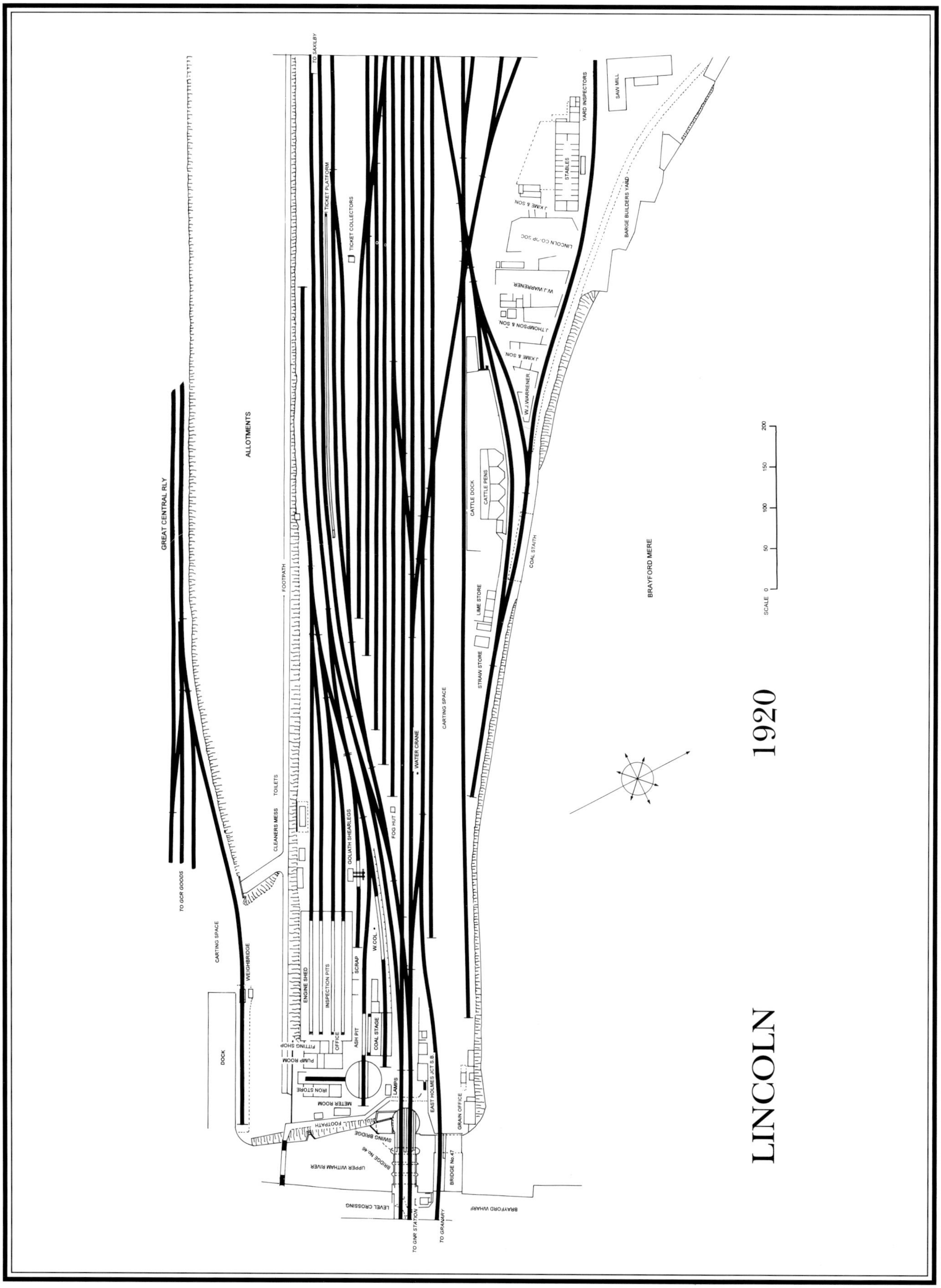
LINCOLN
1920
TO SAXILBY
YARD INSPECTORS
SAW MILL
STABLES
J. KIME & SON
BARGE BUILDERS YARD
LINCOLN CO-OP SOC
W.J. WARRENER
J. THOMPSON & SON
J. KIME & SON
W.J. WARRENER
TICKET PLATFORM
TICKET COLLECTORS
ALLOTMENTS
GREAT CENTRAL RLY
FOOTPATH
CATTLE DOCK
CATTLE PENS
COAL STAITH
BRAYFORD MERE
SCALE 0 50 100 150 200
LIME STORE
STRAW STORE
CARTING SPACE
WATER CRANE
FOG HUT
TOILETS
CLEANERS MESS
GOLIATH SHEARLEGS
TO GCR GOODS
CARTING SPACE
WEIGHBRIDGE
W. COL.
SCRAP
ENGINE SHED
INSPECTION PITS
ASH PIT
COAL STAGE
OFFICE
FITTING SHOP
PUMP ROOM
IRON STORE
METER ROOM
LAMPS
EAST HOLMES JCT S.B.
DOCK
FOOTPATH
SWING BRIDGE
GRAIN OFFICE
BRIDGE No.46
UPPER WITHAM RIVER
BRIDGE No.47
LEVEL CROSSING
BRAYFORD WHARF
TO GNR STATION
TO GRANARY

J69 no.8618, still wearing the austere wartime N E on its tankside, rests between duties on Lincoln shed yard with another of its class in April 1948. These former Great Eastern engines were very popular at Lincoln, indeed throughout the LNER system they could be found going about their business with enthusiastic crew's. *Authors collection.*

Railway, in the latter half of 1876. Louth shed's own sub-depots of Mablethorpe and Grimsby also came into the domain of the District Locomotive Superintendent, Lincoln, therefore.

As befitted a Locomotive District centre, Lincoln was provided with a breakdown train not long after Holme shed opened. The train featured a Doncaster-built 8 ton hand crane, which although inevitably soon rendered inadequate, was to remain in service well into LNER days. Following arrival of the crane, very little happened at Lincoln to be included in the GN archive, until 25th January 1907. That was with regard to a job let three weeks previously, to provide additional accommodation at Lincoln station, at a cost of £3,745. In readiness for the work, the archive noted, among other things that: "...the locomotive turntable has now been taken out..."

At Holme shed, an improvement at a date as yet unknown, but probably in the early 1900's, was installation of a "Goliath" shearlegs in the depot yard. Next, approval was given on 1st October 1914 for an electric water pump, from Messrs. Mather & Platt, at a cost of £91-11-0d. What was probably the last of the company's additions to the engine shed came in November 1920. That was when Gresley requested an electric jib crane, of 1 ton capacity, be provided for Lincoln coal stage. The stage had never been converted to a ramp type because of the aforementioned space limitations, so some form of mechanisation was long overdue. The actual machine requested by the loco engineer was a two-motor type, made by Charteris Engineering Co. available at a price of £592. The cost of erection and connecting up would add another £78 to the final bill. However, Gresley pointed out that: "...the present coaling arrangements require three shifts of two men, one of which could be dispensed with, giving a saving of £225 per year, after allowing for electricity charges, interest and depreciation..." The crane was approved by the Locomotive Committee on 3rd December 1920.

Came the Grouping, at which time Lincoln's allocation stood at 35 engines, compared with 42 and 4 railmotors that were based there (and Louth) in 1912, and 43 and 3 railmotors, seven years before that. The allocation at Lincoln, not including the seven at Louth on that last day of the GNR was as follows:

(LNER classification is used)
C12 1016, 1512, 1514.
D2 46, 1368, 1369, 1392.
D3 1303, 1307.
D4 1313.
E1 867, 883, 887, 1061, 1063, 1067, 1069.
J3 1109.
J4 317, 394, 644, 730, 731, 1039, 1081, 1085, 1110.
J52 1217, 1276.
J54 617, 691, 908.
J55 610A, 638A.
J56 608A.

The presence, on 1st January 1923, of seven Class E1 2-4-0 is notable, these being among the last survivors of the once numerous class, pottering about on Lincolnshire's easy grades and schedules in the twilight of their lives. Three were withdrawn on 3rd February and two more on 28th June 1923, one in August 1924 and 1061 in June 1925, however, but No.4070, transferred in from Retford in October 1924, survived until 1927 and only a year before that, Lincoln turned her out for a last trip to London, with a horse box special. Ivatt's 4-4-0's formed Lincoln's prime passenger power, working to Doncaster, Boston, Skegness and Grantham, and on summer weekends to Mablethorpe. Their numbers increased soon after Grouping, to about ten, mostly D2's at that time, a situation which pertained through the 1930's, with seven remaining (3 D2 and 4 D3), in 1939 and the last three leaving just before nationalisation. A couple of Ivatt's 4-4-2T were normally allocated for local passenger work, but unusually, for a fairly important depot, Lincoln had few Atlantic tender engines on its roster. On 25th June 1936 it was allocated one of only three GN engines to be named, but 3990 HENRY OAKLEY'S stay was brief because in October 1937 it was withdrawn for preservation. Other C2 class to arrive were 3254 on 6th July 1936 followed by 3256 on 7th July 1939 and 3252 on 28th May 1941 but all had left by August 1943 and were replaced by a brace of C1,until early BR times.

On the goods side, Lincoln GN shed seems not to have been very active. Indeed, the 1889 WTT shows that the depot

Pullman car 2992 was a feature of the rear of Lincoln shed from its grounding there in 1925, for use as a classroom for locomens' Mutual Improvement classes. During World War 2 the coach served as a post for the local Home Guard, afterwards returning to its original purpose, as the notice put up by British Railways indicates, in a picture dating from about 1966. *D.Tarpey.*

had no main line goods workings at all, its engines being concerned with shunting Lincoln's yards and trip working between them. Things must have improved though, as by 1905, there were five of Ivatt's J5 and five Stirling 0-6-0's of Classes J6, J7 and J8 operating from the shed. At the same time, however, only one Stirling J17 0-6-0ST was present, with one each of that designer's 0-4-2T and 0-4-4T - these presumably took care of yard shunting duties. By 1912 there were eleven 0-6-0 of Class J5, J6 and J7 classes and six 0-6-0ST - the same J17 having been joined by three of Stirling's J15 and two of his J16, in place of the 0-4-2 and 0-4-4 tanks. At the Grouping, Ivatt's J5 were still predominant, with nine of them being accompanied by a single Stirling J4; at the same time, the six Stirling 0-6-0ST had been supplemented by a pair of Ivatt J13. Ten years after grouping, much had changed. All the saddle tanks had been swept away and replaced by two ex-GE J66 and eight of that company's J69 0-6-0T. Of the 0-6-0 goods engines, a solitary example of GN design remained - a J6, which was shedmate to eight LNER J39, a J10 and no fewer than 15 of the GC's J11 - the latter two classes probably working out of Lincoln's ex-MSLR shed, which also hosted a trio of Robinson's O4 2-8-0. By nationalisation, the MSLR depot had gone, as had all GN goods locomotive types. Six K3, two O4, eight J11 and eight J39 took care of goods work and J66/67/69 still shunted the yards. That was basically the pattern of locomotive events until closure of Lincoln GN shed.

The newly formed LNER found itself the owner of three engine sheds at Lincoln: Holme (GN), East (GC) and Pyewipe Junction (GE) - a blatantly uneconomic situation. Accordingly, plans were quickly drawn up to close Pyewipe Junction four road northlight depot, and transfer its passenger duties and engines to the ex-GC shed, and the goods locomotives and their work to Holme depot. The job was approved on 2nd October 1924, along with expenditure of £789, to provide an additional engine road, with pit, at the former GN shed. On completion of that work, Pyewipe Junction closed, on 1st October 1925, and while the building was largely removed soon after, the turntable and some of the engine roads remained for a number of years. It would seem that staff at Holme did not generally take to the recently arrived ex-GE locomotives, so by 1930 most had gone, to be replaced by the likes of J39 0-6-0. However, as mentioned above, some GE types, namely J66 and J67/9 0-6-0T, were well liked.

Facilities at the Holme were further enhanced in 1925, when clerestory-roofed Pullman car No.2992 was grounded at the rear of the shed, for use as a lecture room for enginemen's Mutual Improvement classes. During World War Two, the Pullman car housed the local Home Guard unit and afterwards survived well into BR times. About 1938 Lincoln's old coal stage was at last replaced by a 200 ton mechanical coaler and extra siding room was created along the southern edge of the loco yard. Nevertheless, space was still at a *(continued on page 50)*

Table 1. **Lincoln pilots.**

Duty	Time	Return
Bardney	8.00 am	circa 4.00 pm
Lincoln Passenger Stn	4.55 am	circa 10.30 pm
Lincoln East Yard No.1	5.50 am MO	circa 9.43 am
Lincoln East Yard No.1	1.00 am MX	circa 12.45 pm
Lincoln East Yard No.2	5.50 am MO	circa 11.30 am
Lincoln Holmes Yard No.1	5.55 am	circa 12.00
Lincoln Holmes Yard No.2	5.55 am	circa 1.30 pm
Lincoln Holmes Yard No.3	3.55 am	circa 2.00 pm
Lincoln Holmes Yard No.4	5.10 pm	circa 2.00 am
Lincoln Holmes Yard No.5	1.55 pm SO	circa 10.00 pm
Lincoln Pyewipe Jct No.1	10.15 am	circa 5.00 am
Lincoln Pyewipe Jct No.2	5.55 am MO	circa 2.00 pm
Lincoln West Yard	10.27 am	circa 1.30 am
Lincoln Pyewipe West	5.50 am	suspended

In addition, there was a Lincoln Holmes Yard Pilot, worked by an Immingham engine, 6.00 pm to 10.00 pm SX.
Key to both tables: ***C.S.*** *- Carriage sidings;* ***MO*** *- Mondays only;* ***MX*** *- Mondays excepted;* ***OP*** *- Ordinary passenger;* ***Q*** *- as required;* ***sdgs*** *- sidings;* ***SO*** *- Saturdays only;* ***SX*** *- Saturdays excepted.*

Table 2. **Lincoln Shed duties.**

Shed dep	Arrives at	Time	Train worked
A.M.		A.M.	
12.02MX	Holmes Yard	12.05	Takes over 10.30 pm Boston-Doncaster SX
1.15MO	Pyewipe Jct	1.20	1.35 am Lincoln-Whitemoor MO
1.40	Pyewipe Jct	1.45	2.00 am Lincoln-Whitemoor Q
2.00MX	West Yard	2.03	2.10 am Lincoln-Mottram MX
2.25	Pyewipe Jct	2.30	2.35 am Lincoln-Whitemoor
3.00MX	Pyewipe Jct	3.05	Takes over 7.35 pm Huskisson-Whitemoor
3.30MX	Pyewipe Jct	3.35	3.50 am Lincoln-Sheffield
4.10MO	Pyewipe Jct	4.15	4.30 am Lincoln-Whitemoor
4.20MO	Pyewipe Jct	4.25	5.00 am Lincoln-Mottram MO
4.38	Pyewipe Jct	4.43	Takes over 2.50 am Whitemoor-Guide Bridge
4.50MX	West Yard	4.53	5.00 am Lincoln-Mansfield C.S. MX
5.43MO	Pyewipe Jct	5.48	6.03 am Lincoln-Sheffield MO
6.00	Passenger Stn	6.05	6.15 am OP Lincoln-Cleethorpes
6.15	Holmes Yard	6.18	6.30 am Lincoln-Firsby
6.45	Passenger Stn	6.50	7.00 am OP Lincoln-Grantham
6.50	Holmes Yard	6.53	7.00 am Lincoln-Horncastle
6.55	Pyewipe Jct	7.00	7.15 am Lincoln-Sleaford
7.00	East Holmes	7.05	ECS to Pass Stn then 7.55 am OP Lincoln-Boston
7.10	Passenger Stn	7.15	7.28 am Lincoln-Sheffield
8.00	Pyewipe West	8.08	8.20 am Lincoln-Langwith Jct
8.15	Passenger Stn	8.20	8.42 am OP Lincoln-Cleethorpes
8.35	Holmes Yard	8.38	8.45 am Lincoln-Barnetby
9.20	Pyewipe Jct.	9.25	9.40 am Lincoln-Spalding
9.20	Holmes Yard	9.23	9.30 am Lincoln-Honington
9.35	Holmes Yard	9.38	9.45 am Lincoln-Doncaster
10.05	Holmes Yard	10.08	10.15 am Lincoln-Doncaster
11.15SO	Passenger Stn	11.20	11.35 am OP Lincoln-Blankney SO
11.40MX	Pyewipe Jct	11.45	12.00 Lincoln-Sheffield MO
11.50	Pyewipe Jct	11.55	12.10 pm Lincoln-Whitemoor
11.50	Holmes Yard	11.53	12.00 Lincoln-Bracegirdle Gas sdgs
P.M.			
12.10	Pyewipe Jct	12.15	Takes over 3.55 am Dewsnap-Whitemoor
12.10	Passenger Stn	12.15	12.45 pm OP Lincoln-Chesterfield
12.10	Passenger Stn	12.15	12.40 pm OP Lincoln-Boston
12.20	Passenger Stn	12.25	12.45 pm OP Lincoln-Chesterfield
12.40	Pyewipe Jct	12.45	1.00 pm Lincoln-Broughton Lane
1.10	Holmes Yard	1.13	1.20 pm Lincoln-Boston
1.25	East Yard	1.35	1.45 pm Lincoln-Grimsby
1.50	Passenger Stn	1.55	2.25 pm OP Lincoln-Retford
2.55	Potterhanworth	3.15	3.52 pm Potterhanworth-Whitemoor
3.20	West Yard	3.23	3.30 pm Lincoln-Mansfield CS
4.00	Passenger Stn	4.05	4.35 pm OP Lincoln-Grantham
4.10	Pyewipe Jct	4.15	Takes over 1.15 pm Whitemoor-Mottram
4.45	Passenger Stn	4.50	5.10 pm OP Lincoln-Cleethorpes
5.00	Passenger Stn	5.05	5.56 pm OP Lincoln-Skegness
5.00	Pyewipe Jct	5.05	5.20 pm Lincoln-Whitemoor
5.50	Passenger Stn	5.55	6.25 pm OP Lincoln-Chesterfield
6.50SXQ	Holmes Yard	6.53	7.00 pm Lincoln-Doncaster SXQ
6.57	Holmes Yard	7.00	7.07 pm Lincoln-Boston
7.55	Pyewipe Jct	8.00	8.13 pm Lincoln-Mottram
8.20SO	Passenger Stn	8.25	8.35 pm OP Lincoln-Blankney SO
9.00SX	Passenger Stn	9.05	9.15 pm OP Lincoln-Blankney SX
9.10	Passenger Stn	9.15	9.58 pm Lincoln-Sheffield Pcls.
9.30	Pyewipe Jct	9.35	Takes over 5.20 pm Dewsnap-Whitemoor
9.40	Passenger Stn	9.45	10.15 pm OP Lincoln-Coningsby
10.00SX	Pyewipe West	10.08	10.25 pm Lincoln-Whitemoor SX
11.30	Holmes Yard	11.33	Takes over 9.45 pm Boston-Doncaster
11.50	Pyewipe Jct	11.55	Takes over 9.00 pm Whitemoor-Mottram
SUN			
A.M.			
12.50	Pyewipe Jct	12.55	1.10 am Lincoln-Whitemoor
10.20	Passenger Stn	10.25	10.40 am OP Lincoln-Retford
P.M.			
1.28	Passenger Stn	1.33	Takes over 12.30 pm OP Doncaster-March
5.05	Passenger Stn	5.10	5.20 pm OP Lincoln-Retford
10.05	Passenger Stn	10.10	10.30 pm OP Lincoln-Woodhall Jct

(left top to bottom) **Yard scenes in the 1940's. D3 no.2140, 14th July 1947. N5 no.9311 and C12 no.7384, 18th April 1948. O4 no.3570, 18th April 1948.** *H.C.Casserley and authors collection.*

(above and opposite) **Two views from the LNER's late 1930s improvements scheme. First we see, in a view which is precisely dated 21st September 1937, the 200 ton capacity coaling tower being formed; it was completed some 18 months later and in the illustration over we see the newly commissioned plant serving J66 no.7282 which required not much more than a shake of the coal 'jiggers'.** *Authors' collection & cty "Lincolnshire Echo".*

L N
726

Space was often at a premium at Lincoln, even into BR times, as this picture from the late 1950's shows. Ex-LNER B1's are now much in evidence as are former LMS types, the latter after the closure of yet another Lincoln engine shed, this time the former Midland establishment at St.Marks shed. *N.E.Stead.*

premium, so the old stage was quickly removed, in order that the area could be used to site a wheeldrop, housed in its own shed; at the same time, the turntable was replaced by a 65 ft model situated between the depot and the new coaling tower. That flurry of activity was the last major work carried out by the LNER, but BR did undertake other works - *see below.*

Further changes came about when Lincoln GC depot closed on 20th May 1939. However, engines continued to stable in the roofless building until about 1946, when it was given over to carriage use. Accordingly ex-GC types were moved to Holme shed and having entered upon the depot's busiest period, and taking on the duties of two other sheds, it would be appropriate to list Holme's pilot duties. These are as given in the October 1946 WTT *(table 1, page 47)*, and are followed by Holme's despatches of light engines, for its other work *(table 2, page 47)*.

Of the ex-GC engines that moved to Holme shed, B4 and B5 were prominent, with one of the latter's duties being the Colchester-York train, which often loaded to 16 coaches; both types had gone by 1947, however. The elegant C4 Atlantics also operated from Holme - again until the dawn of British Railways. In high summer of 1947, Holme turned out 2904 to head a relief fast to King's Cross and return - the only known use of a C4 on a GN main line express. With the exception of N5 0-6-2T - favourites for the Horncastle branch - ex-GC engines were swept away, early in BR times, by an influx of Thompson B1's. Four of these 4-6-0's were present after one year of nationalisation, a figure that reached eleven 4 years later, and peaked at 17 at the end of 1961. In a reverse operation though, five ex-GC "Director" 4-4-0 came to Holme shed about 1953 and stayed for $3^1/_2$ years, being used on Nottingham and Derby stopping trains, over the former MR route.

Other notable classes were K2 and K3 Moguls, which did not reach Lincoln in numbers, until about 1943 (K3), and the early 50's (K2). They were used mostly on ex-GC lines (K3) and over the MR line to Newark, Nottingham and Derby (K2). Other types tried by BR were N7 0-6-2T between 1948-50, seeing use on local goods services, including the Horncastle working. 69694 was even tried on Lincoln - Chesterfield (Market Place) passenger trains, late in 1948, but was not considered a success. A similar failure attended the trial, in February 1948, of ex-LTSR 4-4-2T No.2144 - as in the case of the N7, a limited fuel capacity was the engine's handicap.

Through all this, BR carried out various works at Holme shed, starting in 1950, when the depot's water tank collapsed, due to failure of internal stays. Most fortuitously, the sudden depositing of some 260 tons of water, plus attendant debris about the rear of the shed, did not result in any serious injury or damage. In the period before a replacement was built, locomotives took water at the station, the former MR shed at St. Marks, and at some still extant facilities of GE and GC origin. Next, in 1954, new locomen's accommodation was constructed, as a prelude to the depot's major rebuilding, two years later. By 1956 Holme shed's hipped roofs were in a very bad state, so BR replaced them with its standard light steel frame and corrugated asbestos, in two gables. In addition, considerable reconstruction attended the upper section of the side walls, and much repair work was carried out to ancillary buildings. The result was that on completion of the job, Holme shed was mostly a new structure that would require little else to be done to it, in the years remaining before closure.

Mention of St. Marks shed above, neatly takes us back to 20th April 1953, when that depot was tranferred to Holme as a sub-shed. Its allocation at the time was: 40419, 41060, 41686, 44247 and instructions were issued that those engines should go to Holme for washouts and minor repairs. As it happened, the "Midland" engines did not stay for long, being replaced by the "Directors" mentioned above. But, further, even older ex-MR engines came on 5th January 1959, when Newark GN shed closed and 0-4-4T Nos. 58065 and 58085, working from there, on the Southwell branch, were transferred to Lincoln. Three months later, however, St. Marks shed closed and not long afterwards Holme lost its ex-LMS types again.

Now Lincoln's sole remaining engine shed, Holme's allocation had nevertheless dropped to 51 engines, compared to 64, in 1950. Increasing dieselisation had gradually pared away the shed's steam duties, particularly after 1956, when a diesel depot was opened on the site of the former GC shed and d.m.u's invaded Lincolnshire in large numbers. Even so, as Lincoln always seems to have been a bit of a backwater, its remaining locomotive turns were not completely taken over by diesels until comparatively late in the day. So, it was not until October 1964, that the shed finally succumbed, when its surviving engines were transferred to Retford. After that, on 31st January 1965, the coaling plant was demolished by explosives, but the shed continued to house the steam breakdown crane for a number of years, the drop-pit was used for changing belts on d.m.u's and the coppersmith's shop was used for d.m.u. repairs. The latter closed on the retirement of the coppersmith, the drop-pit was eventually taken out, and despite plans to turn the shed into a wagon shop, the tracks were taken up.

However, even that was not the end, as Holme shed's office block continued to house clerical staff for a time, until they moved to the Station Manager's building. For a while after that the depot still served as a locomen's booking on and off point, with a Running Foreman in charge. It was in use as such in 1978, but when this ceased is unknown. Nevertheless, still today (June 1995), the shed continues to stand, abandoned and increasingly derelict - surely now with a very limited future.

(right) **The view from the coaling plant c1948. The 1930's additions to the shed yard are apparent on the right.** *P.Grey.*

(below) **This portrait of Class K2 61743, taken on 7th September 1958, also shows the loco sidings installed in the late 1930s, and part of the crew accommodation block put up by BR around 1954.** *B.Hilton.*

BR's modernisation of Lincoln GN shed had not long been completed when this picture was taken in June 1958. Between 61828 and an ex-works 63985 some detail is visible of the asbestos roof with its lightweight steel columns and cross braces. *Authors' coll.*

Finally, a reminder of what nature can do to the best laid plans. This was the Holmes during the floods of 1947. Ever susceptible to the whims of the Witham, the railway has learned to live with events such as this over the decades. *R.Tarpey collection.*

LOUTH

Centre of northeast Lincolnshire's agricultural district, Louth was also well known for its carpet weaving industry, in addition to which were lesser involvements in ironfounding, brewing and carriage making. Situated on the River Lud, which gave the town its original name of Luda, Louth has the distinction of being the operational centre of the first section of the GNR to be opened, and also the site of the company's first 'permanent' locoshed.

The line from (Great) Grimsby to Boston was sponsored by the East Lincolnshire Railway, which came into being with the passing of its Act on 26th June 1846. Making its headquarters at Louth, the ELR was leased by the GNR before opening, that lease being regularly extended until the end of the ELR's nominally independent existence at the Grouping. To all intents and purposes though, the East Lincs was pure GNR and with its first section expected to be brought into use in March 1848, the GN Board resolved, on the preceding 3rd February, that: "...a cargo of coke of the best quality, for locomotive engines, be ordered to Grimsby..." Also, on the same day: "...that 5 engines and tenders, 12 carriages for passengers, 1st and 2nd class, 3 for 3rd class, 4 horse boxes, 2 luggage vans, 2 carriage trucks, 20 cattle wagons, 10 sheep pens, 50 goods wagons and 60 ballast wagons, be ordered to be sent onto the East Lincs line at Grimsby or Louth..." (These locomotives were not the first to run on the ELR. Sharp 2-2-2, Nos.1 and 2, had arrived at Grimsby in August 1847 and assisted with construction work, until transferred to Boston). The somewhat disproportionate number of cattle wagons ordered is a reminder that Louth's cattle market used to be one of the most important in the country, with even Irish store cattle being sent, by boat to Liverpool and rail to Louth. Outwards from Louth, special cattle trains could be up to 30 wagons in length.

James Johnson had already been appointed by Benjamin Cubitt to oversee the arrival and operation of the first stock for the ELR, which actually opened on 1st March 1848, from Louth to Grimsby. At Grimsby, the ELR linked up with the Manchester Sheffield & Lincolnshire Railway line from New Holland - opened the same day - and initial services over the whole route were to be jointly worked by the two companies. In practice, however, MS&LR engines rarely ventured south of Grimsby and it was those machines that appear to have been a prime cause of the GN's first unpunctual trains!

The inaugural timetable, Louth - New Holland, consisted of five return trains on weekdays and two on Sundays, as in the table below.

Within a couple of weeks of opening, delays were being attributed to "waiting the Packet at New Holland" or MSL locomotives breaking tender springs! Indeed in the first five months of working, up to 31st July 1848, there is no record of a GN engine failure. Locomotive facilities consisted of GN engines sharing the MSL shed at New Holland, which is briefly described elsewhere in this book, and at Louth, where the shed had opened with the line and where James Johnson and his men were attaining their good record for engine reliability.

Louth engine shed adjoined the Up side station building and consisted of a brick-built two road structure, scaling 170 ft x 30 ft with a slated roof in single-pitch gable style. Engines gained access to the building through individual arched doorways; in later years, the doorway at the southern end, nearest the station, would be bricked up. A 40 ft turntable was installed in the yard, but this survived only for a few years, as a smouldering dispute between the GN and MSL finally flared up and resulted in the ending of joint working south of Grimsby, with effect from 1st July 1851. Consequently, Grimsby became the GN's northern terminus and need for a turntable there was met by taking out that at Louth and re-installing it. Coking at Louth was effected from a simple open platform, while water came from a well, via a steam-powered pump (dieselised in 1951!), to be stored in a 32,000 gallon tank, by the shed.

With successive openings of the ELR, on 3rd September and 2nd October 1848, to Firsby and Boston respectively, a link was made with the northward progress of the GN's Loop line. Accordingly, engines drifted away from Louth, leaving a handful to cope with local services to Grimsby and places like Willoughby and Firsby. So it remained until 1876, when the Louth & Lincoln Railway was finally completed, no less than ten years after being incorporated. In fact, a second Act had to be obtained to complete the line, as the construction period of the first expired. This GN-worked line, meandering across Lincolnshire from Bardney, opened for goods on 26th June 1876 and passengers on 1st December 1876. Part of the agreement for working by the GNR - whose 18 August 1882 Act for absorption of the L&LR, came into force on 30th June 1883 - was that a turntable be re-installed at Louth. This was done in time for commencement of passenger services, with the GN charging the L&LR 10% - later 5% - interest on the cost of providing the 44 ft -6 in table.

Inauguration of the L&LR, which would have entailed additional locomotives coming to Louth, was followed in October 1877 by completion of the GN-worked Louth & East Coast Railway, to Mablethorpe: a sub-shed was provided at the terminus, which probably meant another engine being drafted to Louth. By now, Sharps and Hawthorns were not so commonly seen as Sturrock's later designs and Stirling's first Doncaster products.

Table 1

	WEEKDAYS					SUNDAYS	
	Parliamentry	**Express**	**Ord. Pass**	**Express**	**Ord .Pass**	**Parliamentry**	**Ord. Pass**
Louth dep.	6.00 am	8.30 am	11.15 am	4.00 pm	5.30 pm	9.00am	5.00pm
Great Grimsby	6.39 am	8.57 am	11.54 am	4.27 pm	6.09 pm	9.39am	5.39pm
New Holland arr.	7.20 am	9.28 am	12.35 pm	4.58 pm	6.50 pm	11.00am	7.00pm
New Holland dep.	8.00 am	11.00 am	1.15 pm	3.45 pm	7.00 pm	9.00am	5.00pm
Great Grimsby	8.45 am	11.45 am	1.50 pm	4.29 pm	7.35 pm	9.45am	5.45pm
Louth arr.	9.20 am	12.20 pm	2.13 pm	5.04 pm	7.58 pm	10.20am	6.20pm

There was also a return goods on weekdays; its running times have not been discovered.

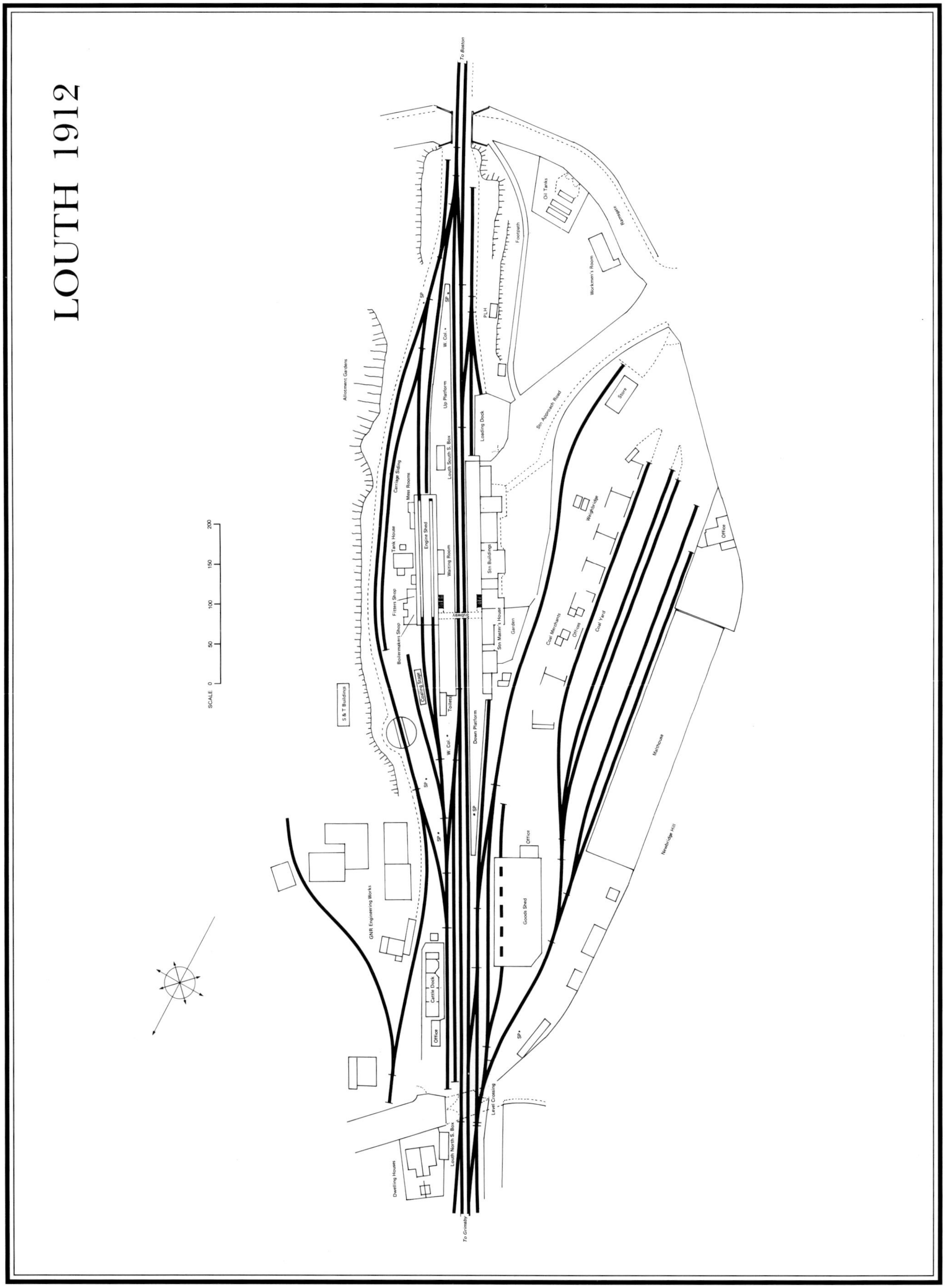
LOUTH 1912
To Boston
To Grimsby
Allotment Gardens
Carriage Siding
Mess Rooms
Tank House
Engine Shed
Fitters Shop
Boilermakers Shop
Coaling Stage
S & T Buildings
GNR Engineering Works
Cattle Dock
Office
Dwelling Houses
Louth North S. Box
Level Crossing
Goods Shed
Office
Down Platform
Toilets
Waiting Room
Stn Buildings
Stn Master's House
Garden
Louth South S. Box
Up Platform
Loading Dock
Footpath
Oil Tanks
Workmen's Room
Stn Approach Road
Store
Weighbridge
Coal Merchants
Offices
Coal Yard
Malthouse
Newbridge Hill
Office
SCALE
0
50
100
150
200

The south end of Louth in 1927, with Class D3 4307 and E1 3814 awaiting their next duties. For the 2-4-0 that duty might well be her last, as she was the only survivor of her class and the writing on the rear of the print claims that this is the last known photograph of that venerable locomotive. *J.E.Kite.*

Doubtless their 2-4-0, 0-4-2 and 0-6-0's were usual, with the odd 0-4-2T or two. Services over the ELR had not changed much by mid-July 1888, when Mablethorpe and Willoughby were connected, via Sutton-on-Sea, giving Louth locoshed a few more duties to undertake.

That ended route development in East Lincolnshire for 25 years (until the Kirkstead-Little Steeping line opened in 1913), so it is hard to visualise what Stirling was referring to, on 18th May 1893, when he reported to the Board: "...With the opening of new lines in the neighbourhood of Louth and a consequent increase in train services, the number of engines that have to be stationed there has been increased to eight. The present arrangement for coaling engines is very defective, the stage being simply a wooden platform, where coal has to be lifted onto locomotive tenders. The work is divided among engine cleaners who have no protection in bad weather and are often complaining. Further, there is no room for the use of enginemen. I recommend the erection of a small covered coal stage with a hand crane and an enginemens' room of 14 ft x 8 ft; the cost of providing these is estimated at £360. I also intend to relieve the cleaners of the coaling duty and appoint a man solely for the work, which will not entail any extra cost..." What "new lines" Stirling meant is not known (unless he was harking back no less than 5 years!), but he got his £360 approved by the Board on 28th July 1893.

In late 1904 Louth's eight sets of footplatemen presented a memorial to Ivatt, which he passed on to the Board on 5th January 1905. The enginemen requested provision of a 45 ft turntable at Willoughby - obviously to eradicate some tender-first running. Ivatt apparently supported his men because he suggested relocating the 45 ft table from the north end of Doncaster Carr locoshed, at a cost of £550, to include foundations and spur line. The proposal was turned down and Willoughby never did get a turntable.

At the end of 1905 - 11th December, to be precise - two Kitson steam railmotors appeared at Louth, to operate the shuttle service to Grimsby. On the following 19th February, the steam cars' duties were extended when a third car, GN-built, was introduced on the Louth - Mablethorpe - Willoughby line. A short time later, on 4th April 1906, Ivatt gave this report on railmotors to the Board: "...The Louth -Grimsby service was run supplemental to the train service, with, for the two months ended 31st March 1906, 13,860 miles run by train and 9,996 miles by railcar. Passengers carried totalled 64,767, of which just under 24,000 were taken by railmotor. Local receipts increased by £186, or 24%, during that period. Between Louth, Mablethorpe and Willoughby, the railcar has largely taken the place of the train service, except on days when the railcar was not sufficient for the number of passengers. For the 6 weeks ending 31st March trains had run 3,611 miles and railmotors 5,452 miles. Out of 15,168 passengers, 8,518 had travelled in the steam cars. Local receipts increased by only £18, however..." It is said the railmotors also appeared on the Spilsby branch, but all in all, they had a brief operating life in East Lincs, due to their limited accommodation, and they were replaced by conventional engines and coaches from September 1914.

Before the end of the railmotor era though, in the latter period of 1911, a fire caused severe damage to the roof of Louth engine shed, and in November, Gresley gave instructions that it should be rebuilt - no other details are known. It was also during this time that Stirling Singles Nos.8 and 1008 came to Louth, to see out their twilight years on the depot's comparatively easy duties; No.8 was withdrawn in August 1907 and 1008 followed in June 1914.

On the eve of Grouping the locomotive allocation was as follows: C12 1503, 1506, 1513; D2 1383; D3 1304; E1 814, 1000A.

The GNR and ELR ended their existences on 1st January 1923 and for two years nothing changed at Louth. By then the shed's most prestigious duty was the Ivatt 4-4-0 from Grimsby sub-shed (4382 and 4383 were 'regulars' for a number of years), rostered for the 5.50 a.m. Grimsby, 6.19 a.m. Louth, to Peterborough, arriving 8.47 a.m. After a trip to Peterborough East and back, the 4-4-0 returned to Grimsby, 10.50 a.m. ex-Peterborough, with a crew change at Louth. At 4.50 p.m. the same engine and crew left Grimsby for Boston, arriving 6.50 p.m., returning from there at 8.32 p.m., on the 7.22 p.m. ex-Peterborough, which arrived at Louth at 9.25 p.m. Some other Louth loco duties at this time were, weekdays only: 7.05 a.m., 9.53 a.m. and 1.15 p.m. light engines to Grimsby to work passenger trains to Louth and Boston. Two morning and four afternoon return workings to Bardney also passenger and freight workings to and from Grimsby, Mablethorpe and Willoughby.

By the end of October 1931 Louth's allocation had increased to no less than 16 engines, the exact number found 'on shed' when a visit was made, on 9th February 1930, the resident locomotives comprised of no fewer than eight classes: **C12** 4015, 4019, 4503, 4506, 4513, 4525; **D2** 4325, 4377, 4383; **D3** 4304, 4307; **J10** 5840; **J11** 6009; **J52** 4217; **J65** 7248; **J69** 7359.

The number of engines stationed had fallen to eleven by September 1934, when it consisted of: 3 **C12;** 4 **D2;** 3 **D3** and 1 **J11**. During the 1930's therefore, there was a period of flux at Louth, with only one class being constant - the C12 4-4-2T, that

Louth's position vis-a-vis the wonderfully ornate East Lincolnshire Railway station is seen in this mosiac photograph, taken from the top of a grain elevator, about 1949. Notice the roof of asbestos sheeting with four glazing panels let in - all provided during the air-raid damage repair. Besides the engine shed area, the view holds many interesting facets of the newly nationalised railway - the goods yard and coal depot; the oil depot; horse landing; underbridge; level crossing and of course those well cultivated allotments. *H.L.Howe.*

first appeared about 1920 and stayed until the end. Other classes were seen at this time, including 1930-5, D7 4-4-0's 5684, 5701, 5703, 5711 at different times, for varying periods. By the start of the 1930's ex-GE class J69 0-6-0T had appeared, to remain until BR days - similarly with two ex-GC classes that came later in the 30's: N5 0-6-2T and J11 0-6-0 - the latter proving very popular indeed. Another ex-GC type was D9 6029, which was present at Louth from December 1938 to April 1942.

Earlier in 1938 another development was the replacement of Louth's 1876 turntable by a 49 ft - 8 in. model, but after that, all else stayed fairly static - with one significant exception, during the Second World War. In the early years of that conflict all of Britain's east coast was front-line territory, even to the extent that small towns like Louth saw their share of action. For example, on 19th February 1941 the German Airforce carried out a sharp attack that encompassed the railway station area. The locomotive shed's north end was extensively damaged, as was the coal stage. Repairs to the shed did away with the north end's arched entrances, by substitution of a steel lintel,

Louth gets a new 50ft turntable in 1938. As was often the case, a railway steam crane officiates - the machine seen here came from Peterborough. *J.White*

supported by a brick column between the tracks. The coal stage was not restored, however, and henceforth coaling was carried out direct from wagons, albeit with the benefit of a shelter.

The war ended and by 1946 it was evident Louth's importance had dwindled somewhat. The 'star' Grimsby - Peterborough duty no longer existed, as the WTT for that year showed the following weekdays only despatch of locomotives from the shed:

Depart	Duties
6.00am	Pilot No.1 - 7.20am to 9.30pm SX, 7.20am to 8.30pm SO
6.15am	FOQ 6.30am Cattle to Willoughby
6.15am	6.30am Passenger to Grimsby
7.10am	SX 7.25am e.c.s. to Sutton
7.30am*	7.42am Passenger to Grimsby
7.30am*	7.44am Passenger to Willoughby
7.30am*	SO Light engine to Sutton
7.55am	8.05am Goods to Bardney
11.30am	12 noon Passenger to Grimsby
11.40am	FOQ Pilot No.2. (Shunt cattle dock and work special to Grimsby)
12.28pm	12.43pm Passenger to Bardney
2.00pm	2.15pm Goods to Grimsby
4.00pm	4.10pm Passenger to Grimsby
4.00pm	SX 4.20pm Passenger to Willoughby

Notes:
Q - runs when required.
* - coupled together off shed.

No other timings were available to the authors.

In BR times ex-GE Class N7 0-6-2T made a brief appearance 1948-50, then A5 4-6-2T right at the end. The first indications of that came with withdrawal of the four weekday passenger trains over the Louth & Lincoln line, on Guy Fawkes Day, 1951. Five and a half months before that, a visit to Louth shed on 26th May, found the following: J6 64274 (Bradford, Hammerton Street), N5 69306 (Louth), O2 63934 (Frodingham) - the allocation at the time was: 7 C12; 1 D3; 2 J11; 2 N5. Just over $5^{1/2}$ years later, on 26th September 1956, the Louth - Donington-on-Bain section of the L&LR closed completely and exactly a month previously another visit to Louth discovered: A5 69816, J11 64320, 64439 (all Louth). The 4-6-2T was one of a pair that, as mentioned above, came to Louth about 1954 and 69812 of the class worked the last steam-hauled Louth - Grimsby local train - the "Motor Train" as it was known locally, in a throwback to steam car days. That train left Louth at 4.10 p.m. on 30th June 1956, a clear indication that the end was in sight, and sure enough, Louth shed closed in December 1956. The remaining engines, C12 67398; J11 64320 and 64328 and their duties, were transferred to Immingham, which had its engine diagrams recast, to continue the dwindlng goods services, while passenger trains were taken over by d.m.u.'s from Lincoln.

Demolition soon followed and although a diesel shunter stabled at Louth for a while, eventually the whole of the GN between Firsby and Grimsby passed into history. Today, the energetic Grimsby - Louth Railway Preservation Society is determined to see through its plan to re-open the original section of the East Lincolnshire Railway. The Society may not rebuild Louth locoshed but we wish them well in their endeavours to return steam to this historic part of East Lincolnshire!

J11's, 64320 and 64372, stable on the turntable road at Louth on Sunday 12th September 1954. Shed room at weekends was fairly sparse and these two, being tender engines, were relegated to the yard. *Authors collection.*

Louth's north end was much more involved, with the coaling stage and turntable in close proximity. In a picture dating from around 1954, the latter-day coaling facility is seen - manhandled from wagons, but at least with the benefit of a shelter. Two Class C12 and a J11 complete the scene. *B.Yale.*

Class C12 4525 stands outside Louth's only remaining arched portal on 9th May 1946. The brickwork in the buttress shows evidence of repair at some time - such remedial works, large and small, were a constant drain upon the resources of every railway in the battle against the depredations of weather, soot and steam. *H.C.Casserley.*

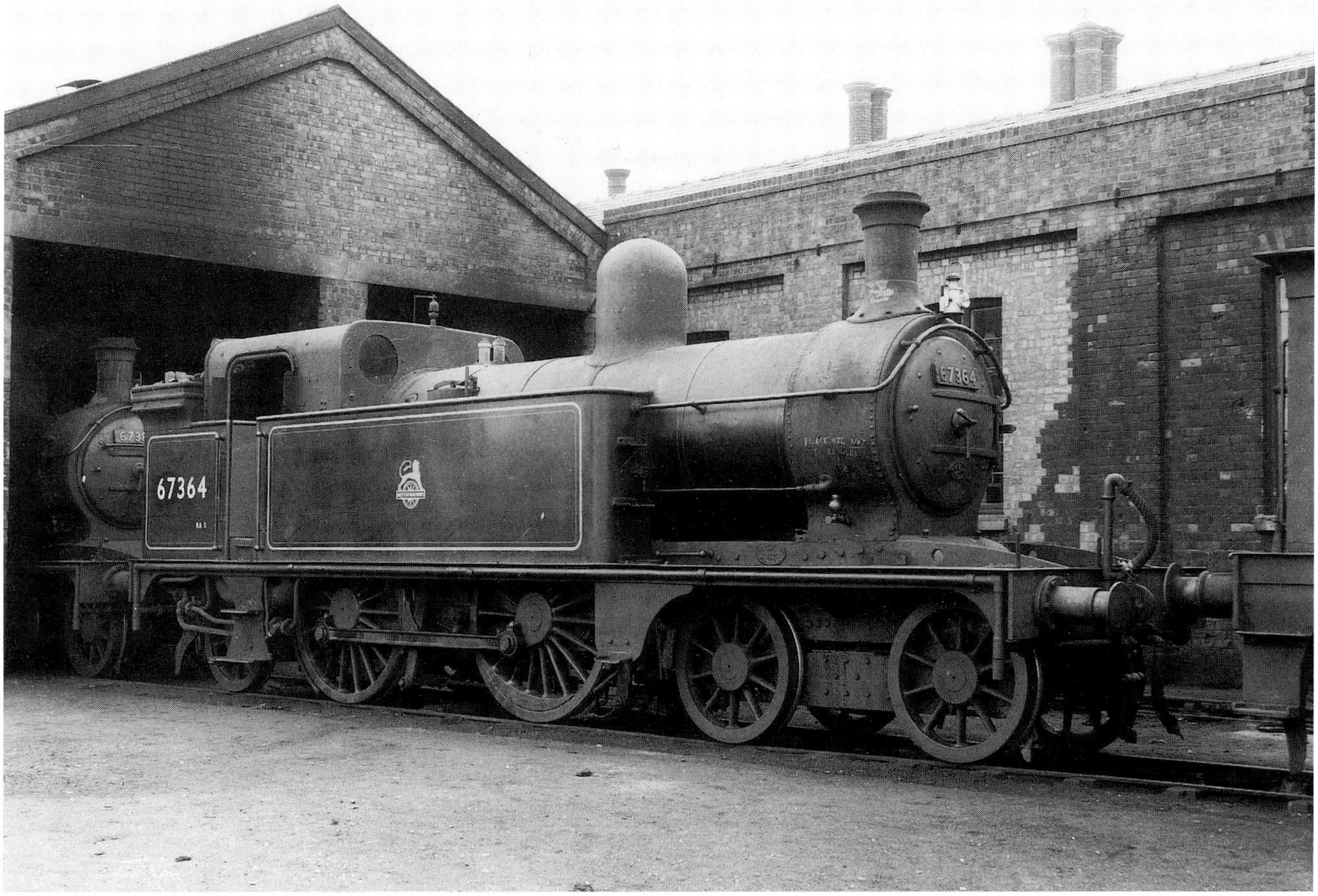

This undated but nevertheless 1950's period portrait of a C12 clearly shows the extent of the repair work needed for station and shed, following the wartime bomb damage. For some reason it appears that black oil was injurious to 67364! *H.Ballantyne.*

The south end of Louth on 12th September 1954, with two of the then-resident ex-GCR 0-6-2T 'on shed'; No. 69322 is at left. Louth's general lack of space is evidenced by the parking of coaches on the fringes of the shed yard. *K.Hoole.*

MABLETHORPE

Mablethorpe like its more southerly neighbours, Skegness and Sutton-on-Sea, owed its popularity as a holiday resort to the miles of excellent beaches fringing the Lincolnshire coast. Mablethorpe's population in 1881 was 640 a figure which had grown to 934 by August 1913, but during the months of July to September in that year, the town also hosted 28,000 visitors plus day and half day trippers - such was the measure of its success.

Such potential had hardly been realised though, when the Louth & East Coast Railway was sponsored, to duly receive its Act on 18th July 1872. The Act included powers for branches to North Somercotes and Saltfleet but all that materialised was the 12 mile line from Louth to Mablethorpe which was worked by the GN from the outset, opening on 17th October 1877. As usual the terminus was provided with a small locomotive shed, brick built with a slated gable roof over the single dead-end road. The building measured 60 ft x 20 ft and was accompanied by a 44 ft 8 ins turntable, coal platform and a 3,600 gallon tank, on its own tankhouse. Water came from a well, later by means of a windmill pump the only example ever employed by the GNR.

Louth provided the locomotive that worked the branch service and stayed overnight at Mablethorpe. This might have been a Hawthorn or Wilson product or possibly a Sharp 2-2-2T, a type which had gravitated to East Lincolnshire in the late 1860s. In time, 0-4-2T and 0-4-4T would have appeared on the route, which early in its history saw a weekday service of seven or eight return passenger trains, plus a goods working.

Mablethorpe became a through station on 14th July 1888, with a southerly connection via Sutton-on-Sea to Willoughby. The company involved, another GN worked independent concern, was the Sutton & Willoughby Railway & Dock Company, incorporated on 28th July 1884 and opened between Sutton and Willoughby on 23rd September 1886. Two days later the S&WR&DC had a further Act granted for its onward extension to Mablethorpe. Both the independent companies were finally absorbed by the GN, the S&WR&DC in March 1902 and the L&ECR from 1st August 1908; purchase prices were £40,500 and £87,000 respectively.

Now situated just over halfway along the $22^{1}/_{2}$ mile loop line from Louth to Willoughby, Mablethorpe continued as a locomotive centre. The basic service to Louth didn't change much, with the exception of the 1905/1915 steam railmotor period, but now of course trains worked in from the south too. Mablethorpe's resident engine was usually employed on the section from Sutton to Louth, though it did make occasional forays to Willoughby and even to Firsby. For example in 1924 Mablethorpe's weekdays only locomotive diagram was as follows - the machine by then employed being a Class C12 4-4-2T, a type which had supplanted the Stirling 0-4-4T a few years before:

Depart	Duties
Mablethorpe	LE to Sutton-on-Sea
Sutton-on-Sea	8.20 am FX Passenger to Louth
Sutton-on-Sea	8.30 am FO Passenger to Louth
Louth	9.53 am Passenger to Sutton-on-Sea
Sutton-on-Sea	10.33 am e.c.s. to Mablethorpe
Mablethorpe	Shunt yard
Mablethorpe	11.43 am Passenger to Louth
Louth	2.36 pm Passenger to Willoughby
Willoughby	4.45 pm SX Pass to Mablethorpe
Willoughby	4.49 pm SO Pass to Mablethorpe
Willoughby FO	LE to Firsby
Firsby FO	7.45 pm Pass to Mablethorpe, through coaches off 6.00 pm ex-Notts

A typical late-Victorian GNR stopping train pauses at Mablethorpe. Among such detail as the interested bystanders, hand barrows of various kinds, barrels and gas lamps, we see in the left distance the single road engine shed. *Authors' collection*

A vivid reminder of the days when all of Britain travelled by train. An early 30s crowd emerges, somewhat thankfully one would imagine, from a rake of ancient carriages, to get their first whiff of Mablethorpe's bracing East Coast air. Of more interest to students of engine sheds though is another rear view of Mablethorpe shed, by this time equipped with the unique windmill for pumping water. *H.L.Howe*

Engines from other depots visited Mablethorpe daily and may, on occasion have needed to use more of the town's engine shed facilities than the turntable and water crane. Again, from 1924, close to the end of Mablethorpe shed's existence come the following details of train workings using "foreign" engines:

Mablethorpe (D - departure; A - arrival)

D 7.10 am MO	Pass to Nottingham (Boston loco)
A 9.10am	Pass from Willoughby (Louth loco)
D 9.25 am	Pass to Willoughby (Louth loco)
A 11.30 am	Pass from Grantham (Boston loco)
D 12.05 pm	Pass to Grantham (Boston loco)
A 12.53 pm	Pass from Nottingham (Colwick loco)
D 1.40 pm SO	Pass to Leicester (Boston loco)
A 1.52 pm SO	Pass from Leicester (Boston loco)
D 2.15 pm SO	Pass to Notts and Derby (Colwick loco)
D 4.23 pm SO	Pass to Notts and Derby (Boston loco)
D 4.23 pm SX	Pass to Notts and Derby (Colwick loco)

In addition, Mablethorpe saw a number of 'through' workings, including a Down goods, in the care of Louth based engines, and a daily appearance of a Wainfleet locomotive, on the 1.10 p.m. Willoughby to Louth service.

As alluded to above, by 1924 it had become obvious that the far from arduous duties undertaken by Mablethorpe's sole locomotive could quite easily be handled by an engine sent out daily from Louth. Accordingly, the necessary rearrangements were made and Mablethorpe engine shed closed, in June of that year. Even so, engines on long distance trains continued to terminate and commence their journeys from Mablethorpe, so the turntable and water facilities were retained in service - despite the very poor quality of the latter. The turntable, incidentally, had been extended to 45 ft 9 ins by 1947 but such was the traffic that built up in the immediate post-war period that on 4th August 1954 the turntable was replaced completely by a 52 ft model recovered from the north end of Doncaster station.

Expanding the turntable's size enabled it to turn locomotives larger than say J6 and J11 because B1, K2 and LMS Class 5's had become increasingly more common on weekend specials. For example, on August Bank Holiday 1951 no fewer than 19 specials visited Mablethorpe and engines too large for the turntable had to be coupled together three at a time to travel to Firsby triangle to turn - a 15 mile trip each way. When such traffic levels were reached - usually on Sundays - coaching stock would be parked on every spare yard of track at Mablethorpe before overflowing onto the "main" line towards Louth, which of course, saw no Sunday trains, up to six rakes of coaches were accommodated in this way. On Saturdays, the daily goods would terminate at Mablethorpe so that the engine could act as a very necessary station pilot.

Louth shed closed in December 1956 when diesel multiple units took over the area's local services, including the Mablethorpe loop. Steam continued on goods though and the many summer specials. As such Mablethorpe would have continued servicing locomotives right up to the end of steam in 1964 the year in which Boston depot closed and Skegness saw its last summer of steam. Mablethorpe engine shed had been demolished many years before that though and today the resort's still numerous summer visitors must all come by road, following complete closure of all lines north from Firsby to Grimsby. However, a late 1991 visit to the site found part of the 1954 turntable pit still visible.

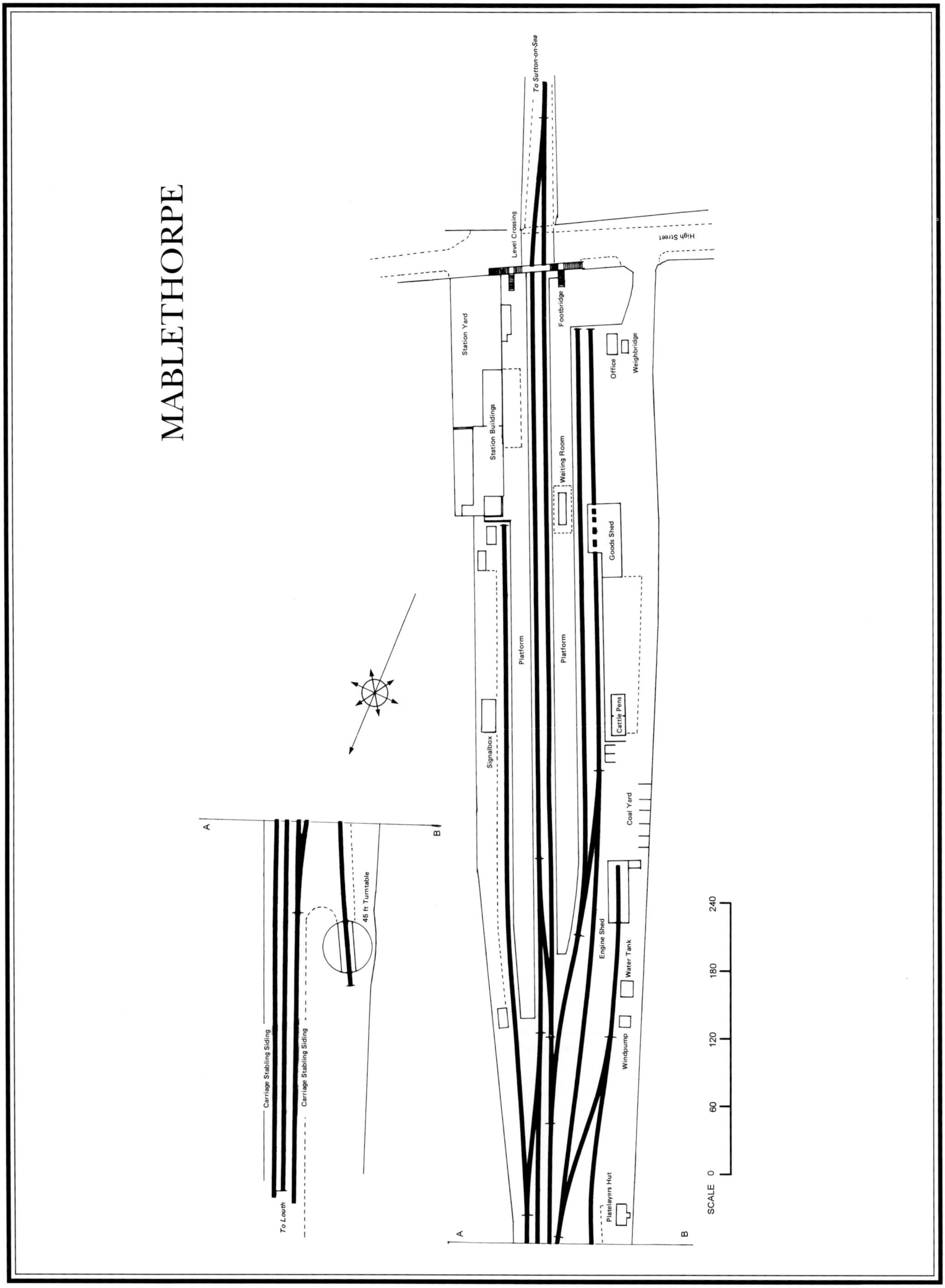
MABLETHORPE
To Sutton-on-Sea
Level Crossing
High Street
Footbridge
Station Yard
Station Buildings
Office
Weighbridge
Waiting Room
Goods Shed
Platform
Platform
Cattle Pens
Signalbox
Coal Yard
Engine Shed
Water Tank
Windpump
Platelayers Hut
SCALE 0 60 120 180 240
A
B
Carriage Stabling Siding
Carriage Stabling Siding
To Louth
45 ft Turntable

Even after its shed closed, Mablethorpe remained an important locomotive servicing point, during the summer months at least. So much so, that BR went to the expense of installing a new 52ft turntable on ground that had to be specially built-up. Actually, the table itself was not new, but was a refurbished machine, formerly sited at the north end of Doncaster station. This view of 4th August 1955 shows the then 'new' turntable, against a backdrop of a large Territorial Army summer camp. *Authors' collection.*

A final look at Mablethorpe, this time in September 1954, with a 'local' headed by Louth C12 no.67379, calling to pick-up its few intending passengers. Within a few years diesel multiple units had taken over the passenger workings and the only steam came on the ever dwindling goods traffic and summer excursions. *Authors collection.*

NEWARK

The Trent-side town of Newark's large trade in corn, malt and flour was first tapped by the Great Northern Railway when its main line opened between Peterborough and Retford, on 1st August 1852. Locomotive facilities in the shape of 40 ft by 15 ft coke platforms and water cranes appeared at Newark at an early stage being sited just beyond the ends of the Up and Down platforms.

Both the GN's Derbys and Staffs Extension and its Joint Line venture with the LNWR in the period 1876/9 had a natural progression. That was in the building of a connection from Bottesford Junction on the Nottingham - Grantham route northwards to join the GN main line, just south of Newark. Sidings were laid down at Newark in time for completion of the line, in April 1879. At the same time a 45 ft turntable was installed at an all-in cost of £312 south of the station on the Up side. The turntable which had been extended to 47 ft 7 ins by 1947 was sited adjacent to an open area of land, earmarked for erection of an engine shed for which tenders were duly invited, late in 1879. The successful offer, of £1,130 came from one Charles Baines with a contract being let on 15th January 1880; there were five other bids the highest being £1,880.

Baines & Co. certainly worked fast because the new engine shed was brought into use during June 1880 but not without some prevarication on the part of the GN in the meantime! In May 1880 with construction at a late phase, Stirling proposed that the shed's coke stage should be moved from its present site adjacent to the turntable spur, to alongside the ashpit on the road leading to the shed. He also advocated that the depot should be four roads instead of two! Though Stirling had gone to the extent of having plans drawn up for his ideas nothing (ever) came of them, but it would seem that in being "messed about a bit" Baines & Co. overspent their budget. Six monthly payments to the contractor by the GN from February to July 1880 totalled £1,230. Then in October came a final payment of £82 so Newark locoshed ended up costing £1,312 - £182 over budget. Regarding coke/coal stages, those by the station went out of use after the shed opened. The stage at the shed, while not moved as the Locomotive Engineer had asked, also went out of use during LNER times with coaling henceforth being done direct from wagons.

As completed the depot comprised a 125 ft by 35 ft brick building with a slated hipped roof, the last example of that roof style to be built by the GN. One shed road terminated inside the building with the other (eastern) road being slightly extended through to the rear, ending in stop blocks. Fuelling and turning facilities at the shed have previously been touched upon above, but no water point seems to have been installed at first. Nevertheless the locomotives' thirst was soon being noticed, as on 4th October 1883 Stirling asked the Way & Works Committee to sanction a new water tank for Newark, at an estimated cost of £1,142. The Committee had other ideas however and Stirling was asked to prepare plans for enlargement of the existing tank which stood at the station. Even so it seems

Newark stood amidst a grassy space and despite the close proximity of the back gardens of a row of houses, it exuded a distinctly rural air for all its existence. This is evidenced by this sleepy-looking picture of the shed, taken around 1936, and doubtless on a Sunday. An assortment of 0-6-0 quietly slumber, awaiting the arrival of the firelighter and preparation for another week's work. *Authors' collection.*

A visit on Sunday 7th May 1950 found the following engines 'on shed':- 63486, 64133, 64335, 9273, 69282, 69294, 69304, 9313 and 90153. Certainly, the allocation was of an ex-GC flavour at this time. The hipped roof is showing signs of wear and tear and is probably a result of blast damage from a locomotive chimney; it was to be some years before this 'minor' damage was repaired and the fact that BR had other larger projects to deal with at the time meant that such monies that were available went onto more important budgets. The doors are still intact and were to remain so up to closure, a tribute to good housekeeping over the years no doubt, although the shed yard was typical of the period with spilt coal littering the ground. *T.J.Edgington.*

as if Stirling got his way because a 29,000 gallon tank did eventually appear at the shed! That might have been as soon as 1884 when a water crane was installed in the shed yard, in the fork of the turntable spur and shed access road.

At first Newark was a sub-shed of Retford which outstationed an average of six or seven engines. Three were usually 0-6-0STs for shunting while the others were 0-6-0 or possibly 0-4-2 and 2-4-0 for local goods and passenger work. One interesting passenger turn around 1900 was a return trip to Burton-on-Trent but this appears to have been a short-lived working. On 1st June 1912 the post of District Locomotive Superintendent at Retford was abolished, resulting among other things in Newark depot being transferred to Grantham main shed but this had little effect upon Newark's duties or engines allocated. Thirty five years later on 13th July 1947, the dying LNER reversed the process and Newark once more became a sub-shed of Retford. That was on the same day that Retford, which now consisted of the ex-GC shed, as well as the former GN depot, moved into Doncaster District. Locomotives sub-shedded at Newark at the time, were transferred from Grantham to Retford too, these being all 0-6-0s viz: J3 4124, 4133; J6 4203; J21 5058, 5070, 5095, 5117. The absence of tank engines is noteworthy so it would seem as if Grantham depot may have used the opportunity of rid itself of a few 'dud uns' including the four former NER waifs and strays

Retford hung on to the J21 until 1951/2 as a matter of fact while in the meantime some of the N5 0-6-2T gained from Retford GC shed were sub-shedded at Newark for shunting. Those duties were dieselised during the mid to late 1950s but the N5 remained and saw occasional use on the former Midland branch to Southwell. That came about with the January 1955 closure of Southwell shed, a sub-depot of Nottingham ex-MR shed. Newark took over workings from Newark Castle station to Rolleston and Southwell operated by venerable Johnson 0-4-4T and push pull trains. Three engines came to the former GN shed: 0-6-0T 41779 which acted as pilot at Castle station and two 0-4-4T, 58077 and 58085. Before long 58077 was replaced by 58065 and, on the odd occasion that neither was available, an N5 substituted though not with push-pull trains of course.

The ex-MR locomotives' sojourn at Newark was destined to be brief as it turned out because increasing dieselisation of decreasing traffic rendered Newark shed surplus to requirements. Accordingly closure came on 5th January 1959 when all remaining duties and engines including the 0-4-4T were transferred to Lincoln *not* Retford. Demolition of Newark engine shed commenced immediately and by the end of January 1959 the roof had gone and a year later everything had disappeared, tracks and all. After lying disused for four years the shed's site was once again built upon when an emergency generator plant appeared as part of a power signalling project.

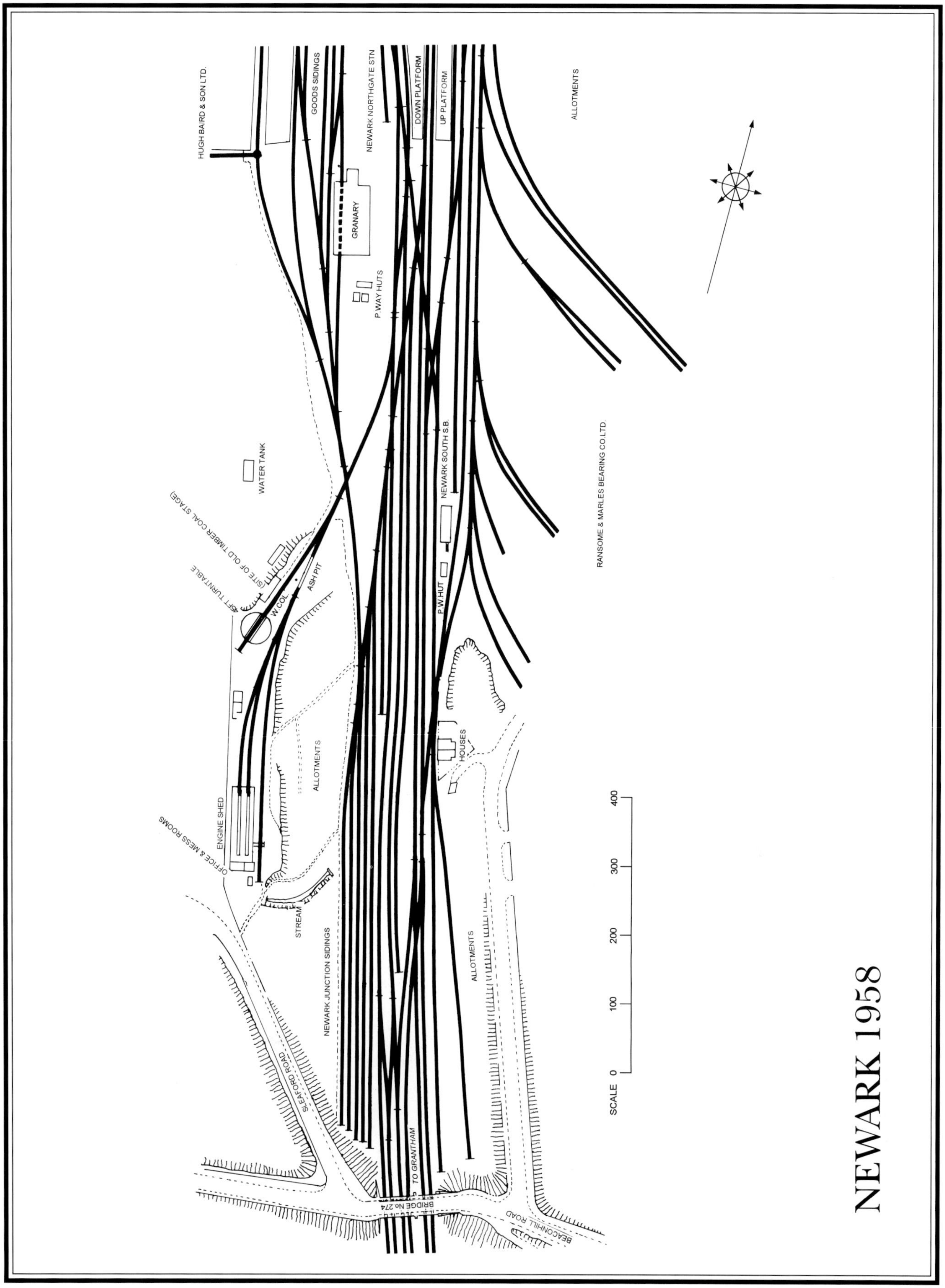
NEWARK 1958
HUGH BAIRD & SON LTD.
GOODS SIDINGS
NEWARK NORTHGATE STN
DOWN PLATFORM
UP PLATFORM
ALLOTMENTS
GRANARY
P.WAY HUTS
WATER TANK
(SITE OF OLD TIMBER COAL STAGE)
45FT TURNTABLE
W.COL.
ASH PIT
NEWARK SOUTH S.B.
P.W.HUT
RANSOME & MARLES BEARING CO.LTD.
HOUSES
ALLOTMENTS
ENGINE SHED
OFFICE & MESS ROOMS
STREAM
NEWARK JUNCTION SIDINGS
ALLOTMENTS
SLEAFORD ROAD
TO GRANTHAM
BRIDGE No 274
BEACONHILL ROAD
SCALE 0 100 200 300 400

41779, a one-time Newark "Castle pilot", resides out of use at the rear of Newark shed in late 1958. Its job had been taken by one of the growing band of diesel shunters. D3612, D3613 and D3614 had arrived at Newark in July 1958. *Sid Checkley.*

Newark shed in its last full year of operation. It is Sunday, 7th September 1958 with a definite ex-GN stud of engines present. J6 no.64178 is nearest the camera. *B.Hilton.*

By 3rd April 1954, a further locomotive siding had been installed beside Newark shed, and the gas lamp in the yard had been converted to electricity. Prominent is ex-MR 0-4-4T 58085, which was on the depot's allocation at the time, following closure of Southwell shed. Others in residence at Newark the same day were: 58077; 64234; 64341, 64403, 64423; 68863; 69282, 69283, 69300. *B.K.B.Green.*

NOTTINGHAM LONDON ROAD (LOW LEVEL)

A share of the potential traffic offered by the population and industries of the City of Nottingham was a considerable attraction to the GN Board. Access to it was denied until 2nd August 1852 and the link up of the GN with the Ambergate Nottingham & Boston & Eastern Junction Railway - Ambergate Railway for short. The latter obtained an Act on lst July 1855 empowering the GN to work all its services: this was after an attempt at securing identical powers, exactly three years previously, had proved abortive. Formal leasing by the GN occurred from 1st August 1861 but the Nottingham & Grantham Railway & Canal Company, as the Ambergate was renamed from 15th May 1860, remained independent, in the legal sense until Grouping.

So on 2nd August 1852 the first GN train steamed into Nottingham and into the history books. Ambergate Railway trains had been using the Midland Railway's station in the city, but the MR would not initially accept the GN presence. This resulted in the famous incident where the engine hauling the GN's first train was "arrested" by the MR and imprisoned in the closed ex-Midland Counties Railway locomotive shed, to the west of Nottingham station. The legal niceties took over nine months to resolve so the Ambergate company's nine locomotives and rolling stock continued working services from Grantham until the GN was formally allowed access to the MR station.

But the East Coast companies had learned a lesson and determined to build an extension of the Ambergate Railway into Nottingham and open their own facilities there. The GN had of course to legally resolve to work the proposed extension and station which the Board did on 17th November 1857, four months before the new works were finished.

Nottingham London Road terminus was built in the grand style and had a large goods shed and an engine shed to accompany it. The last named, a sub-shed of Grantham, was a straight shed with two through roads. The building scaled 145ft x 35ft being constructed in brick with arched entrances and a single-pitch slated gable roof. A coal stage and 23,000 gallon water tank were installed, the latter initially getting its supplies from a borehole and in later years, from Nottingham Corporation. Facilities at the depot were completed by a 38 ft turntable, which was the first of two to give the GN some trouble in Nottingham over the years. Witness on 2nd September 1865 when Sturrock again reminded the Board that Nottingham turntable although only 7½ years old was nearly worn out and not likely to last the coming winter. He recommended a new table incorporating wrought iron girders "...much better than the existing inferior construction..." on 7th October 1865 Sturrock repeated his case and the Board at last sanctioned expenditure of £570 for installing a 42 ft turntable.

Nineteen years later on 2nd October 1884 Stirling commented that Nottingham turntable required replacing and proposed the job be done as part of the recommendation for removal of the locomotive shed and its facilities to a new site to allow improvement of the station. Estimated costs of the shed's removal totalled £17,592 including land purchase and carrying out necessary earthworks. The whole matter was passed to the Board for consideration and it was 30th September 1886 before the subject was again detailed in the archives. Then the Way & Works Committee were proposing to erect a five road shed for 20 passenger engines, on land lying south of the Grantham line, just east of Old Trent Lane bridge and the MR bridge. Costs including land were now to total £23,756 of which £9,400 was for the shed building, £1,300 for a 45 ft turntable and foundations and £1,350 for a coal stage with water tank over. Earthworks and permanent way would have incurred additional costs of course but the price of land was a big drawback. The

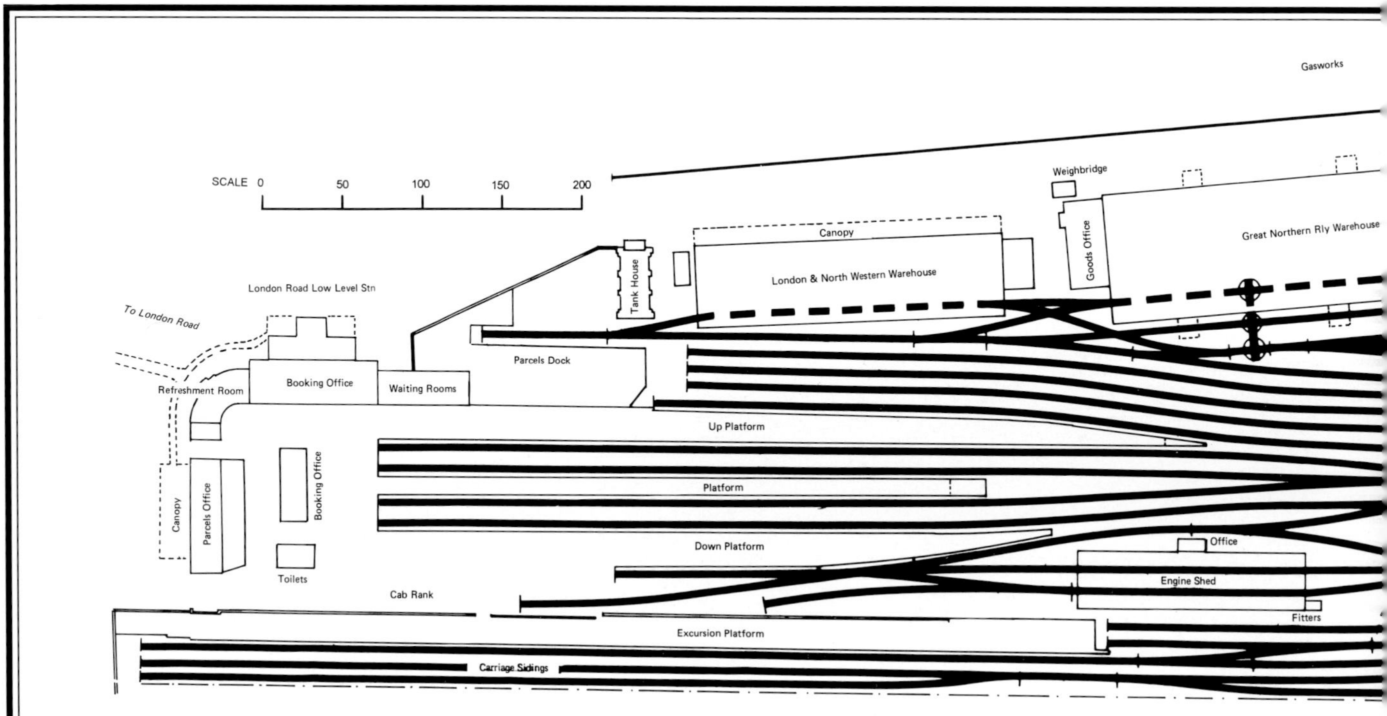

Directors had hoped to purchase just over 9½ acres of Earl Manvers' land at £500 per acre whereas His Lordship wanted £11,000 or £1,186 per acre! The GN's agent was told to offer £1,000 but even though the land requirement was subsequently reduced to 7 acres no compromise was reached and the new locoshed remained a pipedream. Through all these dealings we are left to assume the 42 ft turntable at Nottingham was either repaired or replaced as Stirling had asked in October 1884.

Apart from the niggling problems with turntables, London Road shed was the scene of another noteworthy incident. That was on 1st January 1866 when locomotive no.116 celebrated the New Year with a boiler explosion! Fortunately Sturrock was able to report that no casualties had resulted. 116, an 1850 Hawthorn 0-6-0 goods engine, was typical of the locomotives using the shed at the time. Later after Colwick opened, London Road was dedicated almost exclusively to passenger work, between Grantham and Nottingham and over the eastern end of the Derbys and Staffs Extension. In this way the shed would have been visited by the whole range of classes in the GN passenger locomotive fleet, tender and tank. Also in 1879 by then being a sub depot of Colwick, London Road like its parent shed, was host to LNWR engines, before that company's own shed at Netherfield opened. As an interesting aside in LMS days it remained the practice for locomotives working into London Road off former LNW lines to go to Colwick to turn, even though there was an ex-MR turntable only 100 yards from the terminus!

In retrospect it was perhaps fortunate that the expensive new locoshed at Nottingham never was built. This is because with the opening of the GNR/GCR joint station at Nottingham Victoria, on 2nd May 1900 emphasis of the GN's passenger traffic began inexorably to shift to it and away from London Road. In addition, three years earlier Colwick shed had been extended for the second time so it was only a question of how long it would be before London Road engine shed became redundant. That finally occurred about 1906 when all remaining duties and staff, such as there were, moved to Colwick. London Road station lost all its passenger trains to Victoria and was given over to goods traffic, a duty it performed into the 1970s.

London Road engine shed was shown as still standing on the 1915 edition of the Ordnance Survey although the turntable had by that time been removed, worn out again some years before no doubt! From the next edition of the OS, circa 1924, one can see that the shed had succumbed at some time since 1915 but the bore hole still existed, as it did in 1983!

A photograph of Nottingham GN shed has yet to be discovered, so this view of Stirling Single No.550 standing on the depot's 42ft turntable, of 1865 vintage, must suffice. It is thought the picture dates from the last years of the 19th century and note that water was stored in twin tanks, although according to the gauge, the tank nearest the loco was empty. *Authors' collection.*

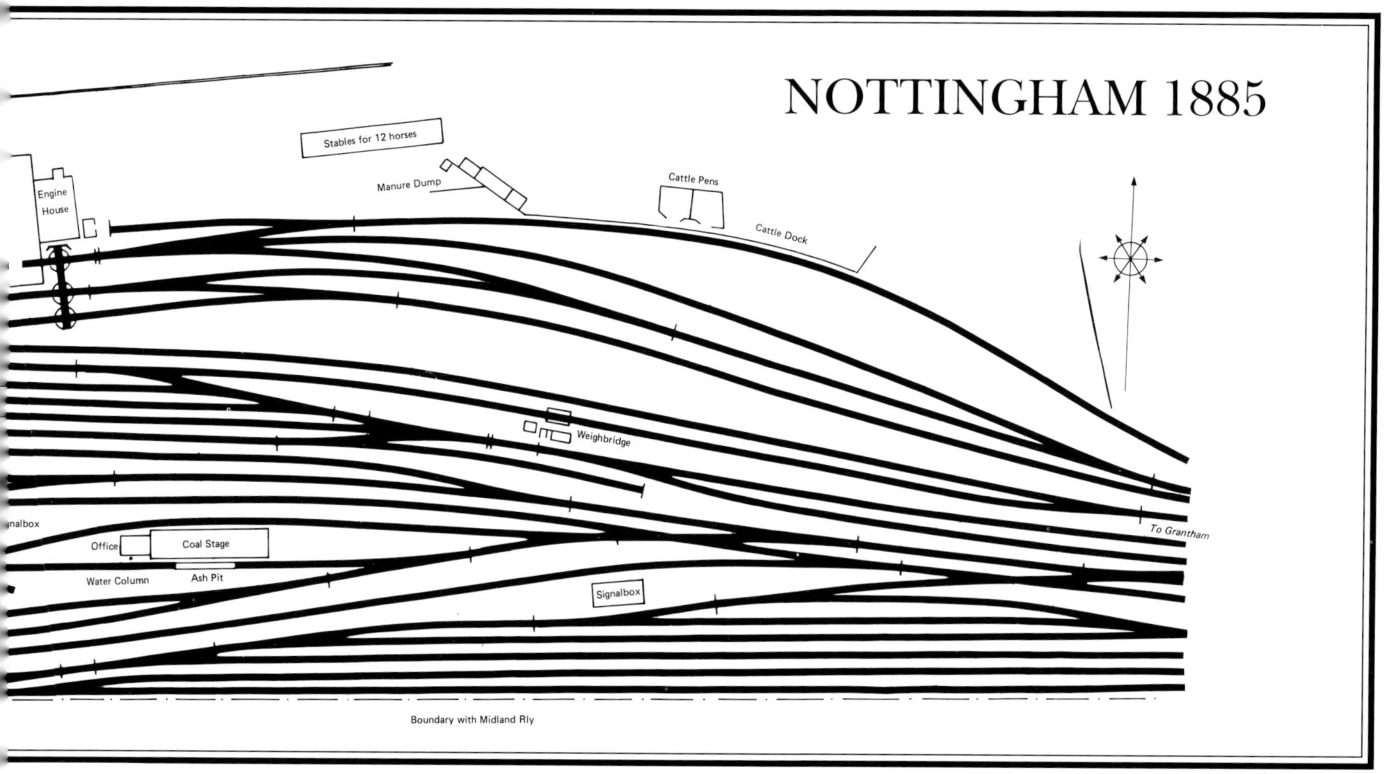

PINXTON

Plans for the GN's Pinxton branch, along the industrialised Erewash Valley, were laid down in the company's Derbyshire and Staffordshire Act of 1872. The line opened for traffic on 1st August 1876, but even though Pinxton was a terminal station, no locomotive facilities were installed initially. Then, soon after opening, a goods train ran down and killed a person walking along the track.

The subsequent enquiry blamed the accident on the fact that the goods train was being hauled by a tender engine running in reverse, with consequently reduced visibility for the footplatemen. Accordingly, the GN were required to install a turntable at Pinxton as a matter of priority, and by early 1877 this had been done, on a site south of the station, on the east bank of the River Erewash. Probably because that time was a period of relative prosperity, the GN complemented the 44 ft. 7 in. turntable with a two road engine shed and also put up three cottages for staff use. In addition, the company dug a well and installed a water crane, but after only a decade or so the increasingly heavy pollution of the adjacent River Erewash, by industrial waste, was affecting the well water, so thenceforward, whenever possible, engines took water at Eastwood.

The 90 ft.x 35 ft. brick-built locoshed followed the then standard pattern in having a tiled hipped roof, with a canopied coal stage, employing a crane and bucket, sited adjacent to one shed road (the eastern one in this case). Apart from the 1947 Working Timetable (WTT) showing Pinxton turntable to have been 47 ft. in diameter, subsequent history is virtually non existent! Even so the 1st November 1897 WTT clearly shows an engine spending the night at the shed, arriving at 10.40 p.m., on the last train from Nottingham, and returning the next morning on a coal train to Colwick. Three years later there had been some changes, inasmuch that the 1st October 1900 edition of the GN's WTT shows the 'overnighter', while still arriving late in the evening (by then, 10.30 p.m.), the return balancing working was not until 1.05 p.m. the next day - a passenger train to Netherfield. In the meantime Pinxton's resident was evidently carrying out some shunting, because the incoming and outgoing goods trains were operating to some pretty smart turnround times! It also seems as if the engine stayed over on Sunday nights as well, viz:

WEEKDAYS

Train	Time	From/To
42	6.20 am	Pass from Basford & Bulwell
58	7.25 am	Pass to Basford & Bulwell
60	9.05 am	Goods & empties from Colwick
152	9.25 am	Coal & empties to Colwick
75	9.27 am	Pass from Grantham
89	9.45 am	Pass to Newark
100	11.00 am	Pass from Basford & Bulwell SO
73	11.05 am	Pick-up goods from Colwick
104	11.16 am	Pass to Notts LR High Level SO
94	11.35 am	Empties from Colwick
154	11.50 am	Pick-up goods and coal to Colwick
155	12.20 pm	Coal to Colwick
138	1.05 pm	Pass to Netherfield
129	1.35 pm	Pass from Notts LR Low Level
158	2.15 pm	Pass to Grantham
166	3.59 pm	Pass from Netherfield
200	5.10 pm	Pass to Notts LR High Level
178	5.14 pm	Pick-up goods from Colwick
197	6.10 pm	Pass from Radcliffe on Trent
235	6.15 pm	Coal to Colwick
223	7.00 pm	Pass to Netherfield
227	8.06 pm	Pass from Notts LR High Level
251	8.45 pm	Pass to Netherfield
243	9.18 pm	Pass from Netherfield SO
267	9.40 pm	Pass to Netherfield SO
260	10.30 pm	Pass from Notts LR High Level
279	11.42 pm	Pass from Notts LR High Level SO

SUNDAYS

4	12.35 am	Empty stock to Basford & Bulwell
37Dn	1.36 pm	Pass from Basford & Bulwell
37Up	2.10 pm	Pass to Basford & Bulwell
44	4.36 pm	Pass from Basford & Bulwell
42	5.10 pm	Pass to Basford & Bulwell

By December 1912, the service had been increased slightly, to 12 Down and 11 Up trains daily, and there were then three trains each way on Sundays. According to a contemporary article, "The GNR in Derbyshire & Staffordshire" carried by *Railway & Travel Monthly*, the timetable shows that there was not then a

This familiar picture of Pinxton shed, dating from April 1912, remains the only known illustration, so the authors make no apology for including it here. Class E2 No.704 takes water after being turned, both functions being the only duties performed by the depot by that time. Certainly the 2-road building seems unused and the coaling shelter, with its elegant columns, smoke trough and vents, appears to cover no more than a supply of fire bricks. Just visible at right is the arched entrance to the coaling shed. *R.Dyer collection.*

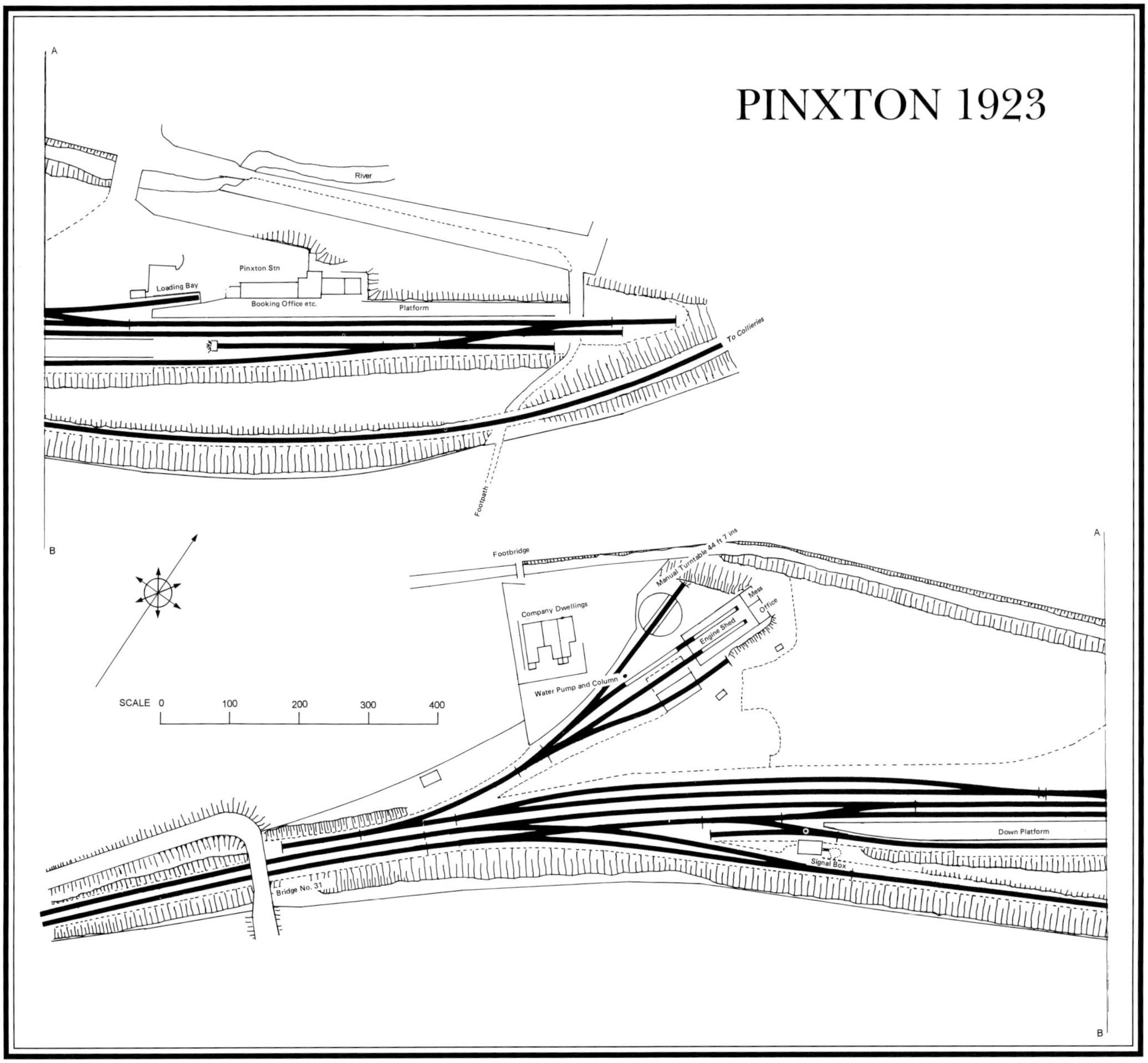

requirement for a locomotive to stable overnight at Pinxton. The article also stated that Pinxton shed had: "...been out of use for some years..." When the actual closure occurred has not yet been discovered but locomotive rostering rearrangements at Colwick had caused the demise of the shed at Nottingham, London Road Low Level in 1906 and the authors suspect that Pinxton closed at the same time. If any reader can supply definite information on this matter, the authors would very pleased to hear from them.

Services that ran over the branch were, in early days, normally in the care of 0-4-2, 2-4-0 and 0-6-0 types, of both tank and tender versions. Then, soon after their introduction, the GN Class L1 0-8-2T commenced working on the Pinxton branch, in an association that would last for nearly 30 years; they handled coal trains and some passengers - usually workmen's services. But, 0-6-0's were the most constant fare with GN Class J21 first appearing in 1908 and remaining a common sight for some 39 years. LNER J2 took their part after 1926 and J5 also had a regular working, on the 7.30 p.m. Nottingham - Pinxton, returning on a goods; this class was also used on summer specials over the branch. Passenger services were probably more the preserve of tank locos, with C12 being prominent before the Second World War. In BR times, N7 0-6-2T took over the work from 1951 to 1954, handing over in their turn to Thompson's L1 2-6-4T, a class which was generally popular with the Colwick enginemen.

The L1's went out of use towards the end of 1962, and that more or less wrote finis to the Pinxton branch as it was closed completely, between Pinxton and Langley Mill & Eastwood on 7th January 1963. The little engine shed had disappeared many years before, at a date as yet unknown. Certainly it still stood, looking very closed, but in good condition, immediately prior to WW1. Someone who knew Pinxton in the 1930's told the authors that only the turntable and water column had been in existence 'for years'. The most reasonable assumption is that the shed was demolished in the 1923/4 period, when the fledgling LNER was carrying through a sweeping programme of rationalisation. When the shed was actually closed may remain a mystery.

RETFORD

Retford or East Retford as it was more properly known, stands on the River Idle some 140 miles north of London and was in the 1800s a centre for ironfounding and paper mills. The town's first rails were those of the Manchester Sheffield & Lincolnshire Railway which opened its Woodhouse Junction - Retford - Gainsborough line on 16th July 1849. Soon after on 4th September in the same year GN trains commenced running into Rétford, with completion of the line from Doncaster. A further GN service through Retford began on 7th August 1850 between Lincoln and Sheffield with the company's trains utilising MSLR tracks from Sykes Junction. Lastly on 1st August 1852 the final link in the GN main line was completed from Peterborough and Retford saw its first direct trains from the capital.

Up to 1850 the GN had not considered provision of an engine shed at Retford, but very soon after the Lincoln - Sheffield service started the Manchester company began to show some reluctance in allowing GN engines to take water on its premises in the town. Accordingly on 19th October 1850 Sturrock sought approval for a shed at Retford to house two 'assistant' engines. It was resolved that Cubitt and Sturrock liaise over provision of a "temporary shed without delay at a spot nearest Retford station".

On what date the shed actually opened is not known but probably this occurred by mid 1851. The two road depot which stood beside the Down station platform was very similar in fact to the engine shed being built concurrently at Lincoln. Constructed in brick and scaling 85 ft x 35 ft it was of the dead end type with arched openings and a single pitch gable roof. A small coke stage was installed at the north end of the yard and water was drawn from a well dug specially for the purpose, thereby ending the problem over use of the MS&L supply. A 40 ft turntable is known to have been in situ in 1864 but the date of its initial installation is unclear - possibly its provision may not have been until 1857 the year in which through Kings Cross - Manchester trains were first promulgated. On 30th June 1857 £900 was approved for 'necessary alterations at Retford station in preparation for the new service'. Most of the money was to be spent on 'rebuilding the engine shed' which however appears to have meant that it was simply converted into a through building. Apart from allowing access from the south (where the turntable was sited) the building retained its basic layout and dimensions which might indicate that provision of the turntable absorbed most of the funds?

Whatever the work involved it was not completed in time for the Manchester trains' commencement on 1st August 1857 which meant they had to reverse at Retford to gain the required access to MSLR tracks. But that awkward manoeuvre was necessary for only one month after which the principal cause of the shed's remodelling, a new chord line, was brought into use. Basically the chord fouled access to the engine shed, so the creation of a through building while not solving the problem, stopped a lot of conflicting light engine movements from the north end of the shed over the chord line. For that first month the trains were reversing, MS&L engines came on and off at Retford GN station, which means that the little shed there would have been housing its competitor's 'crack' main line express engines. After completion of the chord line, GN engines hauling Manchester expresses ran through to Sheffield and Retford depot resumed its former, no doubt quieter existence. Even so the shed's exiting across the chord was tolerated for only a few years, until 28th September 1864 when a plan was drawn up for eradicating the problem. The north ends of the shed's two roads were terminated by a common buffer stop, all access to and from the shed then being via the Down platform road.

In time though Retford's importance increased, to such an extent that on 9th January 1874 provision of a new engine shed, offices, stores etc. was approved as part of a general programme of works estimated to cost £17,000. The West Retford contracting firm of John Wilson & Co. submitted the lowest tender for the loco depot, in the sum of £5,418.3s.11d; there were five other tenders with the highest bid being £6,582.

Retford's original hipped roofs were showing their age when this picture was taken, in 1950. Soon though, the roof and the coaling shed, partly seen at left would be replaced in a modernisation scheme. In fact, a supply of new bricks for that work may be seen between the coal stack and the wagon parked behind Gateshead shed's A3 Pacific 60045, LEMBERG. The Pacific was only visiting and was in fact a 'failure' taken off a southbound train. *Authors' collection.*

Ex-GER J69 0-6-0T 7339 stands beside Retford coaling shed on 3rd July 1932. The hand crane's swivel is seen above the locomotive's cab and a half-ton bucket, loaded and ready to be swung, is visible behind 7339's bunker. Note the delightful brackets for mounting the gas lamps. *W.T.Stubbs collection.*

Adherence to tendered price was very good, with eleven payments by the GN, to Wilson & Co. between May 1874 and April 1857, totalling exactly £5,400. The shed was sited on the down side to the west of the station and opened in March 1875 at which time the original building was closed to be demolished soon after.

For the money invested in its new shed, the GN got a four road, brick building measuring 160 ft x 65 ft. It was dead-end in pattern with stores and offices ranged along the outside east wall and featured twin slated hipped roofs, a style very much in vogue during that period. For the second time coincidentally construction at Retford was mirrored by erection of an identical building at Lincoln. At the north end of the yard was a coaling shed equipped with a crane, but without the benefit of a canopy over the coaling road, while a 44 ft 8 ins turntable was sited at the depot's east side. Another well was dug and its supply to the shed was stored in a 59,000 gallon tank, on a tankhouse that also adjoined the east side of the engine shed. However by August 1899 the well was faltering and that month's dry spell caused the company to have to pump water from the River Idle for the first time. In January 1900 the well was still giving cause for concern so the Way & Works Committee approved that exploitation of river water should become a permanent arrangement.

Around the time of the new shed's opening, or more likely, as a consequence of it, Retford became the 'seat' of a District Locomotive Superintendent (DLS) In the following year a breakdown train was stationed at the shed featuring an 8 ton hand-powered crane that had been built at Doncaster 'Plant'. Then in June 1880 Retford gained a sub-shed when the small depot at Newark opened and henceforth five of Retford's engines on average were outstationed there. In 1901 Muskham water troughs were brought into use and these too fell within the operating area of the DLS Retford. But not for very long as Retford Locomotive District was abolished from lst June 1912 with a Mr J.Ball becoming Locomotive Foreman at Retford which then came under the control of the DLS Doncaster. Newark engine shed and Muskham troughs transferred to the responsibility of the DLS Grantham whose breakdown area was extended to Carlton exclusive while Retford's breakdown area contracted (under Doncaster) to Carlton inclusive.

Throughout its GN existence Retford shed's duties were reflected in the engines allocated there. Earliest days would have been Hawthorn, Sharp, Wilson or Fairbairn goods engines and 0-4-2 on 'assistant' duties with 0-6-0 and 2-4-0 arriving as the depot's workload increased. At the time of opening of the new shed in 1875 the allocation was around 25 engines 0-6-0, 0-4-2 and 2-4-0 with a few 0-6-0ST for shunting; similar types were sub-shedded at Newark. Major duties concerned haulage of transfer traffic from and to the MSLR - mostly coal from the North Nottinghamshire and South Yorkshire coalfelds, taken by Retford engines to Grantham and Peterborough; by 1889 Retford had nine main line goods workings and return empties. Passenger duties were all local in nature, north to Doncaster, east to Gainsborough and Lincoln and south to Grantham and Peterborough. In the westerly direction duties were probably limited only to a few workings to Sheffield but this is not certain. Because of its position on the main line between Doncaster and Grantham, Retford was always an important 'assistant' engine station and there were usually one or two of the depot's fleet earmarked for standby purposes. Generally details of these are lacking but presumably early Singles then 0-4-2 and 2-4-0 had been the norm. In 1895 however it is recorded that 7 ft 2-2-2 Nos.6 and 41 were on Retford's roster and at that time no doubt they were seeing use as main line pilots. Soon after that Ivatt's 0-6-0s started to arrive so that by 1905 the shed's allocation consisted of: E1 - 3, E2 - 5, E3 - 5, F2 - 4, J1 - 1, J3 - 1, J5 - 5, J6 - 5, J7 - 1. Total 28.

By 1912 Ivatt's 4-4-0s had joined the allocation and changed the picture somewhat with 34 locomotives then being made up as follows: D2 - 7, E1 - 6, E2 - 2, F2 - 1, J5 - 13, J6 - 4, J7 - 1.

At the Grouping things had changed yet again and of Retford's 30 engines at that time only two E1 remained, seeing out their days on local trains. D2 had gone to be replaced by three D1 and two D3 while three J4 had appeared. J5 remained the shed's major class still with thirteen of them allocated and the four J6 and one J7 had been replaced by seven J22. Soon all twenty J22 (LNER Class J5) were at Retford and they

RETFORD 1932

Cloth caps and waistcoats were the order of the day in 1900-1, when this picture was taken in the yard of Retford shed. What each man's job was is unknown, but one of them was the father of Mr Norman Bush, who kindly gave permission for this photo's use. The shear legs gains a faintly pagoda-like look from its neat roof. *R.Tarpey collection.*

(left and below) **Some nice detail here of the chain winding gear of Retford's shear legs, with J5 No.303? receiving attention to her rear driving axle. At the time this picture was taken, around the early 1930s, the shed's smoke vents were still largely intact - surprisingly, so were the doors!** *H.N.James.*

D3 no.4074 was a Retford engine when captured on camera on the west side of the shed yard in July 1932. Out of service at the time, 4074 was waiting to enter Doncaster works for a 'general' repair. Up to July 1935, this D3 had been variously allocated between Retford and Sheffield (Neepsend) but a move to Hull (Botanic Gardens) in that month saw the engine leave Retford's 'books' for the last time; after Hull, 4074 served at five other sheds before being withdrawn in November 1946, not quite 50 years old. *W.L.Good.*

monopolised workings to such an extent that they became known as the 'Retford Pacifics' the locomens' somewhat wry reference to the fact that most other main line sheds did have 4-6-2s for their important duties! By the end of the Second World War though J5 had all gone being replaced by J6 and J39.

The allocation as at 31st December 1922 was thus (LNER classification is given):

D2 1324, 1370, 1381.
D3 1074, 1344.
E1 993, 1070.
J3 350, 1130, 1167.
J4 196, 337, 338, 359, 643, 646, 648, 724, 792, 793, 831, 837, 1121.
J5 22, 23, 24, 31, 32, 34, 36.

After the Grouping Retford GC shed was combined with the GN depot but operating two medium sized engine sheds in one smallish town was an obviously poor financial arrangement for the LNER. Accordingly throughout the company's existence there were a number of proposals to rationalise facilities by closing the GC depot and concentrating all duties at the GN shed which would be substantially improved. Among the work proposed was a 200 ton mechanical coaling plant, 70 ft articulated turntable, additional preparation and disposal pits, improved yard layout and connection to the main line and a number of other minor details. The problem was that even in the early 1930s the estimated cost of all this was some £49,000 which the LNER never could get round to affording, so both engine sheds remained, into BR days. A number of improvements were made at the GN shed though as in 1933 when a 7,500 gallons per hour water softening plant was ordered from Horsehay Bridge and Engineering Co. Ltd. In addition by 1947 the turntable's operating diameter had been increased to 48 ft 6 ins presumably by employing extension rails.

The LNER's and BR's administrative combination of both Retford sheds clouded the issue of locomotive allocations - what was where and when. Basically though for the years up to the end of the thirties GN origin engines tended to keep to their own shed as did GC types. This is amply illustrated by the record of engines seen at the ex-GN depot on 5th January 1930: - **D2** 4322, 4324, 4337, 4373, 4381; **J3** 4130, 4167; **J4** 3394, 4090; **J5** 3021, 3023, 3024, 3025, 3027, 3030, 3031, 3033, 3035, 3038, 3039, 3040; **J6** 3561; **J69** 7339; **K1** 4665; **Q4** 5065.

Changes did occur and for the last few years before nationalisation all passenger engines operated from the GN building. This brought such machines as GC Class C4 Atlantics onto Retford's main line pilot duty, a job they performed with outstanding success on a number of occasions when deputising for failed Pacifics. The C4 had replaced D2s of which 3250, 3253 and 3259 came to Retford in the early 1940s. In fact the last surviving member of the class 3252 was withdrawn from there in July 1945.

Light Engines from Retford Loco. to work trains as under:-
6th May to 6th October 1946 inclusive.

(A)	(B)	(C)	(D)	(E)	Train to work:-
am	am	am	am	am	
2.00	—	—	2.08	—	No.4 Pilot Retford MO
3.42	—	—	3.47	—	353 Up, 4.15 a.m. Retford to New England MX
4.30	—	—	4.38	—	No.5 Pilot Retford MX
5.00	5.25	—	—	—	224 Down,5.49 a.m. Worksop to Kiveton P MX
5.10	—	5.15	—	—	380 Up, 5.23 a.m. Retford to New England MO
5.28	5.48	—	—	—	225 Down, 6.19 a.m. Worksop to Kiveton P MO
5.50	—	5.55	—	—	381 Up, 6.30 a.m. Retford to New England
6.05	6.25	—	—	—	176 Up, 6.44 a.m. Worksop to New England
6.10	—	6.15	—	—	6.30 a.m. O.P. Retford to Sheffield
6.55	—	—	7.03	—	MTT, 7.15 a.m. Retford to Scrooby
7.15	—	—	7.22	—	341 Down, 7.30 a.m. Retford to Doncaster
7.15	—	7.20	—	—	7.40 a.m. O.P. Retford to Sheffield
7.50	8.10	—	—	—	MTT, 8.50 a.m. Worksop to Steetley
8.00	—	8.05	—	—	No.1 Passenger Pilot, Retford
9.15	—	—	—	9.40	430 Up, 9.55 a.m. Scrooby to Whitemoor
pm	pm	pm	pm		
12.00	—	12.08	—	—	No.5 Pilot Retford MO
5.10	5.30	—	—	—	294 Up, 5.50 p.m. Worksop to New England
7.15	—	—	7.20	—	505 Up, 7.30 p.m. Retford to New England
11.00	—	11.05	—	—	No.2 Passenger Pilot, Retford

Key:-
(A) - *Time leaves loco*; (B) - *Arrive Worksop*; (C) - *Arrive Retford station*; (D) - *Arrive Babworth*;
(E) - *Arrive Scrooby*; MO - *Mondays only*; MTT - *Mondays, Tuesdays and Thursdays only*; MX - *Mondays excepted*; O.P - *Ordinary passenger*.

Four and a half months before nationalisation Retford regained Newark as a sub-shed and Grantham kindly sent seven of its 0-6-0s with it to join Retford's allocation. Four of those

The remodelled Retford shed is seen from the yard on 19th May 1957. A B1, J11, 04 63736, an O2 and J39 64960 are joined by a visitor from the North Eastern Region - York's B16 4-6-0 61464. The gantry coaler which replaced the coaling shed is just visible behind the latter. Presumably the "Dutch Barn" gave shelter to the coal handlers while they shifted the fuel from wagon to narrow gauge skip. *N.E.Preedy.*

0-6-0s were ex-NER class J21, 5058, 5070, 5095 and 5117 which had come south years before and seen use from a number of former GN sheds. Just before regaining Newark the following were allocated at Retford, divided between both sheds. Those marked * were probably working from the GN depot: **C4*** 2900, 2906, 2919, 2923; **D3*** 2116, 2140; **J3*** 4152, 4155; **J4*** 4125; **J6*** 4205, 4271, 4274; **J11** 4282, 4287, 4295, 4306, 4341, 4347, 4348, 4349, 4380, 4385, 4402, 4410, 4413, 4416, 4421, 4423, 4425; **J39*** 4830, 4886, 4887, 4906, 4956, 4970, 4987; **N5*** 9294, 9321; **O4** 3550, 3637, 3688, 3763, 3774, 3775, 3782, 3785, 3877, 3905, 3907, 3908, 3914; **Q4** 3200, 3210, 3224; **Y3*** 8165.

The Y3 Sentinel had been a resident of Retford for a number of years employed mainly as pilot at Gainsborough Lea Road station but it also saw service on trip work between the Top and Low yards at Retford. The list notes that all J39 were stationed at the GN depot, while all J11 were at the GC shed. Both are assumptions and it is quite possible that either class could be found at both sheds - especially the J11 which were very popular at most GN depots that had anything to do with them. As mentioned above J21 came to Retford in 1947 to disappear again at the end of 1952 by which time a minor revolution had occurred in the motive power scene.

That 'revolution' concerned the working of B1 4-6-0's and Class O1 and O2 2-8-0's from the GN depot - the latter having moved from Grantham in large numbers; ex-GE J69 0-6-0T and J94 'Austerity' 0-6-0ST were to come in later phases of the locomotive change round. Coincident with the start of the 'revolution' - around 1951 - BR replaced the shed roof with a concrete and steel version; the hipped roofs had finally given up the ghost after 80 years service. BR at last also installed a mechanical coaler, but it was only of the half ton skip-loading type, an indicator perhaps that despite new engine types being allocated, there had, in official circles been a change in Retford's status.

In January 1965 Retford GC shed was closed in readiness for the 'dive-under' scheme and all remaining duties gravitated to the GN building, which at the time had some 35 locomotives allocated not including numerous members of Class O2 withdrawn in November 1963 and still lying in store at the GN depot - they had worked out their last days on Worksop - Rotherwood (for Mottram) coal trains.

Last days they were too for Retford GN locoshed, with dieselisation bringing about its closure only five months later. The coaler and turntable were quickly removed but the shed, rebuilt only a decade earlier, survived demolition. It was converted for use as a small factory and formed the nucleus of an industrial estate that gradually built up on the former shed yard and as such exists today.

Being the next shed south of Doncaster, Retford was often used by ex-works locomotives on running-in turns. On the 9th September 1951, New England's 61210, one of the few fitted with a self weighing tender, had just completed a 'general' and waits to work back to Doncaster before completing its acceptance trials and eventual release to traffic. *W.Potter.*

This 22nd July 1960 close-up of the re-roofed shed shows that virtually all the original side walls had been retained - and the doors were STILL intact! Beyond the bomb-shelter, a grounded van body bears some strange annotations. What or who, were "Sprutts" and "Wallah"? *K.Fairey.*

A southerly aspect of Retford shed, dating from 1958, details the original offices with later extension, and the water tank on its lofty tankhouse. Behind that is the even loftier water softening tower, with just a glimpse of a former locomotive tender in use as a sludge carrier. *Authors' collection.*

Another view of the shed in 1958. The place is extremely tidy and quiet but it is a weekday and most of the allocation would be going about their duties. B1 no.61208 spent all of its working life at Retford from its mid July 1947 entry to traffic; re-allocated to Doncaster when Retford closed on 13th June 1965, the B1 was stored until condemned three months later. *Authors collection.*

A final look at Retford shed, this time in July 1960, from the road leading to the bridge over the connection between the ex-GC line from Sheffield and the ex-GN main line (see plan on page 74)**. There was still plenty of work for the shed to do and five more summers would go by before closure.** *K.C.H.Fairey.*

SLEAFORD

Situated on the banks of the River Slea some 17 miles southeast of Lincoln, Sleaford was and still is to some extent, the centre of a large agricultural trading area. It was the potential rail traffic offered by that trade which caused the promotion of the Boston Sleaford & Midland Counties Railway which received the Assent to its Act on 20th August 1853.

The BS&MC arranged for the GN to work all services over its route the first section of which would be that from the GN main line at Barkston Junction, north of Grantham, to a temporary terminus at Sleaford. This section saw opening celebrations on Saturday 13th June 1857 when a train left for Grantham at 10.00 a.m. and returned with the Directors who had travelled from London at 1.00 p.m. Regular services commenced on 16th June 1857 and the WTT from 1st August that year shows the Sleaford-Grantham service comprising four return trains, Monday - Friday with five on Saturday and two on Sunday. All workings commenced and finished at Sleaford, where a turntable of indefinite proportions had been installed. This infers that some sort of engine shed was almost certainly provided at Sleaford as was the norm in those days but no evidence has been found to confirm this. In any case such shed as may have existed would not have been required for long as the next section of the BS&MC on to Boston was opened on 12th April 1859. Grantham trains immediately commenced through running as evidenced by the 1860 WTT so any shed at Sleaford would surely have become redundant.

On 25th July 1864 the GN obtained an Act for absorption of the BS&MC with effect from 1st January 1865. By the middle of that year further developments were presaged by the passing of an Act for the Sleaford & Bourn(e) Railway another concern that would be GN worked from the outset. That particular line opened for goods traffic in October 1871 with passenger trains commencing on 2nd January 1872 and its plans give an indication that the 1857 turntable at Sleaford no longer existed as part of the S&BR's works concerned provision of 45 ft turntables at each end of its route, these being fabricated at the GN's Doncaster Plant.

It seems certain no engine shed appeared as a result of the S&BR's opening as even in 1881 the WTT Supplement carried only a Whistle Code (1 long, 1 short) for access to the turntable at Sleaford West. But just one year later on 6th March 1882 the first stretch of the Lincoln-Spalding line, jointly sponsored by the GN and Great Eastern, opened from Spalding past Sleaford to Ruskington. On the same day junctions were put in between the new line and those entering Sleaford to

Sleaford's sleepy little shed is seen on Sunday 23rd August 1936, by which time the coal stage, seen in the foreground, had been replaced by the simple expedient of coaling direct from a wagon. Access to the shed from the main line was via the turntable which was located behind the photographer. On shed this day were J6 3530 of Grantham and J11 5951 from Tuxford. Of added interest is the little wooden privy next to the stage, and the spur crossing the shed access road on the level, to enter a private siding. This prewar view shows the goods yard was doing good business. *W.A.Camwell.*

Sleaford's pattern of gable roof was unusual, coming as it did during the era of the GN's "northlight" buildings. Perhaps the design had been "borrowed", as there is a faintly Midland - or God forbid, even Churchwardian - air about the structure! Resident on 16th March 1958 was the customary Class J6 0-6-0, in this case, 64229. *B.Hilton.*

enable joint line trains to enter the town. This obviously set things in motion because from 2nd August 1883 comes the one and only official reference to a Sleaford engine shed so far unearthed by the authors. On that date Stirling asked for 'a coke stage, ash pit and store room in conjunction with the new engine shed at Sleaford'. These extras were to cost an estimated £260 which was approved.

When the shed was first mooted and even when it opened are still mysteries but the latter must have been late in 1883 or more likely early in 1884. The building that materialised was a two road dead-end shed in brick with a single pitch slated gable roof. The dimensions were 60 ft x 40 ft which meant it could provide cover only for one tender engine or perhaps one and a half tank engines, on each road - these extended 55 ft into the building and were equipped with 42 ft pits. (During the Second World War, the pit in the southern road was converted into an air raid shelter by the judicious use of sandbags). Adjoining the rear of the shed were an office and stores while in a separate block further to the rear were blacksmiths, carpenters and fitters shops which would also have been used for carrying out repairs to wagons in the adjacent goods yard. Sleaford's remaining facilities consisted of a 50 ft x 15 ft wooden coal platform that stood in the depot yard adjacent to a spur which led to a 45 ft turntable at the extreme west end of the yard. The turntable appears not to have changed during the shed's life but by 1936 the coal platform was out of use though still standing with coaling then being carried out from a wagon which was usually positioned just outside the shed entrance on the southernmost road.

Water for locomotive purposes came initially from a stream on the north side of the station and was stored in a 54,000 gallon tank situated between the turntable and coal platform. However the dry summer of 1896 caused problems with the stream so on 1st October that year the Way & Works Committe approved £300 for Messrs. Legrand & Sutcliffe to sink a 6 inch artesian well with steel piping and all necessary connections. By 1908 a second well had been sunk, these sufficing until 1927/8 when a further borehole was made at Sleaford to maintain a plenteous supply of water for engine use - by then amounting to some 20 million gallons a year.

Locomotives for Sleaford were at first sub-shedded from Grantham, with two (and four sets of men) seeming to have been the normal complement, Diagram No.1 comprised the following workings:

5.08 a.m. Shunt Sleaford Yard.
8.20 a.m. Passenger to Bourne.
10.23 a.m. Passenger to Sleaford.
1.48 p.m. Passenger to Bourne.
3.25 p.m. Passenger to Sleaford.
4.00 p.m. Passenger to Bourne.
5.55 p.m. Passenger to Sleaford.

The locomotive working Sleaford's Diagram No.2 was employed solely on shunting Sleaford Yard, 8.15 a.m. - 5.08 a.m. with a crew from Grantham covering the middle shift. (Incidentally one small item of practice was to normally have the engines facing east i.e. into the shed)

Boston became Sleaford's main shed, with cessation of the Sleaford - Bourne passenger trains, on 30th September 1930, but again two engines remained the usual allocation. At some time the locomotive's duties changed though, with Diagram No.1 then supplying a single engine to act as Sleaford pilot all day. These duties involved working over the spur line to sidings serving Charles Sharpe & Co., the Urban District Council and Messrs R.W. & F. Money (known as Mill Sidings). This work meant that the pilot had to cross the main line to the north side and the enginemen had to open and close two gates - that on leaving the railway's curtilege and the other, upon entering the private siding complex. The pilot engine also served the malting sidings of Bass Ratcliffe & Gretton Ltd. on the south side of the main line at the east end of the station. West end pilot duties often involved the prolonged closure of the level crossing by the West Box, much to the chagrin of the drivers of road traffic, pedestrians at least had use of a subway. Lastly, Sleaford pilot sometimes had an unscheduled duty to perform, that of giving assistance to ailing locomotives. On occasion the pilot 'piloted' failed engines with trains to Grantham, Boston, Spalding or Lincoln where a fresh engine would be available.

One of Sleaford's pilots most interesting duties came about after 1919, the tripping of goods and passengers to and from the Slea River exchange point with the fascinating GN built branch to Cranwell Aviation College. The line was War Department property, the Royal Naval Air Service at first, Royal Air Force later, with its own locomotives but GNR/LNER/BR engines did venture along it on occasions. In fact in more than

SLEAFORD 1940

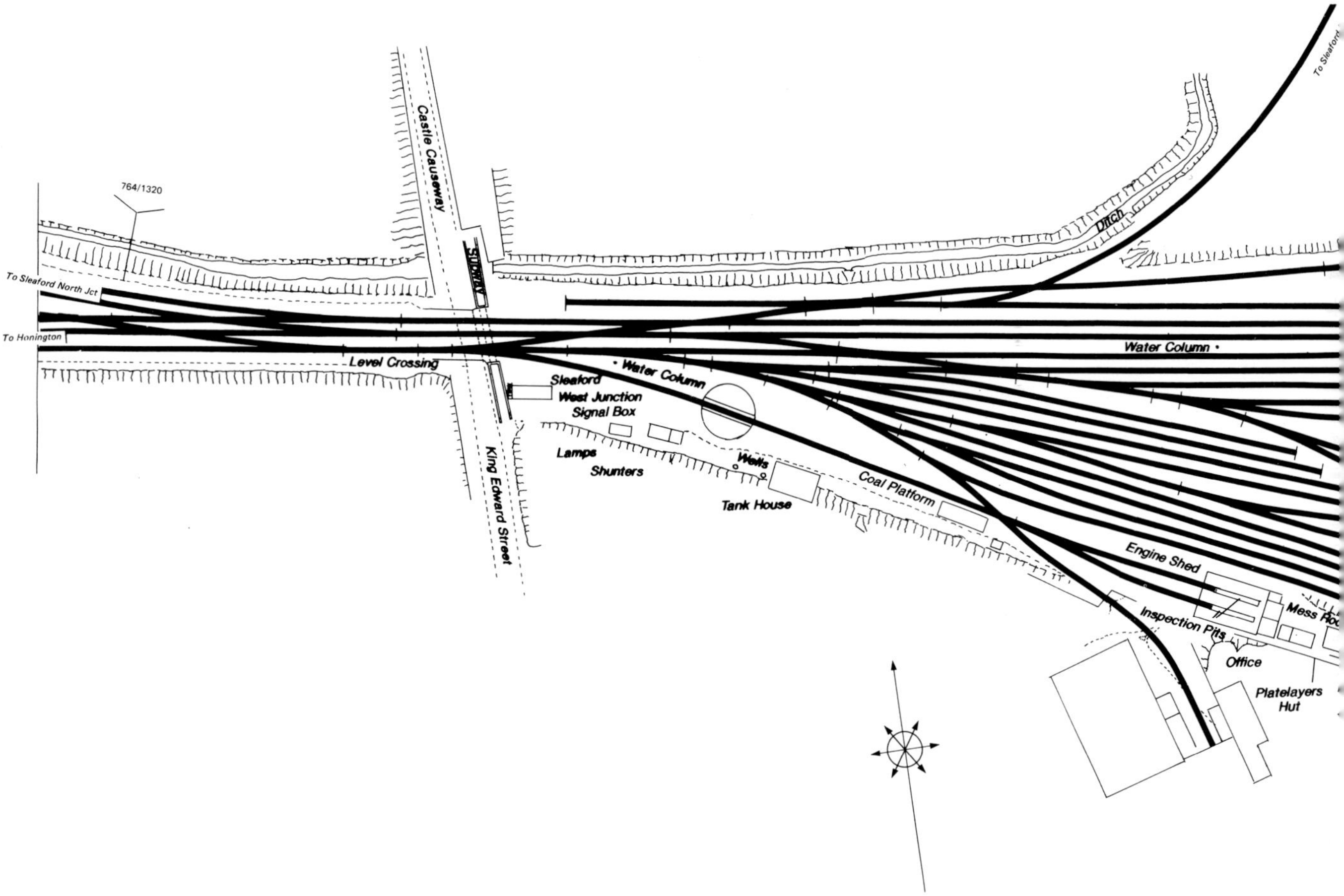

The northern aspect of Sleaford shed at sometime in the early 1960's when it was basically closed but was occassionaly used by interested parties. *Photographer unknown.*

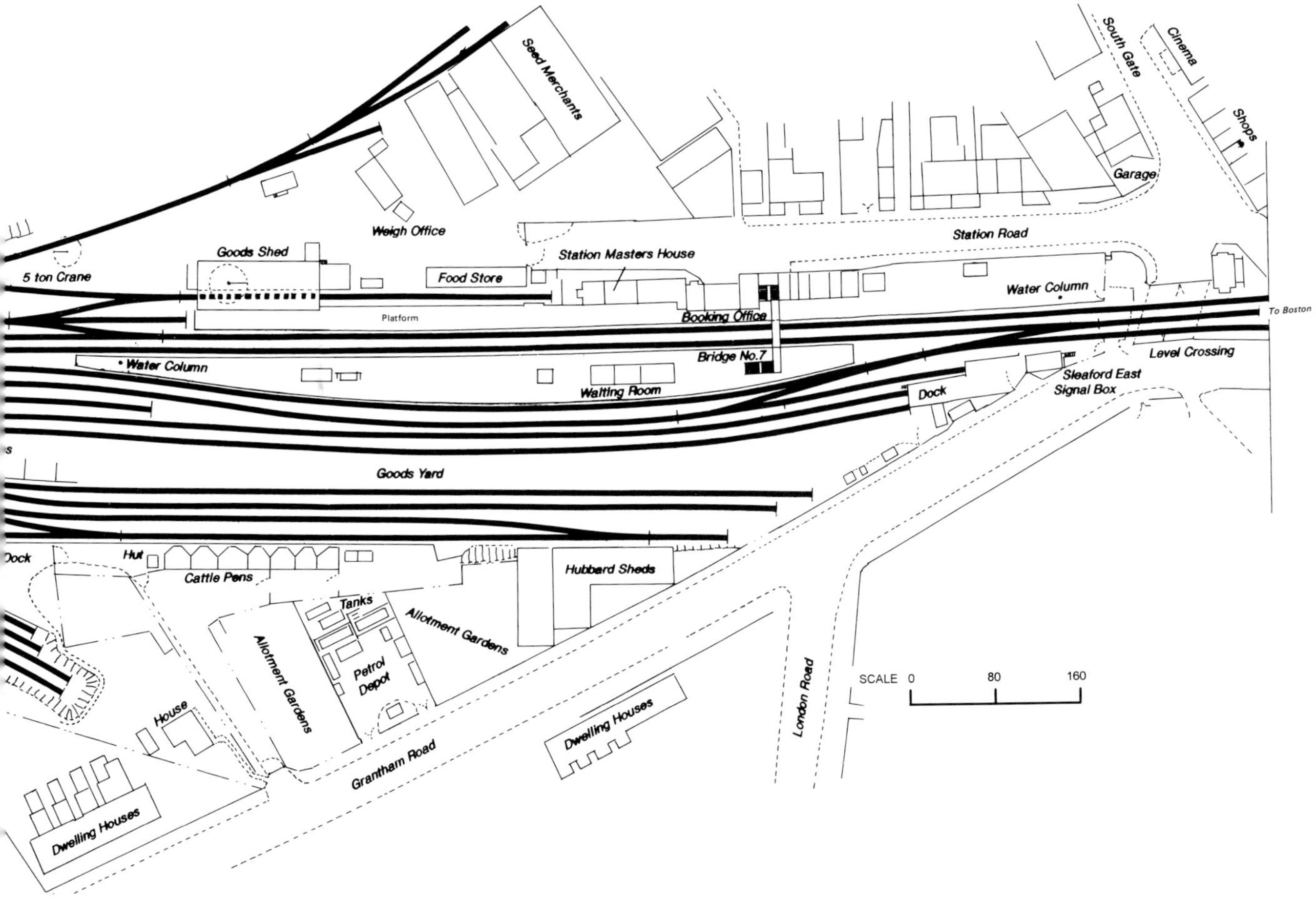

Engine sheds were pretty basic places once the locomotives are removed and the inside of Sleaford was no exception. A fireplace; workbench complete with vice; a cupboard for tools and, a length of hose comprise the fitters lot. The pit to the right, complete with sandbag covering, was used, during WWII as an air raid shelter whilst that in the centre of the frame stables a platelayers trolley. *Photographer unknown.*

Boston J6 no.64214 basks in the sunshine at Sleaford on 15th May 1955. In the background can seen the water tankhouse which served the station and shed needs. The timber coalstage has long gone as had the turntable by this date. *C.A.Appleton collection.*

one instance during British Railways' days the Air Ministry borrowed a J69 0-6-0T from Lincoln shed when its own locomotives were out of use. The Cranwell branch closed to all traffic in August 1956.

Sleaford's No.2 loco diagram entailed departing about 10.35 a.m. with a pick-up goods for Bourne, arriving there at about 1.30 p.m. After shunting Bourne yard for nearly two hours, the engine returned to Sleaford, with another goods, to arrive about 5.15 p.m. On Mondays only - market day at Sleaford - a Grantham engine still ventured over the Bourne - Sleaford line with a return cattle train. By 1946, however, the WTT showed that this cattle train had ceased to run.

The means used to change over engines Boston/Sleaford was by way of the 3.20 p.m. goods from Boston and return. Post World War Two the sequence involved was that after arrival from Boston, the new locomotive worked the yard until about 5.00 a.m. the following day, when it retired to the shed for fire cleaning and servicing, before working the pick-up goods to Bourne. On its return the engine would go on shed until next day, being used then on more yard shunting until tea time when it worked back to Boston.

It is likely that 0-6-0s were staple fare for Sleaford's allocation for most of the shed's life. During LNER days J2 and J3 were common, but J6 became dominant in the latter LNER, and BR periods, during which for a short time Grantham started supplying a third engine for passenger work. By 1954 this duty too was a Boston responsibility with the locomotive, also a J6, returning to its home shed for the weekend. When this duty ceased the allocation at Sleaford reverted to two again e.g. as on Thursday 16th May 1957, J6 Nos.64204 and 64250. On the odd occasion other types could be found 'lodging' at Sleaford. Such visitors were more often than not 'cripples' and a local enthusiast, David Love, has supplied the following examples from the 1950s period:

K1 62065 of Stockton, failed while on a running-in turn from Doncaster.

O4 63762 of Staveley, failed while hauling a goods train.

J50 68965 of Stratford, failed while returning home, after overhaul at Doncaster.

N1 69440 of Copley Hill, failed while running to Stratford.

The busiest time at the shed during this period occurred over the weekend of 3rd/4th November 1956 when following a derailment at Helpringham on the GE/GN Joint line around five additional engines sought refuge in the shed area - one of them being the only named WD 2-8-0 No.90732 VULCAN. Interesting interludes indeed but for the majority of the time most trains passed by, leaving Sleaford shed and its inhabitants to enjoy their peaceful existence undisturbed.

Steam locomotives ceased using the shed in the Autumn of 1958 and on Monday 6th October 0-6-0 diesel mechanical shunter D2025 took over the remaining shunting duties. In 1960 the depot went into the Lincoln District and when Boston closed in January 1964, Sleaford became the somewhat unlikely subshed of Colwick. Some four months later, about May 1964, Sleaford goods yard ceased working so with no work left for the solitary diesel shunter the engine shed also closed. That was not quite the end though as the depot staff were transferred to Boston and travelled there daily by train, although they apparently did no work there! Eventually BR's accountants caught up with this anomaly and the men were made redundant about November 1964. The fate of the engine shed is not quite clear, it was certainly demolished but the exact date of this is unknown.

SPILSBY

It is not widely remembered nowadays that England's second largest county, Lincolnshire, was subdivided into three areas, much in the same way as the Ridings of Yorkshire. Those Lincolnshire subdivisions were known as Holland, Kesteven and Lindsey - the last named having Spilsby as its 'chief' town, because the Clerk of the Peace had his office at Spilsby Court House. The inhabitants of Spilsby had waited nearly 18 years, from the first arrival of the East Lincolnshire Railway at Firsby, to see an Act passed, on 5th July 1865, incorporating the Spilsby & Firsby Railway; Capital was £25,000, with additional borrowing powers for £8,333. The railway would be worked from the outset by the GNR, by an agreement of December 1864, under which the GN was to provide staff and rolling stock, while all construction would be undertaken by the Spilsby Company.

Said construction did not start until March 1867 - the "first sod" being cut on the fourteenth of that month. The delay was due to the slowness with which share capital was taken up, with consequent holdup of land purchases. Opening of the 4¼ mile branch line took place on 1st May 1868, but even so, all was not ready at that time, as a GNR Way & Works Committee Minute, of 30th November 1868, notes that: "...the Spilsby & Firsby Railway is nearing completion..."(!) The Minute then went on to describe one of the last remaining jobs to be the laying of a gravel cart road up to, and around the engine shed.

That engine shed was single road, single-ended, brick-built and had a roof that comprised a slated gable at the front, with a 6,500 gallon water tank at the rear. Measuring some 50 ft x 20 ft the depot was large enough only for one tank engine, which was intentional, as just before the line was completed, Stirling had been told to use "the smallest tank engines" due to the expected light traffic. Accordingly, no turntable was installed and the remaining facilities were scant indeed, with coaling being carried out direct from a wagon and water coming from the shed's roof tank by hose, over the cattle dock spur. That tank also supplied non-drinking water to the station and other buildings and was replenished from a well directly beneath the loco depot. Rather than go to the expense of a pumping engine, a "stationary" injector was provided which got its steam from the branch locomotive's steam heating pipe; a pressure of 40 psi and two hours, were needed to raise the level of water in the tank through one foot.

Initial services over the branch were provided by seven return trains on weekdays only. This had increased to eight trains, weekdays only, by June 1872, but after the Skegness extension of the Wainfleet & Firsby Railway opened, on 28th July 1873, Sunday trains were run from Spilsby. How long they continued is not known - one still ran in 1889, leaving Spilsby at 2.20 p.m. Also, from 6th June 1889, a TThSO evening train ran, in the summer months only: it left Spilsby at 8.50 p.m. and Firsby at 9.23 p.m. In 1897 the WTT shows seven weekday returns only, a figure that had grown again, by 1913, to nine weekday trains. To work the branch, engines were supplied by Boston on a weekly basis, with the crews being resident in Spilsby whenever possible - one driver lived there in 1871, for instance. Locomotives were

The compact layout of facilities at Spilsby is clearly demonstrated in this picture of the station, goods shed and engine shed. It was taken probably just post-World War two, some years after closure of the locoshed, but still it stood in very good condition - it would remain so for some years to come, before finally being demolished. Exactly what function the building performed during that time has yet to be discovered. *W.A.Camwell.*

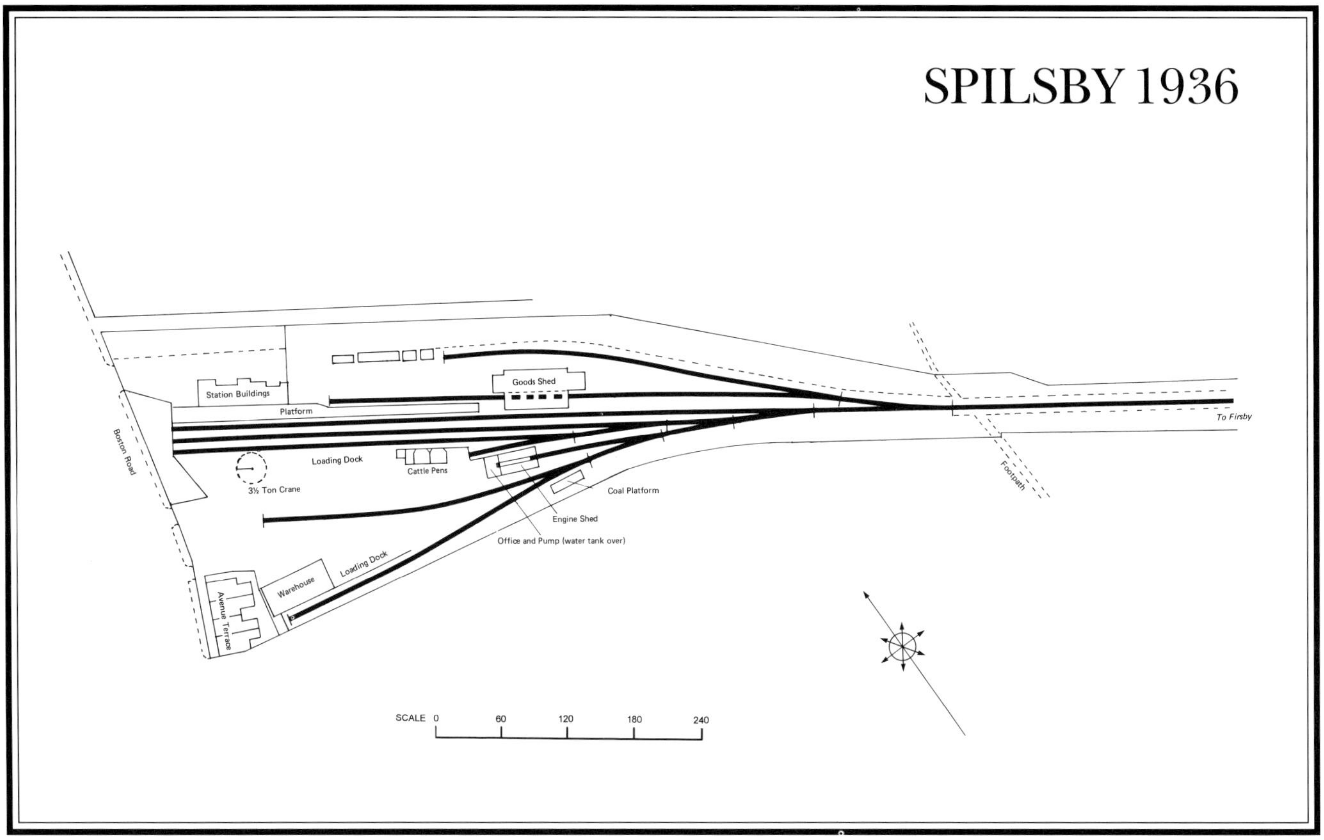

Spilsby terminus 9th July 1954. One can almost feel the summer's midday warmth as you laze in the chair taking in the rural scene at this less-than-hectic location. At the end of the single platform stood the goods shed and to its right we can make out the long disused engine shed with its covered water tank. Passenger trains had long since ceased to serve the place and the days of the branch were numbered although the goods traffic would continue for another four years. *Douglas Thompson.*

In a picture obviously intended to portray the establishment of E.Haw & Sons, part of Spilsby shed nevertheless gets a look in, at extreme right. The photograph may be dated with some precision, as it is known that 0-4-4T No.122A was working the Spilsby branch in 1908. *Hallgarth collection, cty A.Ludlam.*

changed over using the Mondays Only 9.00 a.m. train from Firsby to Boston. In the reverse direction a locomotive left Boston at 7.35 a.m. and ran light engine to Firsby to take up its week's duties.

As directed, successive loco engineers used the smallest available engines for the branch, with Sharps 2-2-2T initially, being succeeded by Stirling 0-4-2T and 0-4-4T, the last surviving for many years. For example, it is recorded that Class F6 Nos.118A and 122A both saw service on the Firsby-Spilsby branch during 1908, and with members of similar 0-4-4T types being resident at Boston until the 1920's, it is certain their use continued until the end. A diversion was provided sometime after the introduction of steam railmotors at Louth, on 11th December 1905. It is reported that those machines worked on the Spilsby branch, but for how long, or whether it was simply a trial, is not known to the authors: anyway, by 1915, the steam cars had been withdrawn from the area, due to their limited accommodation.

In 1886 there was a proposal for the Lincoln, Horncastle, Spilsby and East Coast Railway, one of several schemes in fact, that suggested linking the Horncastle and Spilsby branches - none of which ever came to fruition. Four years later, on 25th July 1890, the GNR obtained an Act for outright purchase of the S&FR; actual takeover occurred on New Year's Day 1891, at a purchase price of £20,000 - sold out at £8 per share, on the £25,000 capital. Nineteen years later, the summer passenger timetable shows that the following service was being provided by the GN, on weekdays only:

UP

Spilsby Dep: AM 6.40 8.15 9.50 10.40
Spilsby Dep: PM 1225 3.25* 3.30 5.50 6.35 8.35
Firsby Arr: AM 6.50 8.25 10.00 10.54
Firsby Arr: PM 12.35 3.35 3.44 6.04 6.45 8.45

DOWN

Firsby Dep: AM 7.10 8.20* 8.47 10.10 11.25
Firsby Dep: PM 12.50 4.25 6.16 7.05 9.23
Spilsby Arr: AM 7.24 8.30 8.58 10.21 11.39
Spilsby Arr: PM 1.01 4.39 6.27 7.16 9.35

* *Runs TThSO, during July and August.*

What is not shown above is the regular TThSO return goods train over the branch, which ran in the period between the 1.01 p.m. arrival at, and 3.30 p.m. departure from, Spilsby. On Mondays Only, a further goods ran as required - leaving Spilsby at 2.15, and extra trains were run during the sheep fairs held in the area, each September. A WTT from 1920 shows the TThSO Goods' timings to have been:

Spilsby Dep: 1.43 pm; Arr: 2.36 pm.
Firsby Arr: 2.00 pm; Dep: 2.20 pm.

Also, the 1920 WTT revealed the first and last workings shown in the 1910 public timetable no longer ran, thereby restoring the service once again to its initial 7 weekday return trips. However, in 1920, the first, third and fifth Down workings and the fifth Up working were by 'Mixed' trains. The remainder were passenger only, with the proviso that horse boxes, or any 4-wheel vans carrying 'passenger' rated traffic, could be attached.

Following the demise of the Stirling's 0-4-4T's, Class C12 4-4-2T became the usual residents of Spilsby shed. Loco staff in early LNER days consisted of one driver, one 'passed' fireman, one fireman and a 'passed' cleaner. They formed two shifts which alternated on a weekly basis. Coaling was carried out by the firemen, at a bonus rate of four pence farthing per ton. They also lit up the engine, washed out its boiler each Monday, Wednesday and Friday and disposed of it at the end of each day's work.

Came the Second World War, with the almost immediate consequence of cessation of passenger traffic over the Spilsby branch, from 11th September 1939, never to be restored (actually the last passenger train to pass over the branch ran on 16th May 1954, with J6 0-6-0 No.64199 hauling a five coach RCTS special. *see over*). The authors have been told that Spilsby shed did not close until 1941, however, after which the locomotive for the daily goods trip along the branch was sent from Boston. In the 1946 WTT this is shown as leaving Boston shed at 7.15 a.m., running light engine to Firsby, arrive 7.45 a.m.: departure from Firsby, with the goods for Spilsby, was at 8.45 a.m. During the 1948-1950 period, ex-GE Class N7 0-6-2T were to be seen on this duty.

Spilsby's little locoshed survived, in very good condition, into the era of BR, which was finally responsible for the eventual closure of the line, on 1st December 1958. The shed was subsequently demolished and today, little trace of it remains.

The aforementioned RCTS railtour of May 1954 with J6 no.64199 running round its train whilst enthusiasts take in the surroundings of this tiny terminus. No doubt one or two of the throng checked the inside of the engine shed, now cut off by rail, for any long hidden occupant; others checked the rolling stock in the yard for rarities. The railtour era had begun; it is such a shame that so many were to branch lines that were ready for closure. *T.J.Edgington.*

STAFFORD

As a logical progression of the Derbyshire and Staffordshire Extension, the GN Board cast its eyes further west, to Shropshire, and the County Town of Shrewsbury. The avenue of approach would be via the Derbys and Staffs to Eggington Junction, then over the tracks of the friendly North Staffordshire Railway, to Uttoxeter. From there the small, ailing Stafford & Uttoxeter Railway would give access to Stafford and thenceforward, Shrewsbury could be reached, not over LNWR tracks, but over those of the projected 'Potteries' section of the Potteries Shrewsbury & North Wales Railway.

As a first step, the GN arranged for the Stafford & Uttoxeter to obtain an Act, empowering the former to run all services. The impoverished S&U, which had been incorporated on 29th July 1862 and completed its 15Z\x mile line on 23rd December 1867, was only too happy for the GN to take over and the Act was passed on 11th August 1879. This gave the GN access to the S&U's sole locomotive shed, sited by the goods yard at Stafford Common station. It was a wooden building, measuring ? ft x ? ft with a tiled gable roof covering the single through road. An ash pit and basic coal and water facilities completed the somewhat ramshackle installation, which never did have the luxury of a turntable.

As is well known, the eccentric PS&NW was a glorious failure, never building its 'Potteries' section and therefore allowing the GN entry to Shrewsbury. There does not appear to have been an approach to the LNWR on the subject of running powers, but the GNR did consolidate its position by obtaining an Act, on 18th July 1881, to totally absorb the S&UR. The price paid was £100,000, plus 'other costs', and it is interesting to go forward slightly, to 1884, when Stirling presented to the GN Board, the following valuation of the S&U's rolling stock: "...there are two engines, twelve carriages, sixteen wagons and one travelling crane and the price to be paid for them is £1,189, as follows: 2 engines - £800; 12 carriages - £215; 16 wagons - £164; the crane - £10. I find that one of the engines, all the carriages and the crane, will have to be renewed before they are of any use. The sixteen wagons and one engine are of such a condition that they can be made available for traffic for 4 to 5 years. The probable cost for renewing the stock is, for 2 engines, say £3,000; 12 carriages - £4,500; 16 wagons - £1,200; one crane, say £300, total: £9,000, less amount paid £1,189 - charging it as Capital, total: £7,811..."

The engines, both built by Beyer Peacock, were an 1860 ex-North London Railway 0-4-4T and a 2-4-0, eight years its junior. Of the crane, nothing is known, but it must have been in a bit of a mess by 1884! Quite what happened about the renewal of S&U stock is not clear, but if Stirling had gone on to give a valuation of ex-S&U buildings, it would not have included the locoshed. That was because after only a short time in GNR ownership, the wooden depot had been totally destroyed by fire, on 22nd November 1881. No replacement was ever made, the GN preferring instead to seek, and get, accommodation at the Stafford locomotive depot of the LNWR, sited adjacent to that company's station. (That depot, consisting of 4 road and 6 road straight sheds, dating back to the LNW's Northern and Southern Divisional days, is covered in detail in *LMS Engine Sheds, Vol.1 The L&NWR* Wild Swan Publications 1981.)

Resorting to the LNW locoshed was a logical step on the GN's part as its passenger services over the Stafford branch - 6 trains each way daily, from Nottingham or Derby, were running over the connection from Stafford Common, into the LNWR's station, where they terminated in the bay at the north end of the Down platform. All in all, a comfortable arrangement and while the authors have no wish to appear slanderous, it does seem as if that locoshed fire did conveniently rid the GN of what must, by then, have been a very dubious asset! Staying with train services for a moment, goods carryings over the S&U were always dominated by milk traffic, especially from Ingestre, Chartley and Grindley, with as many as a hundred 17 gallon churns being shipped daily, from the latter alone. From 1928 the milk was conveyed in 4 and later 6-wheeled tanks, most to the London dairies. Milk trains even ran on Sundays, a feature of the line almost until closure, when road tankers took away the railway's livelihood.

By 1895 the GN had a locomotive foreman, an examiner and one or two labourers at Stafford, in addition to the crews for the two locomotives normally stabled there - Stirling/Ivatt 0-4-2/2-4-0 for passenger work, and 0-6-0 or even 0-8-0 for goods, depending upon the load. By New Year's Eve 1895 the problems of keeping staff at such a remote location were brought to notice, when Ivatt reported on that day: "...the house occupied by the late foreman, at Stafford Common, has been declared unfit for habitation. The present examiner now acts also as the loco foreman and he has found difficulty in getting suitable accommodation. The house he has managed to secure is too far away from the company's premises for a man who is liable to be called out at any moment. I shall therefore be obliged if a house could be built for the loco foreman. I understand that all the staff at Stafford Common have great difficulty in finding accommodation..." This matter took a while to be agreed, but the Way & Works Committee Minutes show that by 25th June 1897, Messrs. J.Jarvis & Co. were "...clearing the site and laying foundations for staff cottages at Stafford, at a cost of £989..." The location of this housing is obscure, but was probably Stafford Common and at that total cost must have entailed 7 or 8 units.

In December 1912, Great Northern engines stabling at Stafford LNWR shed still numbered two, but by then they were in the care of a chargeman from Colwick, stationed at the LNW establishment. He presumably doubled as a fitter and does not seem to have had much in the way of assistance, so there must have been a time or two when his LNW colleagues lent a helping hand - suitable charges duly being raised no doubt. The outstationing of men and machines continued through London & North Eastern Railway days, into the British Railways era. At that time the men were withdrawn, but 'Eastern' engines continued to visit Stafford LM Region shed - Derby Friargate maintaining a couple of Class J1 0-6-0 for working the daily pick-up goods. That working ceased and the old S&U line was closed, between Uttoxeter and Stafford Common, on 5th March 1951; passenger services had ceased on 4th December 1939. Interestingly, just before final closure, Stafford LMR shed's turntable was under repair so Colwick (Derby) Class N2 0-6-2T were used over the old Stafford & Uttoxeter, for the first, and, last time.

(left) **It can hardly be surprising that any sort of illustration of Stafford Common shed has not been found! All that can be offered is this shot of Class J3 0-6-0 3375 resting between duties in the yard of Stafford LMS shed, on 30th April 1933.** *H.C.Casserley.*

WAINFLEET

In early times Waynflete or even more correctly Waynflete (All Saints) as it was then known, had been a quite prominent East Coast seaport with a long history of trade. However the River Steeping gradually silted up the inland harbour and Wainfleet slipped back into a quiet Lincolnshire existence. Until 11th September 1870 that is when the Wainfleet & Firsby Railway opened over the 4¼ miles separating the two communities. Incorporated on 13th May 1869, the company's line was worked by the Great Northern from the outset with the 11th September opening being for goods services only, passenger trains commenced on 24th October 1871.

The W&FR built an engine shed at Wainfleet, where the single platform station was not dissimilar in layout to such places as Horncastle and Spilsby. The engine shed was single road, single ended and measured 54 ft by 20 ft. It was constructed in brick with an arched entrance and single pitch tiled gable roof. Water came from a well and was stored in a 2,500 gallon tank sited on the station platform adjacent to the engineshed. Coal was supplied from a small platform by the shed entrance a location made cramped and awkward by the immediacy of the same station platform. Eventually fuelling was facilitated by provision of a short coaling siding. This had been requested by the local engineer on 2nd March 1908 and approved by the Way & Works Committee, at an estimated cost of £80. For some reason the job was not completed until November/December 1911. At that time the coaling spur installed by the GN's own men had cost a mere £15!

By 1912 the rear wall of the engineshed was being affected by subsidence requiring shoring by application of two timber buttresses. Not long after the problem was cured by creating an arched doorway in the brick wall identical to that at the front and making the depot a 'through' type by extending the track to the rear. This alteration which seems to have been accompanied by a re-roofing would have been appreciated only a few years later when larger tender engines were allocated to Wainfleet *(see below)*.

At first Wainfleet & Firsby services were operated by 2-2-2T sub-shedded from Boston, a type of locomotive made necessary by the need to get around any possible objection from Government Inspectors, about lack of a turntable at either Firsby or Wainfleet. The little tank locos soon had more work to do, for a time anyway, as after only 10 months of operation the W&FR obtained an Act for a 5¼ mile extension from Wainfleet to Skegness. The actual date of the Act was 18th July 1872 and given the level terrain, construction of the single line was rapid with opening occurring on 28th July 1873. Wainfleet shed remained the area's centre of locomotive operations, but a 44 ft 7 ins turntable was provided at the new terminus so presumably the 2-2-2T were soon able to give way to larger types, including tender engines. Whichever, in 1876 the resident engine left Wainfleet at 6.10 a.m. for Skegness and arrived back at 7.45 p.m. after working the Firsby - Skegness 'shuttle' all day. By the early 1890s survivors of classes such as the Great Northern's original 'Small Hawthorns' were being put out to grass at Wainfleet for the final span of their long lives: Nos.67 and 70, by then running as 0-4-2 are known to have been operating from Wainfleet at that time.

A nice study of Wainfleet station, showing the little shed tucked away in its cramped position at the east end of the Up platform. Class D2 3045 was inside the shed on that day, 29th August 1937, while the other engine allocated, Class D3 4357, was out working. *W.A.Camwell.*

But things were changing, presaged by a GNR Act of 30th May 1896 enabling absorption of the W&FR with effect from 1st July that year. This was at a total share redemption cost of £76,500, a bargain, considering the future receipts the GN would gain from traffic over the line. In the year following take-over, six weekday return passenger trains were being run, Firsby - Skegness but the latter's popularity as a holiday resort (in time leading to some of the most successful railway advertising ever), was incurring increasing workings by through trains. So, the GN embarked upon a line doubling programme, already started in a small way by the W&FR and completed it in 1900 together with a large new station at Skegness.

By that time "old dears" like the Small Hawthorns had gone from Wainfleet replaced by Stirling 0-4-2 and 2-4-0 with the occasional tank engine from the same designer or his predecessor. It would seem though that Wainfleet's normal allocation of two locomotives settled down, around the end of the Stirling 0-4-2s in 1921, to Ivatt Class D2 4-4-0s of which 1356, 1358 and 1360 (LNER D4, then D3, Nos.4356, 4358 and 4360) were particularly associated with the shed for some years. At about the same time the practice of changing over Wainfleet engines every three days, with replacements from Boston seems to have ceased. (This frequency was necessitated by the need for boiler washouts given the bad state of water at Wainfleet). In its place engines were changed every weekday using in the outward direction from Wainfleet, the depot's No.2 locomotive diagram which in 1924 went like this:

Wainfleet 6.50 am	LE to Skegness MO
Wainfleet 6.50 am	LE to Firsby MX
Skegness 7.25 am	Pass to Notts MO (to Firsby only)
Firsby 8.40 am	Pass to Lincoln (Lincoln men)
Lincoln 11.20 am	Pass to Firsby (Lincoln men)
Firsby	LE to Willoughby (Wainfleet men)
Willoughby 1.10 pm	Pass to Louth via Mablethorpe
Louth	LE to Firsby via Alford
Firsby 4.20 pm	Pass to Lincoln (Boston men)
Lincoln 6.30 pm	Pass to Boston (Boston men)

Inward to Wainfleet for the engine changeover, the crew working the second half of Wainfleet's No.1 locomotive diagram were involved. In 1924 that diagram was concerned with twelve hours of running the Firsby - Skegness 'shuttle' with a crew change around the middle of the day, ending back at Wainfleet shed for disposal of the engine. The crew then went "on the cushions" to Firsby, to relieve the Boston men on the changeover engine. This then worked back to Skegness on the last down train of the day, returning to Wainfleet shed - engine changeover completed.

In addition to the above Wainfleet shed had a local goods duty to Alford, departing Firsby at 11.52 a.m. and returning on the 1.20 p.m. pick-up goods to Boston, as far as Firsby. This was a Wainfleet crew duty, using a Boston engine.

By summer 1937, if the daily changeover of engines was still normal practice, it is not clear how it was then effected. This was the result of the previous year's large-scale improvements to engine servicing facilities at Skegness, which seems to have left Wainfleet's engines dealing only with the Firsby - Skegness shuttle, which at that time operated to the following schedule:

UP
Skegness dep. 6.35 am 8.00 am 9.50 am
12.04 pm 1.18 pm 3.55 pm 5.55 pm 8.35 pm 10.00 pm
Firsby arr. 6.55 am 8.23 am 10.13 am
12.27 pm 1.33 pm 4.13 pm 6.18 pm 8.58 pm 10.18 pm

DOWN
Firsby dep. 7.10 am 8.42 am 11.12 am
12.50 pm 1.48 pm 4.30 pm 6.49 pm 9.20 pm
Skegness arr. 7.30 am 9.04 am 11.34 am
1.08 pm 2.10 pm 4.53 pm 7.07 pm 9.43 pm

Presumably a crew change took place during the 1.18 p.m. departure from and 2.10 p.m. arrival back at Skegness but perhaps any change of engine was then made at Firsby, after the 10.18 p.m. arrival there, with the new loco then running light engine to Wainfleet. The matter is not too apparent and could do with further investigation.

So also does the final fate of Wainfleet shed require more investigation, as exact details of its last duties and closure date have so far eluded the authors. Apparently the depot survived into the late 1940s for housing locomotives but when such use of the shed ended, crews still continued to sign-on there until the advent of dieselisation 1955/6. Certainly the shed building does not appear on a 1960s OS map but exactly how many years previously it had been closed and demolished remains a mystery. Today its site is incorporated in an allotment garden, with the brick bases of the wall's still clearly visible.

The tender of Boston based D2 no.3045 peeps out of Wainfleet shed on the same August afternoon of the previous picture. This picture shows details of the brick and woodwork of the shed and its arched doors. It does seem something of a surprise that the new doorway created at the other end of the shed was also of arched construction rather than being of a square design with a suitable lintel; perhaps the local authority had some say in the matter. *Authors collection.*

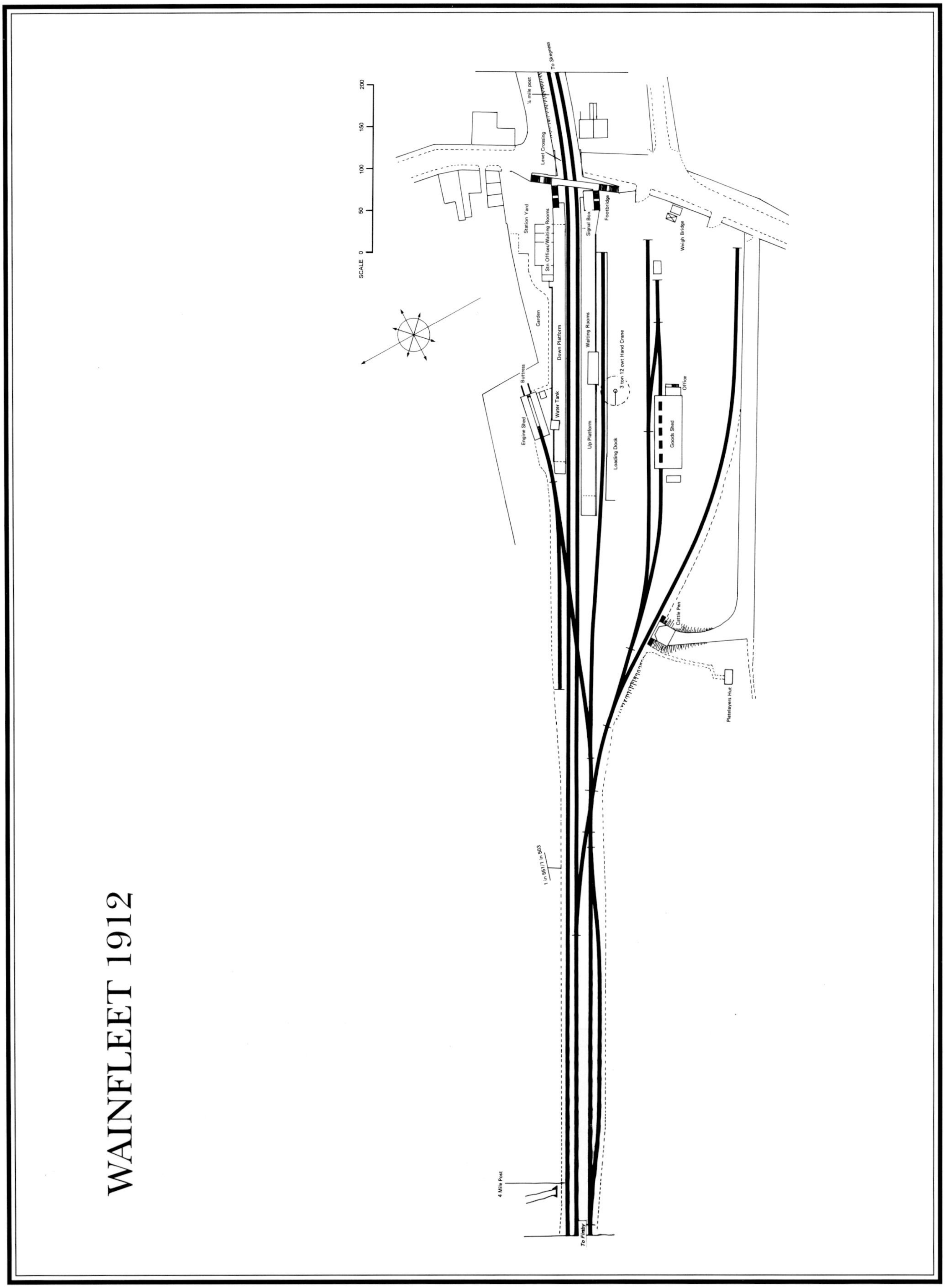

WAINFLEET 1912

This circa 1905 view of Wainfleet shows the original single platformed station and the engine shed with its rear wall intact and unsupported. The line had been doubled by about 1900 and a new Up platform was installed roughly where the goods shed stood in the old layout, necessitating removal of that building to a site further south. *A.Cartwright collection.*

This close up of Wainfleet shed, from an unknown date, clearly shows the arched doorway that had to be let into the rear of the building, as a result of subsidence. The four-square tankhouse, which perforce had to obstruct the platform to a large extent, seems almost too big for the little tank it supported throughout its existence. *A.Cartwright.*

Appendix 1. OTHER COMPANIES' ENGINE SHEDS USED BY GREAT NORTHERN ENGINES

The Great Northern Railway was not an isolated system, so its locomotives had, perforce, to work over the lines of a number of other companies and seek refuge in their hosts' engine sheds. The following list gives all those 'foreign' sheds known to the authors, that at some time accommodated GN engines on a regular basis, and have not been covered elsewhere in this book. The list details only depots where GN engines, whether formally allocated or not, used facilities and/or had space allotted them, with the remainder of the establishment being used by the owning companies' motive power. Where another company provided a shed solely for GN use, e.g. as at York, then those depots are covered among the GN's 'own' premises.

A further qualification is necessary, regarding the engine sheds of Joint Companies, of which the GN was a shareholder, e.g. the Midland & Great Northern Railway, and the Cheshire Lines Committee. It is intended to cover the depots of the former in a separate work, so none that were not of GN origin are included in this volume. With respect to the CLC, as far as is known, GN engines were housed at only two of that railway's sheds: Trafford Park is detailed for clarity's sake with Manchester (Deansgate) GN shed (*volume 3*), while Walton-on-the-Hill (Liverpool), is described below.

BRICKLAYERS ARMS -
Great Northern goods trains commenced running onto SER metals in the 1860's and provision was made for the locomotives to enter Bricklayers Arms shed, but in emergencies only. The GN's 1881 WTT carried the following instruction: "...The engines working the Bricklayers Arms trains will not, unless in case of emergency, require to go to the locomotive yard at Bricklayers Arms, but when that is necessary, a shunter must accompany them from Mercer's Crossing to the Loco. Depot and back to Mercer's Crossing..." It is not known whether the facility ever had to be used by the GNR, but very likely it was.

GRIMSBY -

This town, which grew from a population of less than 1,000 people in the first years of the 19th century, to 100,000, by 1912, can lay claim to having been the world's first major fishing port. The creation of a railway, the Manchester, Sheffield & Lincolnshire Company found new markets to the west. Grimsby also attracted the East Lincolnshire Railway, it forming the northern point of that company's proposed route, which opened on 1st March 1848.

GN engines worked the ELR, transitting Grimsby on their way to New Holland (see below), during the period of initial GN/MSLR joint operation. Inter-company disputes led to the end of joint working on 8th July 1851, leaving the GN with Grimsby as its northern terminus in Lincolnshire. The town was fair and square part of the MSLR, which continued to accept traffic both ways, on behalf of the GN, with the latter installing a 40 ft turntable, ex-Louth engine shed, accessed from Grimsby, Garden Street Junction (Whistle Code: 3 whistles). It took 11 years before the GN arranged to work its own traffic, so on 29th April 1862, approval was sought for the recruitment of eight men and one horse, all to work in Grimsby goods department. This was followed up on 26th March 1863, when the locomotive engineer reported that a well had been dug, at a cost of £12, to supply water to the company's houses, warehouse and stables.

So, no mention in 1862/3 of separate GN loco facilities, with nothing detailed in the 1881 WTT either. Therefore, it could be assumed that nearby Great Northern engine sheds worked all their Grimsby traffic on an 'out and back the same day' basis. On the other hand, how long the 1851 turntable survived is not known - probably not for many years, and no other later record has been found of such a facility. Accordingly, it is equally likely that GN engines were using the MSLR depot at Grimsby. This adjoined the Down side of Grimsby Docks station and was, in later years at least, of six roads, thereby having sufficient space to accommodate the smallish number of GN engines that would have appeared daily.

Certainly, by October 1912, a GN engine was officially allocated to Grimsby - actually J6 0-6-0 No.747 at that time. It is interesting that 1912 was also the year the MSLR opened its new docks and locoshed at Immingham, and reduced Grimsby shed to sub-depot status, housing a handful of dock shunters. Perhaps then, the GN left the premises soon after, because by 1st April 1919, Gresley commented to the Locomotive Committee that there were eight GN engines working into Grimsby daily, from Peterborough and Boston, but no pit accommodation was available to them, at "Grimsby Yard". Two days later the Committee approved expenditure of £112 to provide a 60 ft pit at Grimsby Yard.

In addition, it is known the GN had two drivers and two firemen stationed at Grimsby, in latter days anyway, and their duties included participation in working Louth loco depot's 'star' turn, using an engine stabled overnight at Grimsby. Whether this loco - usually an Ivatt 4-4-0 - was kept at Grimsby Yard, or in the partly defunct MSLR shed is not clear. Its duties took it away from Grimsby at 5.50 a.m. each weekday morning, in the hands of a local crew, to Louth, where they handed over to Louth men, before returning on the 6.44 a.m. Louth-Grimsby Town. Later in the day, the second set of Grimsby men worked the return 'star' duty from Louth to Grimsby, for the cycle to start again the next day.

All this ceased when the grouping ended separate GN/GC working at Grimsby and Immingham shed took over all duties.

HULL -

It seems fairly certain that no Great Northern engines were ever outstationed at Hull, though of course, some GN types did gravitate there after the Grouping. Whether they used Hull locosheds at all, before LNER times, is shrouded in mystery.

Running powers over the North Eastern Railway were granted to the GN in the NER's Hull & Doncaster Act, of 1863. Those powers covered the section of line between Thorne and Hull, i.e., via Goole, a route that did not, in fact, open until 1869. However, a 1912 issue of the NER's "Running Powers" booklet notes that: "...the GN power not to be exercised until Arbitration awards that the NER are not conducting efficiently GN traffic between Doncaster and Hull..." No Arbitration award was ever made in this instance, ergo, the GN never exercised its running powers.

So, did GN engines ever get to Hull in pre-Grouping days? Yes, around the turn of the century, Norwegian Boat Expresses were GN-worked throughout from Kings Cross to Hull on alternate days, during May to August. This facility suited the schedule of sailings and dockings, having been agreed between Henry Oakley and George Gibb, in an exchange of letters at the end of November 1897, and subsequently ratified by a formal agreement. But, all evidence points to the fact that boat train engines and stock worked back to Doncaster immediately after a sailing, or ran up from there, e.c.s, for a docking. Certainly in 1907 these trains worked to and from Riverside Quay station.

The question of whether GN engines ever used NER shed facilities at Hull is therefore, still uncertain. To the authors, it seems incredible that no such visits were made, particularly during the hectic days of the First World War, for example. If they did get there during that time, GN motive power would have been serviced at the North Eastern's Dairycoates or Botanic Gardens sheds. Then, although it seems unlikely, if there should indeed have been incursions into the NER's empire before 1901, GN engines may also have seen the inside of the locoshed beside Hull Paragon station.

Whatever, all of Hull's locomotive depots are well described in Ken Hoole's book on North Eastern sheds, mentioned earlier in this volume, and the authors are grateful to the late Mr. Hoole for his assistance in putting together these few brief notes. It must be said though, that all speculations are those of the authors and not the noted NER historian.

KNOTTINGLEY -

The situation regarding the GN and L&YR at Knottingley is inextricably linked with the same two companies' relationship at Wakefield - in a word - confused! So, for the sake of clarity, the reader is recommended to consult the Wakefield section below, in concert with these paragraphs on Knottingley.

First entry by the GN into Knottingley was on 1st October 1849, when through running commenced over the L&Y from Askern Junction, on the way to Methley Junction and Leeds. By 17th June 1851, Sturrock was making a point about excessive tender-first running by GN engines, due to lack of turntables. The loco engineer instanced Knottingley-Leeds and asked that a 40 ft turntable be put down at the latter place, costs for which were approved on 1st July. However, this was a strange request, as the engine shed at Leeds Central (Low Level) had been brought into use on 15th September 1850, complete with a turntable, so why engines were running in reverse from Knottingley is inexplicable. Most likely the Knottingley turntable was not fitted, as no plan so far inspected by the authors has revealed it, or given any idea where it may have been sited.

Furthermore, if the reader consults the section below, on the GN's presence at Wakefield, it can be seen that the company's engines were probably being housed there in those earliest days. In addition, it must be remembered that the GN and L&Y had reached joint agreements, in March 1851, to rebuild Knottingley and Wakefield stations into grander Joint affairs, with the job at Wakefield including proposals for a new locoshed. Knottingley's contract was let in March 1853 and work was completed exactly one year later. Part of the overall scheme had been replacement of Knottingley's original Leeds & Manchester Railway engine shed by a more substantial structure which, however, was pure L&Y, not joint property.

That single-road, brick-built depot stood in the corner of the goods yard, opposite the station, and was complete with a 44 ft turntable. GN locomotives were certainly in residence there by 1855, as the GN's Rule Book for that year shows Knottingley shed having duties to Wakefield, Leeds and York. The company was still present in 1858, having free use of the shed because the L&Y needed all available space at its Wakefield depot. The ejection from Wakefield became necessary when, for unexplained reasons, no new engine shed was provided as part of the station rebuilding works. Then, on 1st June 1867, when the GN asked if it could store spare locos at Wakefield, the L&Y refused, and instead offered space at Knottingley depot. Whether this means the GN had moved back to Wakefield between 1858 and 1867, is not clear, but the company almost certainly left Knottingley again, soon after 1st July 1868.

On that date, the MR/MSLR Joint engine shed opened at Wakefield (Balne Lane) and it is known that GN engines were using space there shortly after. Which leads the authors to the conclusion that Knottingley L&Y shed ceased housing GN locomotives around 1869, so the depot fades from this history. It continued serving L&Y engines until closure on 1st July 1922, after which it saw private use, until demolition in BR days.

LIVERPOOL (WALTON-ON-THE-HILL) -

This Cheshire Lines Committee depot opened in 1881, along with the nearby Huskisson Goods Station. Initially a four road shed, being expanded to six roads in 1885, Walton saw its first Great Northern engine about 1898, when the company commenced its comprehensive London-Lancashire goods service, to the new Manchester Deansgate complex and Huskisson Goods. This required an allocation of engines at Trafford Park CLC shed, (see previously, under "Manchester"), which shared the duties with Colwick depot.

There has been speculation in the past that a GNR engine was outstationed at Walton and/or the company had some men based there, but after considerable investigation both theories seem to have no basis in truth. Certainly all shunting at Huskisson was carried out by MSLR/GCR engines and it would appear that the GN's sole weekday return goods working to Liverpool was handled by a Colwick engine - invariably an 0-6-0 - which laid over at Walton shed between its inward and outward duties. In addition, study of GN participation in annual CLC locomotive mileages indicates that there was only sufficient distance run to allow of the daily through workings.

All in all, fairly conclusive, but after a quarter of a century, the GN's separate presence in Liverpool was nullified by the Grouping. Walton shed survived for many years after the GN ceased to be, finally being closed, as a four road building again, on 15th December 1963. The depot stood empty for a further 15 years or so, before being pulled down. (The authors wish to acknowledge the invaluable assistance rendered in the preparation of this section by *Mancunian* the journal of the Manchester Locomotive Society).

NEW HOLLAND -

Northern terminus of the very first GNR train services, New Holland was the site of a four road brick-built engine shed of MSLR origin. It is not known if the building was put up for opening of the line, but a turntable certainly was provided from the outset.

Inauguration of New Holland's railway came on 1st March 1848, when both the MSLR and GNR entered the place, over MSLR tracks from Grimsby. The GN's presence was in its capacity as operating company of the East Lincolnshire Railway, between

Grimsby and Louth. Initial services from New Holland, over the ELR, were a GNR/MSLR Joint undertaking, but the Manchester company does not seem to have often exercised its rights, south of Grimsby. In any case, a dispute between the two companies brought an end to joint operation, with effect from 1st July 1851. From that date the GN disappeared from New Holland, and any engine shed that may have existed there at the time.

NORTHALLERTON -

The WTT's from around the mid-1900's show a GN train running from Northallerton, via Cordio Junction and Sinderby to Harrogate; this was a daily turn, in the Up direction only, indicating something like a milk train perhaps. What duty the GN engine undertook to get to Northallerton is not clear, but the locomotive would almost certainly have used the two road NER shed's turntable, although it is just possible the triangular junction to the Hawes line was used. No other details are known.

SCARBOROUGH -

Again, the 1900's (certainly, in the 1907 WTT), saw summer through workings by GN engines from Kings Cross to Scarborough. There can be no doubt the locomotives made use of the NER's large depot at Scarborough, consisting of a turntable shed and an eight road straight shed, before embarking on their return workings. The dates on which such services began and ceased are unknown.

SELBY -

Only reference seen by the authors, about GN locomotives having access to Selby NER depot, comes from the Appendix to the GN's 1881 Working Timetable. In the section titled "Whistle Codes" is given the whistle sequences (2 long, 2 short) necessary for advising signalmen that GN engines wished to enter, or leave, Selby's double turntable shed.

No more can be said, as it has not been possible to discover why the GN would wish to access Selby engine shed. What duties took the company's engines there, when such workings commenced, and when they ended, are each a mystery.

SHEFFIELD -

Great Northern services to Sheffield commenced on 7th August 1850, trains running over MSLR tracks from Lincoln, via Retford. It would seem that GN engines worked through to Sheffield from the outset, and in fact, some were allocated there - almost certainly at the MSL's Neepsend engine shed.

Neepsend was a substantial six road depot, but whether GN locomotives were stationed there, or at some other site, they were not accommodated inside any building. Accordingly, in November 1851, Sturrock asked the Way & Works Committee for cover to be provided for: "...the one or two engines outstationed at Sheffield..." A request from the GN's General Manager was duly sent to the MSLR, resulting in a reply, on 24th January 1852, from James Allport, to the effect that the MSL agreed to provide 'cover' for GN engines, at a yearly rent of 10% of the capital outlaid for land purchase, buildings, etc.

At the Way & Works Comittee meeting three days later, the matter was deferred, apparently never to be resurrected. At a later date, yet to be ascertained, sub-shedding of GN locomotives at Sheffield ceased.

STARBECK -

This two road NER depot at Harrogate began hosting GN engines about 1900, sub-shedded from York GN shed, when a portion of the 1.30 p.m. King's Cross - York train was extended to the spa town. The train departed from York at 6.22 p.m., the locomotive stabled overnight at Starbeck shed, then left Harrogate next day, at 9.47 a.m., with the return working to York.

In 1902, the 11.20 a.m. King's Cross - Edinburgh, and 12.20 p.m. Edinburgh - King's Cross trains were diverted to run via Askern Junction, Knottingley, Church Fenton, Harrogate and Northallerton, a service which, incidentally, saw the first GN expresses passage the Askern - Knottingley line since 1871. Then came introduction of a new train service, the 1.40 p.m. King's Cross - Harrogate, and 10.10 a.m. Harrogate - King's Cross. This, plus the diverted Scotch expresses, replaced the York - Harrogate return working during the winter months, in summer the separate train continued to run. There was also a daily working by a GN engine from Northallerton to Harrogate (see Northallerton, above).

By July 1912, three of York's Class D3 4-4-0, Nos.1071, 1314 and 1344, were subshedded at Starbeck, for the King's Cross train -and probably, another service or two (the Northallerton turn?). How long the York - Harrogate service survived is unclear, but it probably ceased as a result of World War One, never to be re-instituted. As far as is known though, the King's Cross service remained (in later years becoming a Pullman working), keeping at least a couple of GN engines at Starbeck until the Grouping made such separateness obsolete. For how much longer GN-origin locomotives continued to operate out of Starbeck is not certain, but a single D3, 4313, was stationed there up to 22nd March 1933 on which date it transferred to Barnard Castle. It is interesting to note that 4313 was actually exchanged at Starbeck for D17 no.1903 because the Starbeck No.2 N.U.R. objected to the sparse cab on the ex-GN engine.

STRAWBERRY HILL -

A service introduced late in GN days was the cross-London goods workings from King's Cross, via Ludgate Hill, Loughborough Junction, Clapham Junction and Richmond, to the London & South Western Railway's new marshalling yard at Feltham. This service started after the end of the First World War and brought GN engines to the LSWR's nine road engine shed at Strawberry Hill.

The year 1923 saw two things. First was the Grouping, which meant that LNER engines then visited the SR's Feltham yard. That year also witnessed the closure of Strawberry Hill depot to steam, its replacement being a new locoshed, also at Feltham. Thus ended what was perhaps, the shortest-lived example of GN engines using another company's locomotive depot.

VICTORIA STATION (LONDON) -

GN passenger services started running from King's Cross to London's Victoria Station, in April 1867, in a reciprocal arrangement with the LC&DR. Chatham company notices appended to the GN's 1881 WTT contain the following instructions: "...Fantable between 5 & 6 roads. This enables locomotives to run round their trains by a line leading from the fantable to the engine sidings. GN trains must use 5 & 6 roads whenever possible..." This infers that GN engines may have found their way into the engine yard at Victoria, for routine servicing, but any details are lacking.

WAKEFIELD -

Information regarding GN locoshed facilities at Wakefield is, to say the least, thin on the ground! What has been discovered presented the authors with perhaps the most confused series of events of any of the histories contained in this book. Therefore, what follows below is subject to some conjecture, but the writers are reasonably satisfied the story is more or less correct.

Great Northern services from Doncaster commenced on 1st October 1849, at which time there was a five road L&Y shed at Wakefield, opened in the previous year. It seems likely the initial service was worked on an "out and home" basis, from Doncaster and that it was some time before the GN started to outstation engines at Wakefield. However, they were there by June 1851, as on 28th of that month, Sturrock brought to the attention of the Board: "...the great inconvenience caused at Wakefield through having no shed for the two engines stationed there. I would be obliged if some arrangement with the Lancashire & Yorkshire Company can be made, to alleviate this inconvenience..."

It seems the L&Y were willing to accommodate the GN at Wakefield, but with an eye to the future, plans were laid for a new engine shed in the city. These were incorporated in a joint agreement drawn up between both companies, in March 1851, to rebuild Wakefield (Kirkgate) station. The contract also included plans for a new goods shed and granary and was let in September 1853, taking nearly four years to complete.

For some unknown reason, the planned engine shed was not built, so by 1857 there was an acute accommodation problem, exacerbated in 1858, when the GN asked if it could store carriages in its portion. The L&Y, already strapped for space for its own engines, effectively solved the problem by claiming total use of its engine shed at Wakefield, and offering the GN free use of the L&Y shed at Knottingley, in exchange. So, off to Knottingley went the GN, for an as yet uncertain period of time. However, it seems as if the Great Northern may have been back at Wakefield by 1867, as in that year, it asked the L&Y if it could store spare engines there, from 1st June (ex-Bradford, Wakefield & Leeds Railway probably). Again, the L&Y refused, reinforcing the point that the shed was for use only by locos in traffic, of which there were 61 already allocated, with covered standing room for only 20! Once more, Knottingley engine shed was offered, but whether or not the GN moved there is uncertain, particularly as alternative locoshed accommodation was "just around the corner" as it were.

In the mid-1860's the GN had reached an agreement with the MSLR/MR, for a joint station at Wakefield (Westgate), near where, at Balne Lane, the MR/MSL were to build themselves a joint locoshed. It is clear though, that the GN did not at first consider using Balne Lane, as on 13th February 1866, it suggested to the other two companies that they should spend less on the passenger side at Westgate, which the GN would be using. That would enable savings to be made, which could then be diverted to the Goods and Locomotive Departments - which the GN would not be using.

Balne Lane's three road engine shed opened on 1st July 1868 and it is thought the GN moved in soon after, from either Wakefield or Knottingley L&Y sheds. Certainly, the company's engines were at the MR/MSL depot by September 1876, as on the ninth of that month, Stirling gave details of GN coal consumption to the Board, among which was use of 37 tons of coal per week, by engines based at "Westgate". Now, 37 tons of coal a week is not much - 2 tons per day, into three tank engines would fit - those engines being shunters at Wrenthorpe Yard probably, with addition of some local trip working.

Whether "Westgate" actually meant Balne Lane is not entirely certain, but evidence points to this, because on 24th March 1880, Stirling reported to the Board on the serious lack of turntables in Yorkshire District and with reference to Wakefield, suggested that the GN make use of the turntable "already at Westgate". So, assuming the GN was using Balne Lane, it did not have access to the depot's turntable, confirming the above point about only tank engines being sub-shedded there. Stirling's suggestion was quickly acted upon though, as in 1881, the GN's WTT Appendix lists turntable and loco siding facilities as being available to the company's engines, at Wakefield MSLR shed.

Then, seven years later, the situation is both confirmed, and made complicated again by a newspaper announcement. The announcement, of 16th July 1888, was to the effect that Messrs. J&W Beauclaud, whose tender for building turntable foundations at Wakefield had just been accepted by the GNR, were going into liquidation! In reporting this to the Board, on 20th July, the Locomotive Engineer proposed that the next lowest tender, of £412-4-0d, from Walter Binns & Co., of Bradford, should be accepted, subject to prior approval of the MR/MSLR. It looks therefore, as if the GN was paying for a new turntable at Balne Lane depot.

By 1881, L&Y engines stationed at Wakefield had grown in number to 80, reaching 98 only two years later, by which time the five road shed had been extended slightly, as it could then offer cover to 25 locomotives. Very soon after that it was replaced by a ten road shed on the same site, which was itself superseded by a larger ten road depot at Crofton, in 1893. At the same time the L&Y moved to Crofton, the GN had moved out of Balne Lane and taken up residence at the L&Y's older ten road depot where, probably, the L&Y maintained some passenger engines. This is perhaps confirmed by a November 1895 official plan of the shed, which shows it as "GN & L&Y Joint". A year later, in a report to the Board, on Yorkshire District motive power, Ivatt comments that: "...the company keeps five engines at Wakefield GN/L&Y Joint shed, where there is space for five engines..."

Nevertheless, the GN's tenure was short, as a further official plan, dated 1898, shows the ten road engine shed by Kirkgate station as still standing, but trackless. Where had GN locos gone? To Ardsley, almost certainly, but the Great Northern retained right of entry to Balne Lane, for turning purposes. This is confirmed by the 1912 WTT, which shows GN locos having access to the turntable beside Wakefield MR shed (no mention of the GCR!).So, the GN got some more return on its 1888 investment in a new turntable for Westgate.

Balne Lane continued to act as a turning point for GN engines, probably until the depot was closed in the first year of the LNER's regime.At that time, all ex-GCR firemen and engines moved to Ardsley, while the one-time GC drivers continued to book on and off at Westgate station. After a while most of the drivers were relocated to Mexborough shed, thereby ending the very complex history of the GNR and its occupancy of other companies' Wakefield sheds.

Appendix 2.
GREAT NORTHERN RAILWAY LOCOMOTIVE DEPARTMENT
ESTIMATES OF WATER CONSUMPTION, BY LOCOMOTIVE DISTRICT, 1901 AND 1906

KEY: (A) Location (in Departmental number order). (B) Installed storage facilities 1901/6. (C) Estimated annual consumption in gallons 1901. (D) Estimated annual consumption in gallons 1906. (E) Water supplier or source. (F) Analyst's report on water's suitability for use in locomotive boilers. (G) Estimated softing cost per 1,000 gallons. (i) Impossible to say. (ii) Not stated.

SOUTH DISTRICT

(A)	(B)	(C)	(D)	(E)	(F)	(G)
1. Brockley coal yard.	2,000 gal. parachute	390,000	520,000	Kent Water Company	Excellent boiler water, but would form soft scale. Washout every three days recommended.	
2. Bread Street Goods.	Hydraulic power only.	960,000	949,000	London Hydraulic Power Company	No comment	
3. Mint Street goods yard.	4,300 gal. tank	740,000	600,000 + 20.3M Hydc.power	New River Co. (1906-Metropolitan Water Board)	Excellent boiler water, which could be easily softened to reduce soft scale forming.	0.5d.
4. Moorgate	7" standpipe, GN bay.	29M.	26M.	Met. Railway Co.	Ditto, No.3	
5. Farringdon St. goods yard.	1,500 gal. tank	12M. (2.5M. for locos-rest Goods Department)	8.85M.	New River Co. (1906-M.W.B).	Ditto, No.3	
6. Kings Cross Stn..	23,000 gal. tank Traffic offices	104M.	86M.	New River Co. (1906-M.W.B.).	Ditto, No.3	
7. Kings Cross Loco. (Top Shed)	45,000 gal. tank	30M.	20M.	Regents Canal Co.	A bad water forming hard scale, composition varied & polluted; difficult & expensive to soften; probably corrosive when softened.	(i)
-"- Loco Yard	18,000 gal. tank	88M.	85.3M.	New River Co.	Ditto,No.3	
8. Hackney Wick goods yard.	2,393 gal. tank	400,000	400,000	East London Water Company	Ditto, No.3	
9. Holloway.	32,000 gal. tank Clarence Yard	42M.	27M.	New River Co. (1906-M.W.B.).	Ditto, No.3	
10. Holloway Electric Light Wk	—	11.8M.	13.7M.	"	Ditto, No.3	
11. Holloway Oil Gas Works.	—	4.15M.	2.69M.	"	Ditto, No.3	
12. Ferme Park.	2,000 gal. para tank Harringay	27M.	27.27M.	"	Ditto, No.3	
13. Alexandra Palace.	—	Supply under negotiation	1.88M.	Alexandra Park Trustees	Good boiler water, easily and cheaply softened.	
14. Edgware Stn.	13,500 gal. tank.	2.5M	2.45M.	Colne Valley Water Co.	Good boiler water, but may be corrosive if softened.	
15. High Barnet.	15,500 gal. tank stn. yard.	8.5M.	8.67M.	Barnet Gas & Water Company.	Good chalky boiler water which may be softened to make first rate.	0.6d.
16. Hornsey.	50,000 gal. tank locoshed.	21.6M.	24.34M.	New River Co.(1906-M.W.B.).	Ditto, No.3	
17. Wood Green.	2 x 3,000 gal. para	2.8M.	1.78M.	"	Ditto, No.3	
18. Barnet.	12,000 gal. tank pass. yard.	4.6M.	2.9M.	Barnet Gas & Water Company.	Ditto, No.15	
19. Hatfield.	29,000 gal. tank engine house.	30M.	30M.	Two wells.	Very pure chalky water; can be softened to make first rate. Lime-90% CaO, at (1/10)d./lb; 2.07 =	0.2d.
20. Hertford.	4,000 gal. tank stn..	20M.	1.6M.	Hertford Waterworks	Chalky; cheaply softened to make first rate, but for presence of nitrate, which, when softened, may render corrosive to copper/steel boilers.	0.5d.
21. St. Albans.	12,500 gal. tank stn..	No water used by Loco Dept; Traffic Dept only		Well.	No comment	
22. Luton.	17,000 gal. tank locoshed.	8M.	8.85M.	Luton Waterworks Co	Ditto No.20, but washout every three days may obviate.	
23. Hitchin.	12,000 gal. tank locoshed.	100M. (Includes supply for MR locoshed; 2.13M. gal. in 1906).	100M.	Two wells.	Excellent, but liable to form much scale; softening may cause corrosion. 3 day washouts recommended.	1d.
24. Royston.	6,000 gal. tank stn..	3M.	2.29M.	Royston Waterworks Company.	High organic purity from deep chalk well. Should not be softened for locomotive use.	
25. Cambridge.	13,000 gal. tank locoshed (GER property)	2.6M.	3.45M.	Cambridge Waterworks Company	Good chalky water, cheaply softened to make first rate.	0.7d.
26. Biggleswade.	30,000 gal. tank Up yard.	14M.	5M.	Well.	Very bad for locos; much hard scale & corrosion. Expensive to soften, which would cause priming.	4d.
27. Offord.	43,000 gal. tank tankhouse.	21M.	26M.	"	Inferior quality which may be rectified by softening. (The river water nearby is much better [No.281]).	2.25d.
28. Huntingdon.	30,000 gal. tank pass. yard.	10M.	10M.	River Ouse.	Variable, like most river water but can be softened at moderate cost to make first rate.	0.9d.
29. Holme.	15,000 gal. tank pass. yard.	3M.	4.5M.	Drain	Very bad; can be softened satisfactorily, but at high cost.	(ii)
	Total	**602.04M.**	**553.329M.**			

NORTH DISTRICT

(A)	(B)	(C)	(D)	(E)	(F)	(G)
30. Peterborough.	128000 gal. tank New England.	38M.	18.7145M.	Peterborough Corp.	Good chalky water which softening would make first rate.	1.4d.
-"-	45,000 gal. tank Crescent.	+125M.	+165M. (New Eng.)	Well (at Werrington Junction).	May be improved by softening but inherent salts will always cause priming if not washed out often.	1.33d.
-"-	23,000 gal. tank Stn. locoshed coal stage		+50.5M. (Werrington Troughs)			
31. Essendine.	30,000 gal. tank stn..	15M.	16M.	River (plus, in 1906 artesian well).	Ditto	1.25d.
32. Stamford.	10,000 gal. tank locoshed.	3.5M.	6M.	River Welland.	Hard water which can be satisfactorily softened if cost is worthwhile.	(i)
33. Bourne.	19,000 gal. tank loco yard.	(M&GN only, paid for at 5d. a tankful)		Well.	Hard but can be softened to make first rate.	(ii)
34. Grantham.	50,000 gal. tank loco yard.	112M.	102.25M.	Grantham Waterworks Company.	Moderately hard, chalky. Softening would make first rate.	0.75d.
-"- (station)	37,000 gal. tank.					
-"- (Spittlegate br)	29,000 gal. tank.					
35. Caythorpe.	5,000 gal. tank (wood) Up line.	1M.	1M.	Well.	Remarkable soft water containing free soda which will cause priming. Cannot be softened.	
36. Newark (stn)	50,000 gal. tank ..	8.5M.	35,000	Newark Corporation.	No comment.	
Newark (loco)	29,000 gal. tank	+45M.	+109M.	River Trent.	Trent water will make much hard scale which can be bettered by softening. Even so, boilers should be emptied often to prevent priming.	2.25d.
36A. Muskham	Troughs	---	50M.	" "	Ditto	
37. Retford.	50,000 gal. tank loco yard.	80M.	91M.	River Idle.	Good. May be improved by softening if desired.	1d.
37A. Bawtry.	31,000 gal. tank Scrooby Troughs.	--	50M.	River Idle.	Ditto, No.37.	1d.
38. Doncaster.	130,000 gal. tank Crimpsall.	430M. + 2.5M.	430M. + 930,000	River Don. Doncaster Corp.	River Don variable but always polluted. An express loco running wholly on this water will take on 2cwts. of mineral matter per day. Causes much scale, priming & corrosion. Generally speaking it is unfit for locomotive use. Is not capable of being satisfactorily softened.	
-"- Red Bank	130,000 gal. tank .					
-"- New C&W	76,000 gal. tank					
-"- C&W shop	23,000 gal. tank					
-"- Turnery ,Plant	20,000 gal. tank					
-"- Wagon Shop (Plant)	12,000 gal. tank					
	Total	**860.5M.**	**1040.429M.**			

Werrington Junction was the site for the first Great Northern water troughs. Brought into use in November 1900, they were laid just north of the junction of the line from Boston. This fine panoramic view of the area shows the troughs as installed on the fast lines only. In the V of the junction stands the pumping house, with waste steam escaping and forming a cloud. On the right, running parallel to the GN main line, is the Midland route to Stamford and Leicester. *National Railway Museum.*

LEEDS DISTRICT

(A)	(B)	(C)	(D)	(E)	(F)	(G)
39. Wakefield Westgate.	25,000 gal. tank goods warehouse.	9M.	9M.	Wakefield Corporation.	First rate; cannot be improved.	
40. Wrenthorpe.	3 x 2,000 gal. parachute.	13M.	18.5M.	Stanley U.D.C.	Ditto, No.39.	
41. Batley.	12,000 gal. tank stn. yard.	5.4M.	3.9M.	Soothill Urban Council.	No comment.	
42. Dewsbury.	2,000 gal. parachute.	2M.	1.7M.	Dewsbury Corp.	Ditto, No.39.	
43. Ardsley.	200,000 gal. tank locoshed.	16M.	16M.	Well (locoshed).	Always unfit for loco use; cannot be softened.	
-"-	100,000 gal. tank Simpson's Mill.	+ 5.6M.	+ 9.78M.	(For wash-out only) East & West Ardsley U.D.C's.	Cannot be improved but copper/steel boilers sould be emptied every three days. (Applies to Ardsley and Morley Corporation water).	
-"-	100,000 gal. tank Thorpe Lane.	+ 33M.	+ 23.95M.	Morley Corporation.		
-"-	30,000 gal. tank West Yard.					
44. Leeds.	29,000 gal. tank Copley Hill.	50M.	53.21M.	Leeds Corporation.	Ditto, No.39.	
-"- Central Stn	15,500 & 10,500 gal. tanks.					
-"-	6,000 gal. tank Goods.					
45. Bramley.	3,000 gal. parachute.	4M.	4.49M.	" "	Ditto, No.39.	
46. Stanningley.	6,200 gal. tank goods office roof.	Supply not in use.		–	–	
47. Laisterdyke.	31,455 gal. tank top goods yard.	19M.	15.61M.	Bradford Corp.	Ditto, No.39.	
48. Low Moor.	2,000 gal. parachute.	500,000	500,000	" "	"	
49. Morley.	2 x 2,000 gal. parachute.	7.5M.	5M.	Morley Corporation.	"	
50. Bradford.	86,456 gal. tank loco yard.	57M.	49.6M.	Bradford Corp.	"	
-"-	12,431 gal. tank Hydraulic Dept.					
-"-	9,400 gal. tank City Road Goods.					
-"-	2 x 2,000 gal. parachute, Exchange Stn..	+ 19M.	+ 15.61M.	Bradford Corp. (via L&Y).		
51. Shipley.	9,137 gal. tank stn..	1.4M.	1.97M.	Shipley Local Board Waterworks.	"	
52. Clayton.	18,400 gal. tank Bank Top.	6M.	6M.	Clayton Tunnel (by gravity) & Clayton U.D.C (2.18M. in 1905).	"	
53. Holmfield.	46,958 gal. tank loco yard.	1.6M.	1.915M.	Halifax Corporation.	Ditto, No.39.	
54. Pellon.	3,000 gal. parachute.	1M.	1M.	" "	"	
55. St. Pauls (Halifax).	2,000 gal. parachute.	2.5M.	1.5M.	" "	"	
56. Ingrow and Keighley.	50,700 gal. tank loco yard.	20M.	20M.	By gravity, from surrounding hills & Lees Moor Tunnel.	"	
-"-	14,000 gal. tank pass. yard.					
	Total	**273.5M.**	**259.235M.**			

DERBY DISTRICT

(A)	(B)	(C)	(D)	(E)	(F)	(G)
57. Aslockton.	33,000 gal. tank yard.	1.5M.	1.5M.	River Smite.	Very bad. Will cause priming & corrosion. Cannot be softened effectively.	
58. Colwick.	61,000 gal. tank loco yard.	130M.	160M.	Artesian Wells.	Excellent water which softening would make first rate.	0.33d.
59. Nottingham.	30,000 gal. tank stn..	18M.	11.389M.	Nottingham Corp.	Unusual - may be improved by softening but will become corrosive, requiring frequent washout.	
-"-	22,769 gal. tank Goods Dept.		+ 7.481M.	" " (via Jt.Stn. Committee)		
60. Daybrook.	8,585 gal. tank goods yard.	1.25M.	2M.	Nottingham Corp.	Ditto, No.59.	
61. Hucknall.	44,160 gal. tank goods yard.	7.5M.	6.5M.	Hucknall Local Board.	Very good, cannot readily be improved.	
61A. Sutton-in-Ashfield.	Parachute.	–	6.27M.	Unknown.	No comment.	
62. Eastwood.	45,118 gal. tank stn. yard.	9.36M.	12M.	Brook.	Irregular. Always hard but may be improved by softening.	
63. Pinxton.	21,100 gal. tank loco yard.	8.25M.	9M.	River Erewash.	Bad water. Softening would prevent scale but not priming or corrosion.	
64. Ilkeston.	16,360 gal. tank stn. yard.	6M.	12.74M.	Ilkeston Corp.	Ditto, No.61.	
65. Derby.	68,094 gal. tank loco yard.	34M.	28.3M.	Derby Waterworks.	Good chalky water which softening would make excellent.	0.9d.
-"-	12,028 gal. tank goods.		+ 8.245M.	Mickleover springs.		
66. Burton.	8,688 gal. tank goods yard.	2.5M.	4.48M.	South Staffs Water Company.	Hard. Can be much improved by softening should consumption increase sufficiently to justify cost.	(ii)
67. Stathern.	13,371 gal. tank goods yard.	1M.	1M.	Springs (GNR/LNWR Joint).	Good chalky water which softening would make first rate if consumption increases to justify cost.	(ii)
68. Leicester.	56,000 gal. tank coal stage.	10M.	8.25M.	Leicester Waterworks Company.	Good. Could be improved by softening.	1.5d.
	Total	**229.36M.**	**279.155M.**			

At an unknown date during the early LNER period, booster-fitted C1 no.4419 has just finished picking up water from Langley water troughs and although some distance from the end of the troughs there is still a residue of waste water running off the first carriage roof after the Atlantic has obviously topped-up its tank. Langley was the last set of GN water troughs, being brought into operation during October 1918. Notice the photographer, complete with tripod, about to get a soaking. *Authors collection.*

(above) **The 22,000 gallon water tank at Boston station in the early 1960's. At some period after building the tank was raised by about 5ft, no doubt to give it some more 'head'. The 4ft deep plates of the tank can be clearly seen with the aid of the gauge on the front of the tank. Water for the installation was supplied by the Boston Waterworks Co. The additions on top of the structure were recent, the forty gallon oil drum was certainly not a standard feature and remains something of a mystery to the authors.** *T.Henderson.*

(left) **A typical Great Northern water crane at Lincoln Central station, in the 1960's, which had been modified with an extension elbow, probably by the LNER, to give it a higher and longer reach. Fixed alongside is a 'fire devil' for winter operations. The leather 'bag' would not be the original appendage and its replacement would be the responsibility of the 'Outdoor Machinery Department'.** *T.Henderson.*

LOOP DISTRICT

(A)	(B)	(C)	(D)	(E)	(F)	(G)
69. Spalding.	58,000 gal. tank pass. yard.	29M.	22.535M.	Spalding Waterworks.	Good chalky, which softening would make first rate.	1.5d.
70. Boston.	32,000 gal. tank loco works.	35M.	46.5M.	River Witham.	R. Witham at Boston unsuitable as it contains seawater. But, above Langrick Ferry, water is free from this & though hard, it can be softened to make excellent boiler water.	
-"-	22,000 gal. tank stn..		+ 970,000	Boston Waterworks.		
71. Sleaford.	54,000 gal. tank loco yard.	19M.	19M.	Brook and well.	Ditto, No.69.	1.33d.
72. Kirkstead.	17,000 gal. tank tankhouse.	3.5M.	3.5M.	River Witham.	Hard, but softening would make excellent if consumption increases to justify cost.	(ii)
73. Horncastle.	7,500 gal. tank stn. yard.	600,000	410,000	Horncastle Waterworks.	Bad-causes priming and corrosion. Cannot be softened.	
74. Bardney.	27,000 gal. tank yard.	1.25M.	1.25M.	River Witham.	Hard.Softening would make good but never wholly satisfactory while pollution continues in Sincil Dyke & Sth. Delft Drain.	
75. Lincoln.	59,000 gal. tank loco yard.	80M.	80M.	" "	Hard & will cause much hard scale but otherwise good. Softening expensive but would make first rate.	3d.
-"-	19,000 gal. tank stn..					
76. Boultham Jct.	43,000 gal. tank tankhouse.	?	?	Pumped from ballast pit by, and mainly used by, GER.	Fairly good but softening will make excellent.	
77. Gainsborough.	24,000 gal. tank stn..	1.25M.	1.94M.	Gainsborough Local Board Waterworks.	Hard, but softening would make first rate.	
78. Haxey.	13,500 gal. tank tankhouse.	?	320,000	Drain (pumped by GER).	Totally unsuitable for boilers Will cause hard scale, priming & corrosion. Cannot be softened.	
79. Blankney.	43,000 gal. tank tankhouse.	?	?	Brook & well (pumped by GER).	Liable to soft scale & priming when concentrated. Fair water if washed out every 3 days.	
80. Ruskington.	43,000 gal. tank pass. yard.	?	?	Brook & two wells (pumped by GER).	Hard scaling but softening would make first class.	
81. Firsby.	32,000 gal. tank stn..	7.5M.	8M.	Well.	Variable. Sometimes would cause priming. Softening will do harm.	
82. Wainfleet.	2,500 gal. tank loco yard.	325,000	325,000	"	Unfit for boiler use - rapid scale and bad priming.	
83. Skegness.	Standpipe.	400,000	150,000	Skegness Waterworks.	Unfit for boiler use & incapable of artificial improvement.	
84. Spilsby.	6,500 gal. tank locoshed.	127,000	200,000	Well.	Very bad for copper/steel boilers. On no account should it be softened.	
85. Willoughby.	75,000 gal. tank tankhouse.	?	?	"	Remarkable natural alkaline water of high organic purity, but would cause serious priming. Softening useless as already too soft! Recommend mixing with hard water containing calcium or magnesium sulphate to produce good boiler water, after subsidence of precipitated chalk. (See Nos.86 & 87).	
86. Mablethorpe.	3,600 gal. tank tankhouse.	?	?	"	Unfit for locos due to large quantity of salt; boilers should be emptied each day. Locos using should not take water at Willoughby as mixture would aggravate bad qualities of both.	
87. Louth.	32,000 gal. tank loco yard.	12M.	12M.	"	Excellent. Softening would improve but be unnecessary for locos that also watered at Willoughby, which would help inhibit scale.	
	Total	**189.952M.**	**197.1M.**			

MANCHESTER & LIVERPOOL

(A)	(B)	(C)	(D)	(E)	(F)	(G)
88. Deansgate Goods.	72,725 gal. tank goods yard.	2.5M.	1.132M.	Manchester Corp.	(Ordinary water supply). Ideal; cannot be improved.	
-"-				" "	(Pressure supply). Ditto above.	
89. Trafford Park.	CLC metered supply.	12M.	5.13M.	" "	Ideal; cannot be improved.	
90. Dale Street goods.	Hydraulic power only.	320,000	350,000	Liverpool Hydraulic Power Company.	No comment.	
	Total	**25.82M.**	**18.012M.**			
	Grand Total	**2181.172M.**	**2347.261M**			

NOTES: Estimated consumption in South District dropped by 8.09%, 1901-1906, whereas North District expected requirement rose by 20.91%, due largely to the introduction of water troughs at Werrington and Scrooby. Leeds District annual water estimate fell by 5.22% over the same period, but Derby District forecast a massive 21.71% increase - mostly it seems, due to a large rise in workload at Colwick. In the Loop District, with some data missing, a modest rise of 3.76% was foreseen, 1901-1906, but Manchester and Liverpool saw a drop of 30.24%, owing to an inexplicable fall in demand at Trafford Park.

With regard to quality, the GN was very well off for good water in the Leeds District, as it was in South District - with the exception of the Regents Canal supply. North District also was good, spoiled only by the amazingly bad state of the water at Doncaster, which just happened to have by far and away the highest annual consumption on the entire GN system. The Red Bank borehole, made in 1897, obviously had not helped much and it is easy to see why the company went to the cost of laying a pipeline, in 1904, from Bawtry to Doncaster. Strangely, this supply does not appear in the table above. Derby District water was good, generally, with the best quality fortunately at the busiest locations. Such a situation, however, did not pertain in Loop District, which has the widest variation in water quality. This ranged from dilute seawater at Boston, the District's second largest consumer, to the softest (and equally unsuitable) water found on the GN system, at Willoughby. Luckily, the largest consumer, Lincoln, and the next two largest, after Boston-Sleaford and Spalding - all had water that would be very good, albeit after a relatively expensive softening process (£1,000 per annum, at Lincoln).

(above) **The Desrumaux Automatic Water Softener installed on a trial basis at Ardsley in 1902 "for comparison purposes". Sited by the coal stage, the softener discharged the treated water into the tender tank on the left; the water was for the exclusive use of one saddletank locomotive. Whatever happened to this plant or the results of the 'trial' is unknown.** *(right)* **It was left to the LNER to install the larger lineside softening plants such as this huge affair at Langley. The original tank serving the troughs here is visible on the embankment above the softening plant. The by-products (sludge) of the softening process required a dedicated fleet of vehicles for the removal of the sludge and disused locomotive tenders, numbered in the Service Stock series, were employed effectively. In this view one of the Langley 'carriers' is filled from the overhead pipe.** *both National Railway Museum.*

SERVICE STOCK
SLUDGE CARRIER

Appendix 3. BREAKDOWN CRANES & TRAINS

The first accidents involving Great Northern trains were experienced shortly after the various lines in and around Lincolnshire were opened. Even before 1850, the company was having to contend with derailments, some of which were major, at the rate of nearly three a month. The General Manager was quick to point out to the Board that most accidents were caused by indifferent maintenance procedures, some carelessness by the staff and in some cases, the state of the permanent way. No matter what the cause, it was obvious that standards would have to be raised by all concerned but it was realised that breakdowns, collisions and derailments were bound to happen eventually, causing much delay and inconvenience. So, following the lead of other railway companies, the Board decided it would be wise to have tools and appliances set aside with the Locomotive Department, ready to travel anywhere on the system to the scene of an incident. One can only imagine what the first tool (breakdown) wagons were like; in 1851 Sturrock asked for permission to convert some "ballast waggons into tool vans for use at derailments and breakdowns." The tool vans were to be equipped with screw jacks, ramps, levers, chains and ropes.

During 1850 the company had purchased a small number of wagon-borne hand cranes of 5 tons capacity, for use in goods yards and on civil engineering jobs, but it was 1853 before the first purpose-designed breakdown crane was acquired for the exclusive use of the Locomotive Department. This came about after Sturrock had requested that: "....the company should have the means of dealing with a breakdown or an accident in the shortest possible time, so as not to delay traffic and therefore lose revenue...." The directors saw the wisdom of this and promptly approved the order of an 'accident crane' from the Kirkstall Forge Co. This first crane was of 8 tons lifting capacity and had a fixed jib. It was coupled to a travelling van containing tools, blocks, levers and cutting gear. Although this ensemble was not numbered, it became part of the Locomotive Department inventory and was stationed at Peterborough. In December 1857 Sturrock asked for a small siding to be laid in at the north end of the coke stage at Peterborough, "....to accommodate our accident crane and van, so they may be readily available whenever accident or breakdown occurs...." The cost was estimated at £65 and the work was sanctioned. The breakdown train was stationed at Peterborough Station (North) engine shed, rather than at New England, for it was conveniently sited alongside the wagon repair shop and therefore handy for picking up carriage and wagon repairers as well as locomotive fitters, in the event of a

The 'preserved' example of an early GN hand crane housed at the National Railway Museum, York. This one is of 4 tons capacity and although in need of complete renovation, it appears to have all the necessary components. *Terry Henderson.*

This 8 ton capacity, 6-wheel crane allocated to Bradford Hammerton Street in 1954 was probably the same one that came there during the 1880's although the Gresley Brake would have been a recent addition to the ensemble. *S.Outram.*

turn-out. On 10th April the following year Sturrock requested the provision of two more travelling cranes "....for the London and Grantham Locomotive Stations, similar to the one ordered in November 1853 for Peterborough, which cost £160...." London at this time was without a breakdown crane and Grantham was considered to be conveniently halfway between Peterborough and Doncaster, where a four-wheel crane was stationed, also of 8 tons capacity and similar to the Peterborough appliance. In the event, only one crane was purchased and it went to London, King's Cross.

In December 1857, Sturrock comments to the Board: "....because of the recent arrangement with the Midland Company, to have their trains running between Hitchin and London, I consider that an accident van and travelling crane should be stationed at Hitchin...." He went on to say: "....at the moment, if an accident occurs at Hitchin, we have to send to London or Peterborough, with a great loss of time and a delay. The cost of a crane for Hitchin would be £265 and would be of similar construction to the last one supplied by the Kirkstall Forge Company. I could fit up one of the present covered goods waggons with the necessary tools for about £120...." The crane and tool van were supplied to Hitchin, possibly after some arrangement had been reached with the MR for sharing costs. In February 1865, a crane and tool van was, according to Sturrock, "....required at Hatfield, as traffic there is so important...." but this time he met with a refusal. It was left to Stirling to further expand the accident crane fleet and in late November 1875, he requested four at Retford, Grantham, Hatfield and Colwick, "....because of the lack of these appliances at these places...." Estimated costs were £250 each. The last named shed in this group was of course, newly built but its predecessor in the centre of Nottingham had no such equipment to deal with accidents. These four cranes were constructed in the company's own workshop at Doncaster in the early part of 1876. They were as usual, hand operated and of 8 tons capacity, with one-piece wooden jibs; earlier cranes from private workshops had girder jibs. By mid-1881 breakdown train facilities of one form or another were situated at the following sheds:

Boston (Crane)	Bradford (Crane)	Colwick (Crane)
Doncaster (Crane)	Grantham (Crane)	Hatfield (Crane)
Hitchin(Crane)	King's Cross (Crane)	Leeds (Van)
Lincoln (Crane)	Peterborough (Crane)	Retford (Crane)

It is assumed each crane was part of a breakdown train that included tool vans and in some cases, a crew travelling van as well.

When Ivatt took control of the Locomotive Department, he immediately saw the need for breakdown cranes with a greater lifting capacity. He also realised the advantages to be gained by using steam-powered cranes and in December 1898 reported to the Board: "....the travelling breakdown cranes at the various locomotive depots are all of 8 tons capacity and I would like permission to obtain prices for two steam breakdown cranes from Messrs. Cowans Sheldon of Carlisle, similar to the cranes they make for other railways...." Two weeks later Ivatt told the Board that he had been in touch with Cowans Sheldon, who had quoted a price of £1,795 for each crane, but because of the amount of work the firm had on hand, it would be later in 1899 before they could promise delivery. At the same meeting, Ivatt, who was by his own making, something of an authority on breakdown matters, asked the Board for a further crane to be ordered, as he wanted to station one each at Peterborough, Doncaster and Colwick. In the event only two steam-powered cranes were purchased from Cowans Sheldon, each of 15 tons capacity and a massive improvement on the four and six wheel hand-powered 8 tonners. With his special interest in breakdown matters, Ivatt was responsible for standardising the make-up of a typical breakdown train of the period - a travelling van, runner for the jib (if necessary), crane, tool van and finally a break travelling van. In the early days the latter were obtained from redundant four wheel passenger stock until from 1900, six wheeled coaches became available, many of these seeing service with breakdown trains well into the BR period.

In 1892, some years before Ivatt's first 'skirmish' with the Board over breakdown cranes, the Civil Engineer's Department had acquired two 15 ton steam cranes from Smiths of Rodley

A TRILOGY OF INCIDENTS

(top) **An accident at Gamston near Retford in the summer of 1907 required the services of three cranes, one steam and two hand cranes. The 15 ton capacity steam crane came from Doncaster and did the bulk of the clearing up and can be seen at work in the top right of the picture. Retford depot's 8 ton hand crane appears to be 'stowed' in front of the left hand loco.** *R.Tarpey collection.*

(centre) **Retford again but some sixteen years later when the Locomotive Department was better equipped with larger steam cranes. Visible in this view of the accident in February 1923, involving passenger and goods trains, are two 15 ton steam cranes from Colwick and Doncaster, and the 35 ton crane based at Peterborough. The number of parallel tracks enabled the cranes to get nearer to the wreckage during the early stages of the 'clear-up'. However this was not always the case and operating conditions were usually ackward and restricted, prolonging the incident.** *R.Tarpey collection.*

(left) **A343, the 35 ton Peterborough crane, is called out to a 'local' incident involving a locomotive and residential property circa 1922.** *R.Tarpey collection.*

Standing in the yard of its 'temporary' home, the ultimate in Great Northern breakdown cranes shortly after delivery from the manufacturers, Cravens, in 1914. It had been suitably labelled with its owning shed name but Gresley wanted this useful piece of equipment at the centre of the GN system where its shorter turn-out time would be better utilised. Shortly after this portrait was captured on film, A343 was transferred to Peterborough from where it could better serve the needs of the company. The crane went on to serve the LNER and then BR until 1966 when it was withdrawn. *P. Tatlow collection.*

and Ivatt brought this fact to the attention of the Board shortly after his appointment. He did so again in January 1903, through the Locomotive Committee, understandably somewhat aggrieved that the Engineers should have at their full time disposal two such modern and useful machines. Ivatt pointed out that the Locomotive Department's breakdown cranes were still insufficient, with the exception of the two 15 ton specimens at Doncaster and Peterborough. He asked for a third such crane stating that: "....an instance of accident at Royston was attended by 8 ton hand cranes and they proved not very good for the work involved...." The Locomotive Committee approved purchase of another 15 ton crane, but the Board, in their usual parsimonious manner, turned down the proposal.

The following year, Ivatt tried yet again to obtain a larger capacity crane, this time "....for the London depot at King's Cross...." The proposed appliance was to be of 20 tons rating, but hand-powered, with an auxiliary petrol engine, to be supplied by Messrs. Ransomes & Rapier of Ipswich, at a price of £1,550. This too was rejected, basically on the grounds of cost. As a consolation, the two Smiths cranes belonging to the Civil Engineer's were effectively brought under the control of the Locomotive Department, and were allocated to engine sheds, but were to be used, "when required" by the Civil Engineer, as before. It must be remembered that cranes allocated to the Locomotive Department might be called into use only once or twice a week, whereas the Civil Engineer's Department worked its cranes virtually seven days a week and on some jobs, much shunting would be required by the crane in use. The Smiths machines were ideal for such duties, being unlike conventional steam-powered cranes as far as drive to the wheels was concerned. It was usual to have inside gearing, connected to the gears of the crane, but the Smiths machines were fitted with outside connecting rods and jackshaft drive, thereby enabling travel over fairly long distances, at a faster than walking pace. With their outside framing and connecting rods they were ungainly looking machines but they served the company well. The LNER took the connecting rods off them and fitted a more conventional drive and in this condition they were inherited by British Railways for further use as breakdown cranes. Numbered, in Great Northern days, 6 and 7 (in the Engineer's list), the Smiths cranes were allocated to Ardsley (No.6) and Kings Cross, where the latter supplemented the six wheel 8 ton hand crane already in residence.

In 1914, Colwick finally got its long-awaited steam crane. It was in fact the 15 ton Cowans Sheldon machine from Peterborough which, in exchange, had acquired (through the Board and Gresley's guile) a brand new 35 ton crane from the Stockport firm of Cravens Brothers. To secure this fine machine for the Locomotive Department, Gresley had first approached the Board in April 1913, telling them that: "....A new 35 ton crane is required and I have already got prices from the major manufacturers and although all the cranes have some operational problems, the Cravens machine is by far the best at £3,795. The Lancashire & Yorkshire Railway have a very similar crane and are very pleased with it. The crane can be hauled at 40 to 50 miles per hour and if purchase is sanctioned, I intend to station it in the Peterborough District and transfer the 15 tonner there to Colwick...." To back up his case, Gresley reported that the Peterborough crane had been called out 62 times in the last twelve months and Colwick's 8 ton hand crane no less

The Peterborough breakdown train out on the main line circa 1914. This was a typical 'train' which could be hauled to the location of an incident either 'jib in front' or 'trailing'. The 6-wheel brake is numbered 272A. The middle van contained packing timbers. *Authors collection.*

than 65 times. The purchase was sanctioned and the crane was duly delivered in 1914 but at the Board's insistence, to 'Top Shed', where it seems, the Directors wanted to show off their powerful new acquisition. Gresley, however, was both more resolute and more knowledgeable on breakdown matters than the gentlemen of the Board, so shortly after the 35 tonner had posed for photographs with its very 'temporary' home shed name painted on the side tanks and runner, it was discreetly worked back down the main line to Peterborough, where it was to stay for the next 21 years.

In 1917, the allocation of GNR breakdown equipment was as follows:

Steam Cranes

Smiths 15 tons, Class F No.6 - Ardsley
Smiths 15 tons, Class F No.7 - Kings Cross
Cowans Sheldon 15 tons, Class E No.150a - Doncaster
Cowans Sheldon 15 tons, Class E No.152a - Colwick
Cravens 35 tons, No.A343 - Peterborough

Hand Cranes

Six wheel 8 tons No.59 - Grantham
Six wheel 8 tons No.61a - Boston
Six wheel 8 tons No. ? - Bradford
Four wheel 8 tons No.6a - Retford
Four wheel 8 tons No.8a - Hitchin
Four wheel 8 tons No.18a - Lincoln
Four wheel 8 tons No.33a - Hatfield
Four wheel 8 tons No.35a - Leicester

Vans Only

Copley Hill
Hornsey
Louth

There were five other 4 wheel, 8 ton cranes held in reserve: Nos. 44a, 65a, 71a and two unnumbered examples. Allocations for these have not been discovered.

All the Great Northern steam cranes saw service into BR days, but most of the ancient 8 ton hand cranes were either pressed into non-motive power related work, or were retired and consigned to scrap. One of these 'small fry' did fare better than the rest and miraculously survived, to become part of the National Collection at York. This particular example of a GNR travelling crane was actually one of the first purchased by the company for service in goods depots and although of only 4 tons capacity, it embodies all the features of the earliest breakdown cranes.

For additional information about steam breakdown cranes, their working, design, construction and operation, the reader is wholeheartedly recommended to consult *Railway Steam Cranes* by John S. Brownlie (Glasgow 1973).

BR Eastern Region breakdown crane No.109. based at Grantham and seen there in June 1958. Built by Cowans Sheldon in 1899, the crane, of 15 tons capacity, was withdrawn in 1961. *Authors collection.*

DE 941538, the Copley Hill (Leeds) shed breakdown van in March 1958. This former Great Northern 6-wheel passenger break entered the service of the GN Locomotive Dept. at some unknown date but probably before the First World War. A breakdown van was allocated to Leeds by 1881 but would have been an even more ancient vehicle than this one. *D.Butterworth.*

Appendix 4. REPAIR FACILITIES.

Running an efficient public railway service has always required an effective repair organisation. In other words, there must be sufficient quantities of men and machinery, strategically placed, so as to keep to a minimum the rolling stock's period of inactivity and, therefore, inability to earn revenue. All the more surprising then, that the early years of the GNR were marked by not a little prevarication about where the main workshops would be situated. In fact, it was not until the beginning of the twentieth century that Doncaster emerged finally, as the GN's primary repair facility.

On 25th February 1848, the GN Board authorised Messrs. Cubitt and Bury to provide workshops at Boston. In early May the same year, they were asked to prepare the necessary plans, which job was completed in June - one month later! When instructed on 22nd June to install workshop fittings and machinery in the new works, without contract, Bury was again prompt and never one to miss a commercial opportunity, he supplied equipment from his own firm of Bury, Curtiss & Kennedy! In August 1848, Frederick Parker became the GN's first Works Foreman at Boston, at a salary of £350 per annum; his duties were to extend, in Bury's absence, to be over the whole Locomotive Department of the Loop and East Lincolnshire lines. Parker was a former colleague of Bury's, with the London & Birmingham, and London & North Western Railways, and had been offered the GN job by the Board, on the direct recommendation of Bury. Despite the speed of construction, however, Parker did not get his locomotive repair shop into service before October 1849, as evidenced by another detailed record book, meticulously prepared by Charles Sacre - "The Ledger of Boston Locomotive Department, 1848 - 1850," viz:

The last locomotive rebuilt at King's Cross workshops was Stirling 7ft. 6in. Single no.872. Here inside the shop in May 1901, 872 has a typical Ivatt cab and now sports a domed boiler and other new parts supplied by Doncaster. In this condition the engine worked for another 12 years before withdrawal as the last of class. The paint finish can be described as nothing but immaculate. *Authors collection.*

From:
"The Ledger of Boston Locomotive Department 1848-1850:"
January 1849:
Locomotive Depots:
Peterboro (as written), Boston, Louth and Lincoln.
Locomotive repair costs and staff costs, May- October 1849:

Month	Loco Depot	Repairs £ s d	Wages £ s d
May	Peterboro	20-19- 7	
	Boston	87-14- 1	
	Lincoln	19- 2- 5	
	Louth	60- 3- 5	
	Total:	**177-19- 6**	**310-15- 4**
June	Boston	20- 6-10	
	Louth	17-19- 4	
	Total:	**38- 6- 2**	**304-13-11**
July	Peterboro	11-11	
	Boston	33- 9-11	
	Gainsboro	14- 5- 3	
	Louth	7-16- 4	
	Total:	**56- 3- 5**	**333- 9- 6**
August	Peterboro	1- 2	
	Boston	32- 0- 1	
	Gainsboro	6-13- 2	
	Louth	8- 7- 9	
	Total:	**47- 2- 2**	**425- 7-11**
September	Peterboro	11- 3- 4	
	Boston	43- 5- 6	
	Gainsboro	56-15- 4	
	Doncaster	27- 3- 7	
	Louth	4-11- 9	
	Total:	**142-19- 6**	**411-13- 9**
October	Peterboro	38-11- 9	
	Gainsboro	4-17- 0	
	Doncaster	17-19- 5	
	Louth	2- 5-11	
	Boston Shop	65- 7- 3	
	Total:	**129- 1- 4**	**471- 0-10**

With regard to loco repair costs, it will be noticed they were much lower in June, July and August, than the preceding and succeeding months. This was probably due to the summer season during those three months, with traffic requirements keeping locos in service when, in quieter times, they would be stopped for minor repairs. Staff costs, however, rose inexorably to the tune of more than 51% over the five months records. Assuredly though, this was entirely due to the needs of a rapidly expanding service and not some mid-19th century precursor of that late-20th century blight, inflation! However, even at this early stage, the future of Boston workshops was already overshadowed. This was because in May 1848, Bury and Cubitt

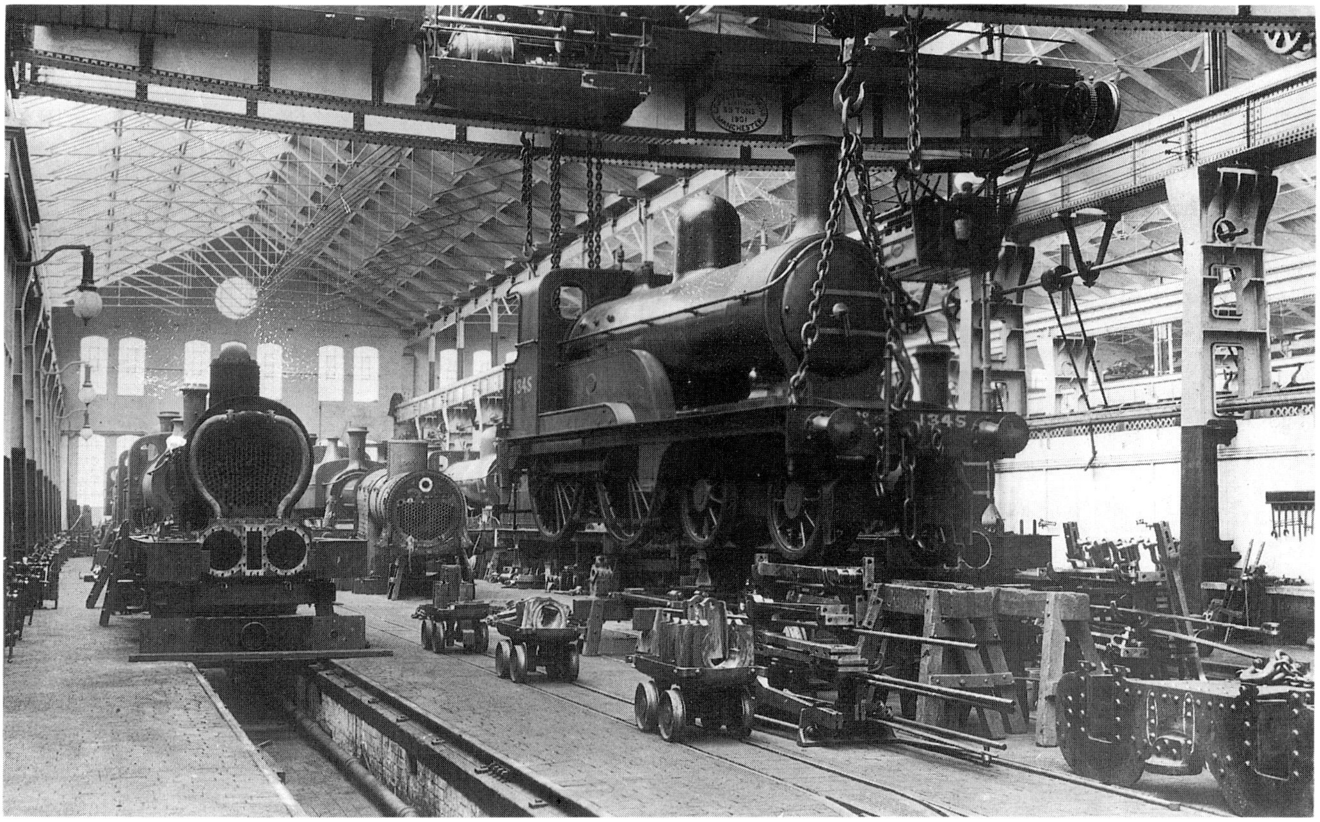

Doncaster's Crimpsall shops in late Great Northern days. They were equipped to deal with all types of steam locomotive repairs as well as new building. *Authors collection.*

had been asked to prepare plans for a locomotive workshop and an engine shed, at Doncaster. By early 1849, Bury had the plans ready, but little was done about the workshop before he resigned, in early 1850.

Bury's successor, Sturrock, had yet another alternative idea! As far as he could foresee at the time, Sturrock quite naturally thought of Peterborough as more or less becoming the centre of the GN's theatre of operations and therefore, the most logical place to site a works complex. He pursued his case to such an extent that on 27th August 1850, the GN Board resolved to purchase 28 acres of land at Peterborough. This was in an area called "Walton Field" - and which eventually became known as New England - and Sturrock was asked to obtain estimates for the erection of workshops there. The land was duly bought, but the mists of time conceal what may have transpired to cause the Board to decide, on 3rd June 1851, that the locomotive workshops would after all, be situated at Doncaster. The fact that the GN's Chairman, Edmund Denison, was Doncaster's leading citizen, might have been a cause of the change, but one can only speculate. Once the decision to build the works was taken, the locomotive building firm of E.B.Wilson & Co., which was undertaking some heavy repair and rebuilding work for the GN, offered a comprehensive repair contract. This, and a subsequently improved offer, were both turned down.

So it was that the famous "Plant" came into being, to a new design by the Cubbitts and Sturrock, at a cost of around £45,000. Construction was undertaken by A. & G.Holmes, a Liverpool company, and most of the workshop machinery was supplied by Messrs. Nasmyth. Locomotives were being repaired by June 1853, with the Plant coming into full operation two months later. Frederick Parker moved from Boston, to be Doncaster's first Works Manager, at the same salary of £350, plus a free house; he brought with him 300 men and their families, some 800 people in all.

Development of the works continued apace, with the first extension being made in 1855. Following this, on 3rd February 1866, Sturrock had the honour (!) to report to the Board that Doncaster's boiler and erecting shops were no longer of sufficient size and he asked for extensions costing £1,200 and £1,800 respectively. However, when Messrs. Kirk & Parry were awarded the contract, on 10th April 1866, the costs had risen to £1,887 and £3,239! As a lead up to this expansion a considerable number of new machine tools were ordered, as follows:

<u>24th January 1865</u>
Riveting machine for boiler shop: £370
<u>7th June 1865</u>
Smith, Beacock & Co. shearing machine: £120
2 Whitworth shaping machines, 10" stroke: £190
2 Nasmyth shaping machines, 5" stroke: £150
<u>3rd February 1866</u>
Boiler plate planing machine from Messrs. Fairbairn, Kennedy & Naylor of Leeds: £115
<u>10th March 1866</u>
Bar Cutting machine: £625
Small bar cutting machine: £250
Screwing machine: £137-10-0d
2 Drilling and punching machines for fastening on steel tyres: Price not stated

Another view inside the King's Cross repair facility, this time in April 1936, when J3 no.4137 was having attention to its centre driving wheels. *H.C.Casserley.*

On 10th July 1866, Sturrock asked for more machine tools for Doncaster and London workshops. The following £811 order was approved and although there is no indication as to what went where, it may safely be assumed that most went to the Plant, then in course of being expanded: One Messrs. Hardings tube cutting machine - £12; Two Messrs. Smith, Beecock & Co. radial drills - £180 each; One Platt single fan - £16; One Messrs. Smith & Co. 14" screw lathe, with side rests - £710; One Messrs. Smith & Co. 10" screw lathe, with side rests - £148; One Messrs. Nasmyths & Co. double bolt lathe - £65. Purchase of furnaces for steam hammers, from Messrs. Wilson, was deferred.

Then, in 1876, the original erecting shop was pulled down, to enable expansion of the station area and the works were extended onto a piece of land with the well-known name of "Crimpsall." A further major extension was effected in 1891/2, when the contracting company of Arnold & Son built another erecting shop at a cost of £13,500.

However, this capacity was absorbed so quickly as to cause Ivatt to report to the Locomotive Committee, on 24th July 1896, about the lack of accommodation for locomotives at Doncaster works. He pointed out that there were only 62 working pits, which meant that as each locomotive occupied a pit for an average of 3z\v months, every one of the company's 1,000 engines could visit the shops only once in every four years, instead of the customary two years. Therefore, more pits were required. In addition, because of this shortage, Peterborough and London workshops were undertaking heavy repairs, at uneconomical rates, when they should be engaged on light work only. Ivatt added that there was also no paint shop at Doncaster, with the consequence that engines were painted standing on the repair pits, amid all the dust and dirt. He then instanced the repair pits and painting facilities provided on three other railways, to compare with the GNR, viz:

N.E.R.	1869 locos	134 repair pits
G.W.R.	2000 locos	214 repair pits
L.& Y.R.	1230 locos	112 repair pits + 31 in a paint shop.
G.N.R.	1030 locos	62 repair pits. No paint shop and 15-16½% of locomomtive fleet out of service at any one time for repair

Ivatt's impressive case had its effect - in 1900, Arnold & Son secured their second contract, for a massive £129,000, to expand Doncaster works. This involved construction of a further erecting shop (the famous "Crimpsall"), plus tender, paint shops and other ancillary buildings. The task was completed in 1901/2 and this more or less brought to an end the major growth of Doncaster works, but of course, in later years, the GNR, LNER and BR Eastern Region, were to make many minor changes. Today Doncaster Plant's future seems assured, although BR's requirements for the late twentieth century do not see it as a locomotive building works, but as a "Level 5 Maintenance Depot" for locomotives, and central stores depot, with alas, a much reduced workforce.

Moving back to the 1850's, the general exodus to Doncaster, of men and work from Boston, naturally caused concern in the Lincolnshire town. Accordingly, Boston Corporation were regular petitioners of the GNR, for more repairs to be carried out in their town's workshops. However, Boston's moment of glory had gone and though the repair shops continued to function for many years, their workload never regained anything like its former impetus and finally, the buildings became part of the locoshed complex. As a sop perhaps, in 1897, the GN did try to keep some favour in the town by purchasing the sleeper creosoting works of Messrs. Bethal, an installation that was later replaced by a larger one at Hall Hills, Boston, which lasted well into BR days.

At Peterborough, the 28 acres of land at New England saw the first section of a locoshed erected in 1851, to be expanded upon on several subsequent occasions. Then, in 1858, Sturrock's stubborn insistence on siting a works in the city was finally rewarded, when an erecting shop and stores were built at New England. These were joined by a boiler shop and gasworks in 1863, while in a large development, only three years later (Sturrock's swan song perhaps?), a spare loco/paint shop and tender, turning and coppersmith's shops were added. In this way New England became the GN's second most important locomotive centre, with 600 men being employed there in the mid-1860's. In fact, it was not until Doncaster's large expansion in 1901/2 that New England's heavy repair activities ceased, but the works continued in constant use, in the execution of the more usual running repairs, until the end of the steam era.

At the London end of the line, King's Cross locoshed had, from the outset, a large repair shop at the rear, complete with a smithy and various shops. Additional machinery was installed in 1857, and again in the early 1860's, in what was by now officially known as "King's Cross locomotive Works." Like New England, King's Cross continued heavy repairs, down to repainting, until 1901, when Doncaster was more able to take over all such work. The last locomotive turned out from King's Cross Works was a Single, No. 872, in particularly resplendent condition. However, soon afterwards, many artisans were made redundant and the repair facility henceforth dealt only with normal day-to-day work, until the closure of "Top Shed" in 1963.

Of course, running repairs were carried out at most of the GN's locosheds from the very earliest days, but it was not until Doncaster (Carr) shed was erected in 1876, that a purpose-built repair shop formed part of a depot's facilities. This two road edifice was repeated, on a larger scale, at Bradford (Bowling Back) and Colwick, in the 1880's and at Ardsley, in 1892. In fact, that at Ardsley undertook considerably heavy work in the few years prior to Doncaster Crimpsall shop's opening. Elsewhere, at places like Hornsey, Lincoln and Grantham, shearlegs were provided for engine repairs al fresco and, in later years, wheel drops were provided at a number of sheds, details of which are given in the individual shed histories.

Before moving on though, it is interesting to study another "Comparative Statement," this time of locomotive repair costs. Featured is the month of July, for the three years, 1872-1874, and the statement gives details of engines repaired in the various locomotive Districts, the amounts expended and the number of locomotives on hand for repair, at the end of each month:

GREAT NORTHERN RAILWAY

Statement shewing the number of Engines repaired in the various Districts, the amount expended and number on hand for repairs at the end of the month of July in 1872, 1873 and 1874.

		A		**B**		**C**		**D**
		-1-	**-2-**	**-3-**	**-4-**	**-5-**	**-6-**	
London District	1872	3	25	3	7	547- 5- 2	101- 1- 7	18
	1873	2	18	2	7	551-19- 3	108- 1- 9	11
	1874	5	21	5	7	610- 8- 3	122-18- 2	14
Peterboro District	1872	3	40	3	19	684-14- 9	87-12- 5	21
	1873	3	38	3	15	672-11- 0	85-16- 6	23
	1874	2	19	2	8	659-15- 5	79- 9- 3	11
Doncaster District	1872	-	-	-	-	388- 5- 8	77- 2-11	-
	1873	-	-	-	-	371-16- 6	53-19- 4	-
	1874	3	4	3	-	383-18- 3	18- 0- 3	4
Doncaster Shops	1872	-	69	-	18	2052-16- 5	4534-15-11	51
	1873	-	65	-	14	2004-16-11	4409-19- 3	51
	1874	-	58	-	11	1994-16- 7	4205-10- 8	47
Totals	1872	6	134	6	44	3673- 2- 0	4800-12-10	90
	1873	5	121	5	36	3601- 3- 8	4657-16-10	85
	1874	10	102	10	26	3648-18- 6	4205-17-10	76

Key: **A.** Number sent in for repairs, including those on hand from previous month. **B.** Number turned out. **C.** Amount expended in repairs. **D.** Number of engines on hand. **1.** Slight; **2.** Thorough; **3.** Slight; **4.** Thorough; **5.** Wages £.s.d; **6.** Stores £.s.d.

NOTES: A number of interesting facts emerge from the above. The first is that the total of locomotives being presented for repair fell steadily over the three years. This was probably due to increased reliability or, looked at another way, it was the result of more efficient repair work, but at what a cost! Overall, the average cost of repair, per locomotive turned out, increased from £169-9-6d., to £223-6-0d. The worst contributor was Doncaster shops, where costs rose from £365-19-7d., per loco turned out, to £563-13-5d., a massive 54%. Peterborough District, which turned out more "thoroughly" repaired locomotives than Doncaster shops, in 1872 and 1873, was seemingly having its activities reduced, with 43 locos arriving for repair and 22 being turned out, in 1872, compared to 21 and 10, respectively, in 1874, this wind-down must have affected efficiency as the average repair cost rose from £35-2-2d., to £73-18-6d., a 111% increase. London District's work pattern stayed fairly static but between 1872 and 1874, the average cost actually fell, from £64-16-8d., to £61-2-3d. This was despite a sharp rise, 1872-1873, to £73-6-9d., so some strong measures of efficiency must have been applied, 1873-1874. Little can be said about Doncaster District's performance when no details of the turnover of locomotives seems to have been recorded during 1872 and 1873. Perhaps there was something to conceal, with 1874's three "light" repairs costing £134-0-0d., each! Working days equated to 1872 - 27; 1873 - 26; 1874 - 25.

Two 20th-century views inside New England repair shops. *(top)* Former M&GN 4-4-0 C class (LNER class D53) no.050 awaits attention circa 1937. Up to 1936 these 4-4-0's were repaired at their parent workshop at Melton Constable but after closure of that works they were sent to Stratford for major repairs. New England was 'handy' for this Peterborough East allocated engine because that workshop could still perform enough 'surgery' without resort to a visit to Stratford by the engine for 'non-classified' repairs. *(below)* One of New England workshops' last tasks was to store steam locomotives and in February 1962, with chimneys suitably covered, L1 no.67795 and two J50 0-6-0T's wait out the winter traffic lull. *K.C.H.Fairey.*

Appendix 5. TURNTABLES & OTHER TURNING DEVICES

In the early years of the GNR, as with many railways, when an engine required turning it was common practice to separate locomotive and tender and turn each independently, on coaching stock turnplates which on the GN, were 16ft. in diameter. Larger turntables were fairly rare in the 1840's, but naturally, the important sheds, like King's Cross, Doncaster and Peterborough featured 30-40ft. models from the start. Louth, however, apart from being the first 'GNR' shed opened, was unusual in that for such a small depot, it was equipped with a 40ft. turntable from the outset: the East Lincolnshire Railway was either very forward looking - or it had grandiose ideas!

Not every location was initially provided with a turntable though and on 17th June 1851, Sturrock commented to the Board thus: "....tender first running for any distance is dangerous. At present I am obliged to run trains tender first, one way to: Leeds and Wakefield, in consequence of there being no turntable of any description at Knottingley; Royston and Hitchin trains, there being no turntable at Royston; on the Lincoln and Gainsborough branch, there not being any large turntable at Lincoln and the timetable not allowing sufficient time to turn the engines (referring presumably to the need to 'split' engine and tender and turn each separately); also the trains from Grimsby to Louth in consequence of there not being any large turntable at Grimsby...." The Board concurred with Sturrock's recommendations and on 1st July 1851, authorised provision of 40ft. tables at Hitchin, Lincoln (in lieu of the existing 16ft. turntable), and Knottingley, with 16ft. tables for Hatfield (not immediately installed), Biggleswade, Huntingdon, St. Ives (never fitted, due to the GN's working of the East Anglian Railway being short-lived), and Shepreth. Sturrock's request for a 40ft. turntable at Grimsby was met by moving Louth's (in exchange, Louth got a 16ft. model, so on reflection perhaps, in the short term, the ELR's provision *was* grandiose).

Very soon, turntables became standard items for most terminal and interchange points - indeed, the Railway Inspectorate usually made their provision mandatory for the sanction of many a line's opening. Generally, the 16ft. turnplates were soon superseded by 30ft. or 40ft. types and by the last quarter of the nineteenth century, 45ft. turntables seem to have become the norm for the busiest locations. Ivatt's Atlantic locomotives made 52ft., then 60ft. tables a minimum requirement for the years up to the First World War, with Gresley's 2-8-0's heralding a 65ft. necessity immediately before the conflict started. Four years after the war, Gresley's Pacific's made provision of 65ft. and later 70ft. versions mandatory at many places.

Turning power on the GNR was provided by man himself, until well into LNER times, when in 1935, the first vacuum-tractor powered installation appeared at King's Cross. Such operating methods were gradually extended to all locations that sported 65 or 70ft. tables, but this exercise was not completed until BR times. As far as is known, no electrically powered turntables were ever employed by the GNR, or indeed on the GN section of either the LNER or BR. However, every table employed seems to have been of the "under girder" type, with open pits. There were two exceptions to the latter feature; those odd ones out were the "Derby" roundhouse at King's Cross, and Doncaster station (Down side) both of which had the pits boarded over.

Mostly, the GNR's turntables were supplied by such well known companies as Cowans Sheldon, or Ransomes & Rapier, but Doncaster shops did undertake fabrication of some numbers of the smaller sizes. The very first tables used by the GN came from an obscure company, however. Tenders for the supply of the first 16ft. models had been obtained on 8th February 1848, from the following firms:

Ransomes & May of Ipswich; Fox & Henderson of Birmingham; Lloyd, Forster & Co. of Wednesbury; J. Ellis & Co. of Manchester; W.M. Thorold of Norwich

The third named was selected to supply 12 turntables, 16ft. in diameter,

A 1930's view of Skegness turntable with what appears to be a problem J6 on board. Provided for the opening of the station in July 1873, the turntable was only of 44ft. 7ins. diameter which sufficed for most engines of the period but in LNER and BR times the nearby triangle was used for larger locomotives. *T.Henderson collection.*

The 52ft. turntable at the north end of Doncaster station in 1911. This view looking out from 'B' signal box shows the board covering to advantage and two access hatches can be seen set into the timber work. Many North Eastern Railway roundhouse turntables had this feature which can only be put down to safety reasons. The fact that NER locomotives used this table may have some bearing on it being boarded over; the extra expense of providing such elaborate measures was probably funded by the NER. *Authors collection.*

12 tons weight, at the following locations: Boston £161-10-0d; Doncaster £161-0-0d; Lincoln £161-10-0d; Spalding £160-0-0d. (Also included was an order for 40 turntables, 13ft. in diameter, 8 tons weight, at £111, £110, £111 and £110-10-0d, at the above mentioned places, respectively).

Maintenance of turntables was usually carried out by the company, on site, whenever possible, but if the required work was too heavy, the turntable would be dismantled and transported to the works for attention.

Lastly, the GNR was unusual for a British railway in pioneering and retaining the use of a triangle specifically for the turning of locomotives. That was at New England, one of the largest depots, which had a turntable for only the first 6 of its 113 years of steam service. Amazingly, the triangle was perpetuated by the LNER, at Skegness and Doncaster. The latter was laid down at Carr shed in the mid-1940's, eventually to be replaced by a turntable again, in 1960. Even more amazing, British Railways, Eastern Region, also laid a new triangle. That was at Grantham, where a 70ft. turntable was replaced by a triangle of unique design, in that it incorporated a scissors in its make-up - necessary because of space limitations.

The Appendices to the GNR's (and LNER's) Working Timetable (WTT), are a mine of information, part of which gives the location of every turntable to which company locomotives had access. The following lists of turntable sites are taken from the 1877, 1912 and 1947 WTT's, and it is interesting to note the increases in size that were made over the years, plus the locations that came and went:

Location	**1870**	**1912**	**1947**
King's Cross Passenger	40 - 0	52 - 0	70 - 0
King's Cross (Top Shed)	40 - 0	52 - 0	70 - 0
Holloway Carriage sidings	-	49 - 7	-

table continued

(opposite) **The new 70ft. articulated turntable, complete with vacuum tractor, installed at Ardsley in 1937.** *National Railway Museum.*

Ferme Park (Down)	-	44 - 8*	-
Hornsey Engine Shed	-	52 - 0	65 - 0
Edgware	40 - 0	-	-
Hatfield Loco Yard	40 - 0	44 - 7	46 - 0
St. Albans	40 - 0	-	-
Dunstable (LNWR) Station	-	44 - 7	44 - 7
Hitchin Loco Yard	40 - 0	60 - 0	60 - 0
Cambridge Loco Yard	44 - 10	44 - 10	-
Peterborough Loco Yard	40 - 0	60 - 0	60 - 0
New England	Triangle used 1858 - 1965		
March	44 - 0	-	-
Grantham (south side of E.S)	40 - 0	-	-
Grantham (west side, new E.S)	-	52 - 0	-
Grantham (NW of coal stage)	-	54 - 9	-
Grantham (Loco, north end)	-	-	70 - 0
Newark Loco Yard	-	45 - 4	47 - 7
Retford Loco Yard	40 - 0	44 - 8	48 - 6
Doncaster Carr (south end)	-	52 - 0	-
Doncaster Carr (north end)	-	45 - 0	-
Doncaster Carr Triangle	-	-	Yes
Doncaster Station (north)	40 - 0	-	-
Doncaster Station (south)	45 - 0	-	-
Doncaster Stn (west of Down CS)	-	60 - 0	-
Doncaster Stn (front of 'Plant')	-	60 - 0	60 - 0
Doncaster Stn (near 'B' signal box)	-	52 - 0	52 - 0
Bourne	-	45 - 0	60 - 0
Spalding Station	23 - 0	44 - 7	45 - 6
Boston Stn (north end, Down side)	-	52 - 0	52 - 0
Boston Loco Yard	40 - 0	45 - 6	54 - 0
Sleaford	-	45 - 0	45 - 0
Bardney (south end, Up goods yd)	-	44 - 7	48 - 0
Lincoln Station	40 - 0	-	-
Lincoln Loco Yard	-	45 - 0	65 - 0
Louth Loco Yard	-	44 - 6	49 - 8
Skegness (entrance to goods yard)	-	44 - 7	45 - 6
Mablethorpe (north end stn yard)	-	44 - 8	45 - 9
Colwick (Old Loco Yard)	-	54 - 9	-
Colwick (by coal stage)	-	55 - 0	70 - 0
Nottingham London Rd (LL)	42 - 0	-	-
Nottingham Vic Stn (north end)	-	49 - 10	54 - 11
Nottingham Vic Stn (south end)	-	49 - 1-	54 - 5
Basford & Bulwell (Down side)	-	54 - 10	54 - 9
Newstead Station	-	44 - 7	46 - 7
Pinxton Loco Yard	-	44 - 7	47 - 0
Ilkeston Station (north side)	-	44 - 7	46 - 7
Derby Loco Yard	-	44 - 6	46 - 6
Burton Goods Yard	-	44 - 7	46 - 7
Stathern Station (north side)	-	44 - 6	47 - 6
Leicester Loco Yard	-	45 - 0	47 - 0
Wakefield Westgate (MR shed side)	40 - 0	49 - 6	50 - 0
Ardsley Locoshed (south end)	-	44 - 6	70 - 0
Ardsley Up Yd (in line from loco)	-	44 - 6	-
Leeds Central Station	40 - 0	55 - 0	55 - 0
Leeds Wortley Junction	Wortley triangle used 1857 - 1899		
Leeds Copley Hill Loco Yard	-	51 - 9	52 - 0
Hunslet Goods Yard	-	51 - 10	52 - 0
Bradford Adolphus St.	St.Dunstan's triangle used 1867 - 1880		
Bradford Exchange Stn	-	49 - 9	50 - 0
Bradford Loco Yard	-	50 - 0	55 - 0
Ingrow Loco Yard	-	45 - 0	-
St.Pauls (Halifax) Station	-	45 - 0	45 - 0

Note: * 65ft from 15/12/1913.

Some of the differences in size, particularly between 1912 and 1947, are hard to explain. A number, changed by only a few inches, are surely due to different methods of measurement, but others, usually around two feet, seem to be too small for a complete renewal of turntable to be made and so presumably extension rails were being employed.

New England based D3 no.4344 is positioned on Leicester's 47ft. turntable circa 1936. When laid down this table was of 45ft. diameter but 1 foot extension rails were added to each end at an unknown date after 1912. The deck cladding of the turntable was also extended and evidence of this can be just made out, below the leading bogie wheel, where the lip of the turntable is proud of the pit. In the background can be seen the shed Smithy stood next to his outside forge. *W.Potter.*

Another variation on the vacuum tank theme was to be found at Lincoln where the turntable reservoir tanks were fitted beneath the deck of the table. O2/2 no.63945 provides its own vacuum to turn in this early 1960's view. *M.Whatmough.*

Another view of the Mablethorpe turntable from the approach road in 1956. *Authors collection.*

Finally a story with a happy ending. The 60ft. turntable at Hichin was assured a new lease of life when it was purchased by a preservation society and removed. However, before that event, the table was used during 1975 to stable an independent snowplough fashioned from an old steam locomotive tender. When this turntable replaced a smaller example in 1905, a vast amount of chalk had to be excavated from the adjacent high-ground to make the required space. The former engine shed occupied the open ground next to the station platform. *Authors.*

ERRATA to Volume 1.

In a work containing so many facts and figures as *Great Northern Engine Sheds* it is usual for a few gremlins to strike. However, in *Volume 1* we had, it seems, more than a reasonable number although many were thankfully typographical. We would like to take this opportunity to thank those readers who took the trouble to write in, pointing out the various mistakes. Below we list the corrections to those mistakes of significance.

Page 1, Col 1, line 16: GWR should be GNR.
Page 18, Col 2, line 7: Barton should be Gorton.
Page 19, Col 2, line 8: Barston should be Garston.
Page 24, Col 1, line 28: B15s should be B1s.
Page 26, Col 1, line 4: H12 should be H2. **line 23**: 3447 was never a King's Cross engine - it was at Hitchin. **line 29**: 3.40 a.m. should be 3.40 p.m. **Col 2, line 10**: The *Flying Scotsman* was introduced in 1862.
Page 30, Col 2, line 5: 2682 is duplicated. **line 16**: should read..Just on the formation...
Page 33, Col 1, line 23: should be....improvements costing £400-£500 be carried....
Page 43, Col 1, line 21: 343/5 should be 3434/5.
Page 49, Col 1, line 32 and 34: Lovatt should be Lovett; 4-4-2 should be 4-2-2.
Page 51, Caption: Stirling should be Ivatt.
Page 53, Col 2, 4th para: There was no railbus No.4. One was intended but never delivered.
Page 57, Col 2, line 19: Y3 66 should be 8185.
Page 64, Col 2, line 15: 5412 should be 5452.
Page 79, Col 2, various: J6 0-6-0 should be J39; O1 2-8-0 should be O2 2-8-0; O2 2-8-0 should be O4 2-8-0.
Page 86, Col 2, line 7: 445 should be 4445.
Page 109, Col 2, line 17: B1 Nos.56 and 62 should be D1....
Page 117, Col 1, line 23: 9/1-2/ should be 9½ miles....
Page 123, Col 1, line 20: armoured loco was 7784 not 7748.
Page 130, Col 2, Acknowledgements: Peter Townsend should be Peter Townend.

ACKNOWLEDGEMENTS

Whenever a work of the size of *Great Northern Engine Sheds* is researched and written there will inevitably be a number of experts and like minded people consulted so that their knowledge can be welded onto all the 'other bits' and also to the vast amount of primary material unearthed along the way.
During the many years that we spent meeting, and interviewing, these 'like minded people' we have made many new friends and sadly we have also lost a number of them too. Here we would like to acknowledge their help and hospitality which was always forthcoming and for which we will be eternally grateful for without their input this work would be somewhat incomplete. Photographs form a large part of this book and many photographers supplied prints of their own taking whilst others loaned prints from their valuable collections.
A simple list of names never seems to be enough in the way of extending our thanks, however, we will take this opportunity to humbly do so. Gentlemen - wherever you are - we value your help and input. Alex Appleton, Bill Camwell, Adam Cartwright, H.C.Casserley, Richard Casserley, Sid Checkley, Jim Davenport, Ron Dyer, Bob Elwell, Leslie Franks, A.R.Goult, Brian Green, Terry Henderson, Harold James, John Kite, Kenneth Leech, Alf Ludlam, Eric Neve, Sid Outram, Les Perrin, Nick Pigott and other members of the Engine Shed Society, Neville Stead, Bill Stubbs, Dick Tarpey, Peter Tatlow.
To give us some credibility, with locomotive matters, after the mini disasters in Vol.1 *(see above)*, Willie Yeadon read through the various proofs, adding and correcting where necessary. Thanks Willie.
Finally, in the background, but always there when needed were Christine and Jane - two very patient ladies.